THE CINEMA OF ME

Nov 23rd 2020

Dear
Alessandra,

for your continuing
explorations of the
'self' and her
spirit in

moving Image.

Your significant talents
continue to shine...
Best wishes
Pratap.

Nonfictions is dedicated to expanding and deepening
the range of contemporary documentary studies.
It aims to engage in the theoretical conversation
about documentaries, open new areas of scholarship,
and recover lost or marginalised histories.

General Editor, Brian Winston

Other titles in the *Nonfictions* series:

Direct Cinema: Observational Documentary and the Politics of the Sixties
by Dave Saunders

Projecting Migration: Transcultural Documentary Practice
edited by Alan Grossman and Aine O'Brien

The Image and the Witness: Trauma, Memory and Visual Culture
edited by Frances Guerin and Roger Hallas

Films of Fact: A History of Science in Documentary Films and Television
by Timothy Boon

Building Bridges: The Cinema of Jean Rouch
edited by Joram ten Brink

Vision On: Film, Television and the Arts in Britain
by John Wyver

Chavez: The Revolution Will Not Be Televised – A Case Study of Politics and the Media
by Rod Stoneman

Documentary Display: Re-Viewing Nonfiction Film and Video
by Keith Beattie

The Personal Camera: Subjective Cinema and the Essay Film
by Laura Rascaroli

THE CINEMA OF ME

The Self and Subjectivity in First Person Documentary

EDITED BY ALISA LEBOW

WALLFLOWER PRESS

LONDON & NEW YORK

A Wallflower Book
Published by
Columbia University Press
Publishers Since 1893
New York • Chichester, West Sussex
cup.columbia.edu

A complete CIP record is available from the Library of Congress

ISBN 978-0-231-16214-2 (cloth : alk. paper)
ISBN 978-0-231-16215-9 (pbk. : alk. paper)
ISBN 978-0-231-85016-2 (e-book)

Design by Elsa Mathern

CONTENTS

ACKNOWLEDGMENTS

This book has been several years in the making, so I would first like to acknowledge the patience and forebearance of the authors who kept the faith, through all of the ups and downs that characterise academic publishing, that their work would one day appear in print. It has been an honour to work with each and every one of you. I also want to thank Wallflower Press's commissioning editor, Yoram Allon, and the *Nonfictions* series editor, Brian Winston, for seeing the potential in this volume. Special thanks also to Jodie Taylor who kept the book's production on track, and to our tireless copy-editor, Ian Cooper, who had to be vigilant against the wanton mixing of English and American spellings that I wasn't able to catch.

CONTRIBUTORS

PROFESSOR MICHAEL CHANAN, Roehampton University, UK

When I was a philosophy student, someone remarked that all philosophy students write poetry in secret and really want to be filmmakers. I stopped writing poetry when I made my first film. A few years later, since independent filmmaking is not a secure way to make a living, I got a job which made me feel like an unemployed filmmaker employed to teach people to become unemployed filmmakers. I also started writing books, then went back to making films, and after that returned to teaching. Now, I'm glad to say that as a Professor of Film in the digital twenty-first century, it's just about possible to do all these things at once, sort of. Anyway, my last long film was *Chronicle of Protest*, composed from video blogs I was posting on the *New Statesman* website, and my latest book, *The Politics of Documentary*, was published by the British Film Institute in 2007. I also run a blog called Putney Debater.

DR. EFRÉN CUEVAS, University of Navarra, Spain

I am an Associate Professor of Film Studies in the University of Navarra, Spain. One of my main research areas focuses on home movies, family memoir and autobiographical documentaries. On these topics, I have co-edited the books *The Man without the Movie Camera: The Cinema of Alan Berliner* (2002), and *Landscapes of the Self: The Cinema of Ross McElwee* (2008); and in Spanish, I edited *La casa abierta. El cine doméstico y sus reciclajes contemporáneos* [*The Open House: Home Movies and Their Contemporary Recycling*]. I have also dealt with these issues in chapters for the books *Documental y vanguardia* (2005), *El cine de los mil años. Una aproximación histórica y estética al cine documental japonés* (2006), *and Cineastas contra el espejo* (2008); and in journals such as the Spanish *Archivos de la Filmoteca and Secuencias*, and the American *Biography*.

ANDRÉS DI TELLA, Independent filmmaker, Argentina

I am an Argentinian filmmaker, based in Buenos Aires. My feature documentaries include *Montoneros, una historia* (1995), *Prohibido* (1997), *La television y yo* (2003), *Fotografías* (2007), *El país del Diablo* (2008) and *Hachazos* (2011). My work also comprises installations, video-art and performance pieces and a book of narrative non-fiction, *Hachazos* (2011), as well as documentaries made for TV both at home and abroad (PBS, Channel Four). Addressing the lack of venues for independent cinema in Argentina, I created the Buenos Aires International Festival for Independent Cinema (BAFICI), considered one of the principal film events in Latin America, which I directed in its first editions (1999 and 2000). I am currently the Artistic Director of the Princeton Documentary Festival at Princeton University, where I have also been visiting professor. I have been the recipient of numerous grants and fellowships including the JS Guggenheim Fellowship. My work is discussed in several books in Spanish, including *Cine Documental en América Latina*, edited by Paulo Antonio Paranaguá (Editorial Cátedra, 2005); *Andrés Di Tella: cine documental y archivo personal*, edited by Paul Firbas and Pedro Meira Monteiro Siglo XXI, Argentina); and *Inventario de regresos: el cine documental de Andrés Di Tella*, edited by Casimiro Torreiro (Cines del Sur, 2011). Retrospectives of my work have been held at the Filmoteca de Catalunya (Barcelona), Filmoteca Española (Madrid), Cines de Sur (Granada), Museo Nacional de Artes Visuales (Montevideo), It´s All True Festival (Sao Paulo, Rio de Janeiro and Brasilia), Festival de Lima, and Centro Cultural Ricardo Rojas (Buenos Aires).

DR. LINDA DITTMAR, University of Massachusetts, Boston, US

For a professor of English teaching film and literature at the University of Massachusetts, Boston since 1969, mine is an unusual biography. I grew up in Israel before and after its founding in 1948, served in the Israeli army, earned a Stanford University PhD in English, and came of age politically at the cusp of the Civil Rights, Vietnam War, and Second-Wave feminist movements. My teaching reflects these concerns, as do my articles, book chapters and two edited books, *From Hanoi To HollywoodL: The Vietnam War in American Film* and *Multiple Voices in Feminist Film Criticism*. Though I am now an Emerita Professor, I continue these activities, including ongoing service on Radical Teacher's editorial board and a photo-text in progress, documenting what is still visible of pre-1948 Palestinian life inside Israel.

DR. ANGELICA FENNER, University of Toronto, Canada
I hold a cross-appontment at the University of Toronto as Associate Professor of German and Cinema Studies. Broadly speaking, I have been pursuing two distinct research strands over the years, which sometimes also overlap with one another: on the one hand, the politics of migration and mobility in European cinemas, and on the other, autobiographical or first person non-fiction film-making. I am the author of *Race Under Reconstruction in German Cinema: Robert Stemmle's Toxi* (University of Toronto Press, 2011) and am developing a second book project on first person filmmaking in contemporary Germany. I am also co-editing with Robin Curtis a second volume of essays titled *The Autobiographical 'Turn' in German Documentary and Experimental Film,* and have published chapters in several film anthologies and in the journals *Camera Obscura, Feminist Media Studies,* and *Women in German Yearbook.*

SABEENA GADIHOKE, Jamia University, India
I live in New Delhi, India where I teach Video and TV production at the AJK Mass Communication Research Center, Jamia University. Besides being an independent documentary filmmaker and camerawoman, I am also a photo historian and curator and I enjoy the mesh of theory and practice in my work. Starting my career in 1986 as a producer/director of educational films, I was a founder-member of an independent women's video collective that made three films on gender and religious fundamentalism in India. The Mediastorm Collective did not make any films after 1991 but we have remained close friends since and continue to collaborate with each other in our professional lives. During 1995–96 a course that I audited on women and photography during a Fulbright fellowship at Syracuse University would have a decisive impact on my research interests. My documentary *Three Women and a Camera* (1998) won awards at Film South Asia in Kathmandu in 1999 and the Mumbai International film festival in 2000. The film was the beginning of a long association with India's first women press photographer Homai Vyarawalla, one that has continued for 14 years. I published a book on her entitled *Camera Chronicles of Homai Vyarawalla* in 2006 and have recently curated a retrospective exhibition of Vyarawalla's work at the National Gallery of Modern Art in three Indian cities. Much of my academic writing since then has focused on trying to map a cultural history of post-independence Indian photography.

DR. JOSÉ GATTI, Universidade Federal de São Carlos in São Paulo, Brazil
I once thought of becoming an actor; I turned out to be a teacher instead. I guess that was the way I found to secure a permanent leading role on the stage.

I was born in 1951, built two houses in the woods, planted numerous (now huge) trees, had two wonderful (now grown up) children, lovers (of both sexes), wrote and edited books (mostly on audiovisual media), helped found Socine (the Brazilian Society for Cinema and Audiovisual Studies) and after all these years I've come to the conclusion that my best works were done along with my friends. I presently live in São Paulo, a frantic, stimulating, ever-changing metropolis.

DR. PETER HUGHES, La Trobe University, Australia

As a Senior Lecturer in Strategic Communication at La Trobe University, Melbourne, my teaching and research has been concerned for some time with the place of the documentary project in the 'post broadcast' mediascape. The main threads in my work concern documentary, new media, and cultural theories of trust and privacy.

DR. ALEXANDRA JUHASZ, Pitzer College, US

I am a Professor of Media Studies at Pitzer College, teaching video production and media theory. My books include *AIDS TV, Women of Vision, and F is for Phony* (co-edited with Jesse Lerner). I produced Cheryl Dunye's first person fake documentary feature films *The Watermelon Woman* (1995) and *The Owls* (2010) as well as my own autobiographical works on AIDS, feminist families and the Iraq War. I recently published an online born-digital 'video-book', *Learning from YouTube* (available for free from the MIT Press, 2011) about my experiences learning on and about YouTube with my students and day-to-day YouTubers. I blog about activist media at www.aljean.wordpress.com.

DR. ELSPETH KYDD, University of the West of England, UK

I am currently a Senior Lecturer in Film Studies and Video Production and I have a PhD in Radio/TV/Film from Northwestern University. As both a practicing documentary video-maker and a publishing scholar I have a strong commitment to the integration of theory with practice. This commitment has led to the development of a film studies textbook, *The Critical Practice of Film* (Allyn and Bacon, 2006) which introduces students to film studies and practice from this approach. My research specialisation is in film and particularly the interaction between discourses of race, post-colonial theory, queer theory and feminism. My earlier work theorises the representation of inter-racial sexuality in classical Hollywood cinema, a topic that by nature explores the intersection of discourses of race, gender and sexuality. My current project on passing in science fiction television uses as its theoretical base the fluidity of the idea of racial passing to deconstruct essentialist notions of (fixed) identity. My video work has included the award-winning *Exile's Complex* and the two documentaries *Lick Bush in '92* and *Drag in for Votes*. These projects, co-directed with Gabriel Gomez in the early 1990s, followed the political career of drag queen activist Joan Jett Blakk as she ran for Mayor of Chicago and then President of the USA on the Queer Nation ticket. My current project is *Stone Street*, a first person documentary about Caribbean diaspora family experiences and the complexity and displacement of ideas of home. It incorporates home movie footage and engages with the fragmentation of memory and identity within the context of diaspora.

DR. ALISA LEBOW, Brunel University, UK
I have asked everyone to submit their bios in the first person, and I now see how awkward a task it is. It forces a more confessional, less professional address, yet one feels somehow bound to also assert a professional stance, however improbable. I am a film theorist as well as a practitioner, originally from New York, relocated to London via Istanbul. My scholarly interests are generally in the area of documentary studies, broadly conceived. I have written a book on Jewish first person films entitled, appropriately enough, *First Person Jewish* (University of Minnesota Press, 2008), and have organised several symposia and conference panels on the subject of first person documentaries worldwide, out of which this volume arose. I am particularly proud to be one of the founding members of docIstanbul, a centre for the promotion of documentary film based at Bosphorus University in Istanbul, where we organized the XVII Visible Evidence Conference in 2010. My current work revolves around questions concerning 'the political' in documentary, first person and otherwise.

DR. PETER LIMBRICK, University of California, Santa Cruz, US
A New Zealander who left for a PhD in Australia before landing on still another Pacific coast, I am an associate professor of film and digital media at the University of California, Santa Cruz, where I teach critical studies in film with an emphasis on postcolonial and transnational cinema, film and video from the Middle East, and gender and sexuality. My first book, *Making Settler Cinemas: Film and Colonial Encounters in the United States, Australia, and New Zealand* (Palgrave, 2010) examines the relationships between settler colonialism and cinema in the wake of the British empire and under the transformations of Hollywood. Related essays appeared in *Screening the Past*, *Camera Obscura*, *Journal of Visual Culture* and *Cinema Journal*. My most recent research and publication is on Arab cinemas and I am working on programming and writing projects related to film and history in the region.

DR. SOPHIE MAYER, Cambridge University, UK
I work between academia, journalism and poetry on feminist, queer and transnational intermedia, writing regularly for *Sight & Sound* and *The F-Word*. *The Cinema of Sally Potter: The Politics of Love* (Wallflower Press, 2009), my first book, led to adventures in curation: firstly, a 2009 retrospective of Sally Potter's work for the BFI, and then first-ever festival programme of feminist documentary for Punto de Vista in Pamplona in 2011, with documentary blogger Elena Oroz. For Punto de Vista, I also edited *The Personal is Political*, a collection of classic essays on feminist documentary, and, with Corinn Columpar, also co-edited the collection *There She Goes: Feminism, Filmmaking and Beyond* (Wayne State University Press, 2009), which includes an essay by Michelle Citron. My poetry collections *Her Various Scalpels* (Shearsman, 2009), *The Private Parts of Girls* (Salt, 2011) and *Kiss Off* (Oystercatcher, 2011) all contain meditations/remediations of filmic texts, particularly examining the tensions between the lyric and the cinematic 'I' where it speaks gender and desire.

DR. LAURA RASCAROLI, University College, Cork, Ireland
I was born in Italy but now teach and live in Ireland. My research often focuses on realism, communication, self-representation, authorship and spectatorship, as well as on questions of identity, space and movement. I have written three books in collaboration with Ewa Mazierska: *From Moscow to Madrid: European Cities, Postmodern Cinema* (2003), *The Cinema of Nanni Moretti: Dreams and Diaries* (2004), and *Crossing New Europe: Postmodern Travel and the European Road Movie* (2006). Currently, I am particularly interested in first person, essayistic non-fiction; my monograph *The Personal Camera: Subjective Cinema and the Essay Film*, was published by Wallflower Press in 2009. Most recently, I co-edited two volumes of essays: *The Cause of Cosmopolitanism: Dispositions, Models, Transformations* (with Patrick O'Donovan; Peter Lang, 2011) and *Antonioni: Centenary Essays* (with John David Rhodes; BFI, 2011).

INTRODUCTION
Alisa Lebow

'The Cinema of Me' is something of a deceptive title for a collection of essays about first person documentary films. Deceptive in that it preys on the all-too-readily accepted impression of first person films as self-absorbed, myopic, ego-driven films that only a mother could love, despite the fact that the films discussed in this book, almost without exception, defy such expectations. The title does, however, point to the levity, humour and playfulness with which a filmmaker may approach her or his self-representation, further debunking the myth of the stultifying seriousness with which a filmmaker might choose to represent herself. And yet in this volume we take a serious look at the implications of this mode of representation, examining a broad range of first person filmmaking from around the world in order to both expand the ambit of what may constitute its practice(s), and to analyse the contribution such films make to the documentary form and to the very notion of self-represen-tation.

First person films can be poetic, political, prophetic or absurd. They can be autobiographical in full, or only implicitly and in part. They may take the form of self-portrait, or indeed, a portrait of another. They are, very often, not a cinema of 'me', but about someone close, dear, beloved or intriguing, who nonetheless informs the filmmaker's sense of him or herself. They may not be about a person, self or other, at all, but about a neighborhood, a community, a phenomenon or event. The designation 'first person film' is foremost about a mode of address: these films 'speak' from the articulated point of view of the filmmaker who readily acknowledges her subjective position. Whether this is done in the first person singular or in the first person plural, is in part, the concern of this book.

As anyone who has ever attempted to ascribe a grammar to film knows, cinema is a somewhat recalcitrant object, refusing to cede to the rigid demands of the form: language has grammar; film – in its proliferating semiotics, its indeterminate syntax, its ultimate resistance to rules – does not. As James Monaco quipped many years ago, it's 'impossible to be ungrammatical in film' (1981: 119). However, I cling to the grammatical formulation for two reasons. Firstly, it allows me to identify a documentary mode or classification, under which can fall a broad range of related yet divergent practices: the self portrait film, the essay film, the video diary, as well as any other documentary form that endeavours to articulate rather than occlude or suppress the position of the filmmaker. In saying this, of course, I open a can of worms. Must the filmmaker's voice literally be heard? Is not their perspective always, implicitly at least, available to be read? In other words, is not this designation too broad to be useful? Would not all documentary, if not all filmic and indeed artistic practice fall under this classification then? My answer is yes, and no. We can, of course, if our tendency is toward the pedantic, argue that all film can ultimately be read as first person, in the same way we can admit, as Christian Metz once did, that every film is a fiction film (1982: 44); or conversely, as Bill Nichols later volleyed back, that every film is a documentary (2001: 1). All of these claims hold true simultaneously and yet do nothing to further a discerning enquiry into the subject at hand. It is far more useful, not to mention more intriguing, to limit the sphere of debate to a broad enough set of practices that admit for a diversity of aims and approaches, while not so broad as to obviate the relevance of the category entirely. Like all categories, it is imperfect. Yet I would argue that it is less imperfect as an umbrella term, than 'autobiographical' documentary, the term preferred by several authors writing on the topic until now (see Lane 2002; Renov 2004a; Gabara 2006). For it should soon become clear, as I have already intimated both here and elsewhere (see Lebow 2008), that first person film is not primarily, and certainly not always explicitly, autobiographical. Subjective as it may always be, the exploration of the filmmaker's own biography is a much less centrally important pursuit in these films than one might expect.

The second reason I cling to the grammatical designation 'first person', and just as pertinently for the study at hand, is for its own formal dualism. The first person grammatical structure can be either singular or plural. By not specifying which form is to be privileged, we allow the resonances to reverberate between the I and the we — to imagine indeed, that the one doesn't speak without the other, that in fact, the 'I' inheres in the 'we', if not vice versa. I find myself increasingly persuaded by Jean Luc Nancy's (2000) formulation of the singular plural, wherein the individual 'I' does not exist alone, but always 'with' another, which is to say being one is never singular but always implies and indeed embodies another. That means the 'I' is always social, always already in relation, and when it speaks, as these filmmakers do, in the first person, it may appear to be in the first person singular 'I' but ontologically speaking, it is always in effect, the first person plural 'we'. The grammatical reference reminds us that language itself, though spoken by an individual, is never entirely our own invention, nor anyone else's. Despite the fact that we believe it to express our individuality, it nonetheless also expresses our commonality, our plurality, our interrelatedness with a group, a mass, a sociality, if not a society. This is as true about the expression of individuality and subjectivity in first person films as it is in language itself. And that is precisely what I find most arresting and fascinating about first person films. They are quite the opposite, in most cases, of the singular 'I', and can even be understood to be a 'cinema of we', rather than a 'cinema of me'. Had that not presented itself as such a ghastly clunker of a title, in fact, it would likely have supplanted the current title of this book, which takes as its premise that the speaking, and in this case filming, subject is neither solipsistic nor monologic, but is always already in dialogue or as Nancy might have it, always already 'speaking with'.

The very act of communicating, whether writing or filming, implies an other, at the very least an interlocutor or audience. Indeed, many times we find that first person filmmaking goes further, well beyond the self, focusing its sights on another as the 'protagonist', the main attraction, and 'subject' of the film, be it a lover, icon, nemesis, relative, friend or some larger collectivity (affective, proximate, imagined community, clan, group, and so on) or phenomenon. This necessarily implies a dialogue between subjects, rather than insisting on the subject/object relations of the traditional documentary. And of course, beyond any notion of traditional dialogue, it also entails the dialogic splitting of subjectivity, as suggested earlier.

Thus, articulating an address in the first person emphatically does not imply an autonomous and autogenous 'speaking self' as if the Cartesian subject had never undergone review. Although it is true that some filmmakers may share an enlightenment conception of the 'rational' and knowable unitary self, it is less true to say that self-representation in film (or otherwise) is ever such a straightforward and singular pursuit. Not only is the constitution of subjectivity a much more complicated endeavour than such a model would imply, its representation further co-implicates others in the process of mediation.[1] Additionally, we should remember, that there is no such thing as a universally apprehended or accepted model of subjectivity. In fact, one of the justifications for promoting a version of subjectivity that belies the individuality so touted in Western conceptualisations of the self is to create a context in which other modes and models of subjectivity may be explored. That said, my own dependence on mostly Western contemporary philosophical thought reveals the limits of my intellectual training that I nonetheless hope for this volume to begin to redress, if only preliminarily. Ideally it can spark further enquiries. Thus one of the aims in surveying cultural paradigms is to excavate different conceptions of the self, to imagine multiple and even competing models of subjectivity itself.

The matter of knowing ourselves or coming to consciousness about ourselves is not only a central ontological question, ultimately unknowable yet endlessly surmised by philosophers but it is also at the centre of the project of self-representation. What is this self that is being represented and is the desire to represent this self (in language, through images) a formative one, constituting rather than re-presenting this self? Do we become ourselves and come to know ourselves in the process of self-representation? Surely if this is the case, then the process of self-representation is also constitutive of an illusion, that of the unified self, as it is obvious upon reflection that this act of representation itself implies a splitting, and it is here that we should be reminded of the second term in the subtitle of this volume: subjectivity.

When a filmmaker makes a film with herself as a subject, she is already divided as both the subject matter of the film and the subject making the film. The two senses of the word are immediately in play – the matter and the making – thus the two ways of being subjectified as, if you will, both subject and object. Let us briefly note that in the Middle Ages, the Oxford English Dictionary indicates, the meanings of these two words were the reverse of what we now know them to be, but only 'subject' still retains both possible significations. There is the important philosophical notion of subjection put into play here, where one only becomes a subject (in the sense of an individual with rights, needs and desires) through the process of subjection to an order, social, political and, of course, symbolic. One becomes oneself as a subject, subject to laws and powers beyond oneself, which are nonetheless constitutive of that self. Inherent in this formulation is the somewhat troubling idea that before we can imagine ourselves at all, before we can think of ourselves as independent or autonomous, we are already subject to another's will, to other powers and forces not of our own making, and indeed, subject to another's gaze as well. Linking notions of subjecthood and subjectivisation, then, inextricably ties the concept of the individual to entire systems of relation, interdependency and power. If we then link the process of subjective representation to self-representation as the title implies, it quickly becomes clear that it entails a process of becoming both subject and object of the gaze, a somewhat antinomous position that is nonetheless constitutive of being able to reflect upon and represent the self.

There is no simple subjectivity, and even deceptively simple representations of the self nonetheless imply an impossibly multiple positionality of subject/object. Thus the project of first person filmmaking (or rather, mediamaking) always carries with it a challenge to the notion of the unified subject.

This doubled position is implied in Michael Renov's cleverly titled book, *The Subject of Documentary* (2004a). Renov teasingly concludes his introduction by observing 'that the subject in documentary has, to a surprising degree, become the subject *of* documentary' (2004a: xxiv). That it should be a surprise has more to do with documentary's own repressions, but indeed it is not a transition, a move from one modality (subject in) to the next (subject of), as implied in this formulation. Rather, it is an awkward simultaneity – being the subject *in* and *of* at the same time – that makes first person filmmaking so complex, co-implicated and, indeed, so compelling.[2]

It is important to consider the challenge that first person filmmaking poses within the documentary field. Subjectivity is by no means a new documentary modality, yet the traditional posture of the theatrical and television documentary around the world has been historically that of objectivity. The personal point of view of the filmmaker was typically elided, left to languish on the cutting-room floor, while more positivist assertions have always taken preference. Prior to the 1980s, with a few notable exceptions, the first person address remained mostly within the purview of avant-garde filmmakers.[3] The artist's vision could be foregrounded at a time when the documentarian's had to be suppressed. The emergence of the subjective voice in documentary had long been hampered by the burden of disinterested objectivity, an impossible ideal that required innumerable evasions and repressions to effect.[4] However, for the past quarter of a century, especially but not exclusively in the West, incursions into the first person mode of address have become increasingly common, with the field of first person filmmaking gaining steady momentum. In the first person film, the filmmaker's subjectivity is not only brought back into frame, it permanently ruptures the illusion of objectivity so long maintained in documentary practice and reception.[5] In truth, first person film goes beyond simply debunking documentary's claim to objectivity. In the very awkward simultaneity of being subject *in* and subject *of*, it actually unsettles the dualism of the objective/subjective divide, rendering it inoperative.

* * *

Several years have passed since a US film distributor friend of mine warned me that European festivals had tired of what they perceived to be an American epidemic of first person films. It was the first time it had dawned on me that first person filmmaking might be perceived as peculiarly American and it was at that point that I began to enquire of friends and colleagues around the world, filmmakers and film scholars alike, if first person filmmaking was emerging out of their own cultural contexts or if it constituted yet another American imperialist invasion. The likes of Michael Moore and Morgan Spurlock might incline us to the latter view (albeit of the friendlier face of cultural imperialism, if such a thing can be imagined), but without investigating further it was impossible to know. Not surprisingly, I quickly learned that first person film, though perhaps most elaborated in the context of North American filmmaking at least in the 1990s, was indeed making its presence felt in geographical regions as diverse as India, Brazil, Australia, China and Guinea. While this emergence has not been uniform in all places, nor does it necessarily imply an autonomous cultural context, free from the influence of North American media and education, it did intrigue me enough to pursue the idea that subjectivity in documentary cinema might indeed find varied expression, not only due to individual filmmaker's idiosyncrasies, but also due to differing cultural conceptions and configurations of the self. After all, the proscription against it, in the form of this anonymous distributor's informal warning, had come before anyone had properly considered the phenomenon with any serious attention.

In the past decade, first person film has arrived on the scholarly scene, with several monographs dedicated to its various permutations. As indicated earlier, some authors take autobiography as their starting point (Lane 2002; Renov 2004a; Gabara 2006), some take the question of subjectivity in documentary as an organising principle (MacDougall 1998; Renov 2004a), still others analyse individual modes of address, such as the 'essay film' (Rascaroli 2009), vernacular video (Dovey 2000) or the home movie (Moran 2002; Ishizuka and Zimmerman 2007). Other designations abound: auto- or domestic-ethnography (Russell 1999; Renov 2004a); performativity (Bruzzi 2000; Nichols 2001); and prior to these the preferred designation was reflexivity or self-reflexive film (Ruby 1988; Nichols 1991; MacDougall 1998). I believe the term 'first person' is uniquely able to include and incorporate the range of these related yet at times distinct practices all of which in one way or another find their way into the pages of this book.

The majority of the studies into various aspects of first person filmmaking focus on films from North America and/or Europe. This collection distinguishes itself in several ways. It is the first edited collection to approach the question of international first person filmmaking. Rather than focusing on one filmmaker, mode or region, it instead attempts to take a rough survey of the field internationally. It asks, in implicit and sometimes explicit ways, what are the conditions for the emergence of the first person mode of address in various parts of the world and what are its consequences? With essays written about first person practices in India, Brazil, Argentina, the Caribbean, Palestine, Israel, Lebanon, Italy, Spain, Australia, the United Kingdom and the United States, this volume takes a broad look at a phenomenon that, though articulated differently in every instance, has become truly global. There is also the consideration of the emergence of first person practices on the internet, a digital medium that defies geographical borders and further complicates the already problematised notion of an integrated, embodied subjectivity. The breadth of the volume's purview does not compromise its depth, however, as each essay examines its subject in a theoretically challenging and innovative manner. With essays by practioners, theorists and practitioner-theorists, the style and approach to the work is also varied and operates in productive dialogue, as the assertions of a talented filmmaker such as Andrés Di Tella, suggesting that his essayistic film form is a matter of trial and error[6] rubs up against the certainties proposed by the eloquent theorist of the essay form, Laura Rascaroli, as she identifies the masterful strategies of Antonioni's complex final identifications. The volume as a whole explores a range of first person iterations emerging at this moment in history, examining the role of geopolitical contexts as well as ethnicity, cultural identity and personal history in the construction of subjectivity in contemporary first person documentary.

This book asks, what is the nature of the interplay between the individual and culture and how is this tension played out in representational terms? How, or in what ways, can culture and ethnicity and even geopolitics be said to 'construct' the first person character on screen? In what contexts and for what reasons do we find first person filmmaking flourishing, and where is it still an unknown or unwelcome practice? We might even begin to ask why it emerges in certain contexts and not others.

The volume is divided into four sections: first person singular; first person plural; diasporic subjectivity; virtual subjectivity.

First person singular explores first person films that, in the main, directly attempt to represent an individual filmmaker's own subjectivity in relation to his or her larger collectivities, including several reflexive essays where the authors discuss their own first person films. This volume welcomes the critical reflections of makers' own first person filmic (and other media) articulations – in this section and elsewhere in the book. UK filmmaker and scholar Michael Chanan's essay begins the section by situating his own first person film in relation to some of the better known first person filmmaking practices in the field. Argentinian filmmaker Andrés Di Tella also tells of his own process of self-narration, identifying ways in which the endeavour is implicitly public and political, a social rather than a selfish act. Both Chanan and Di Tella would find their stories impossible to tell without engaging a range of historical and political phenomena. The next two essays, by Jose Gatti and Laura Rascaroli, in some sense also tarry unavoidably with the historical and political, as they discuss world-renowned auteurs' incursions into first person filmmaking. Gatti gives us a perspective on the always engaging yet ever unpredictable Glauber Rocha, as he stages himself multiply in one of his lesser known films, *Claro* (1975). Rascaroli's essay looks at the final film of Michelangelo Antonioni, as he casts himself in the shadow of the even better known Michelangelo's work. Digital enhancements allow Antonioni to portray his preferred vision of himself, taking tremendous creative licence, as any master might do, in the representation of the self. The filmmaker in Efrén Cuevas's essay, Mercedes Álvarez, ties her history in with generations that came before, as she contemplates the cyclical time in the town of her birth. In her film, *El cielo gira* (*The Sky Turns*, 2004), it is not the filmmaker but the town that takes centre stage, however, while there is an even further displacement at work in Kamal Aljafari's film, *The Roof* (*Al Sateh*, 2006). In *The Roof*, as explored by Peter Limbrick, Aljafari's family stands in for the thousands of Palestinian families who stayed behind as Palestine was forcibly transformed into the State of Israel, while also retaining the particularities of their circumstances as formative of the filmmaker's own memory and identity. Limbrick thus engages the interventions posed by queer theory to read Aljafari's radically displaced and non-normative first person film. This section includes discussions of films where the filmmaker's presence is apparent and his or her identifications are made manifest.

First person plural enters somewhat more fraught territory, wherein the films could be said to engage in a more circuitous route to self-representation, and the films under discussion here take many avenues to the self. Angelica Fenner details the myriad positionalities of the self that US filmmaker Jennifer Fox deploys in her six-hour documentary project *Flying*. While Fox herself may have an uncritical approach to her own subjectivity, Fenner ably deconstructs the layers of identification in the work and the uneven distribution of authorial power. Sabeena Gadihoke's essay examines three Indian first person films in the context of a documentary film tradition that, prior to this century, appeared to have little place for overt subjectivity. In one of the films discussed, Shohini Ghosh's *Tales of the Night Fairies*, we see a different approach from Fox's to the question of surrogacy of the self, that is also at issue in Fenner's essay. Ghosh's film involves a first person dissembling of sorts, as the filmmaker attempts to position the subjects of her film as a series of surrogate selves, identifying with their sexual rebelliousness and outcast status, while deftly avoiding her own embodiment of such a socially reprobate position.

The final essay in this section focuses on Israeli first person representation in relation to the Palestinian *Nakba*. Linda Dittmar weaves her own first person narrative into her investigation of a selection of challenging films that detail aspects of the decades-old occupation that have indeed become a profound preoccupation for the filmmakers in question. It may be worth noting that Israel has a preponderance of first person filmmakers, something not nearly as common for filmmakers in the rest of the region. Not surprisingly, and perhaps not unrelatedly, we do find a higher degree of first person filmmaking also in Palestine and Lebanon, suggesting that the drive toward subjective filmmaking in the region is, directly or indirectly, tied to the political. Within documentary practices of the Middle East, those most inclined to take up first person film-making are precisely those who have experienced both an excess of mediation (predominantly via the news media), and in direct proportion, an excess of violent conflict. That is to say, in our contemporary world, war-zones beget not only mass mediation, but more recently a rash of self-mediation. However, the forms of first person address may be said to differ considerably and deserve further individual and comparative attention.

Diasporic subjectivity takes diasporic identities as its organising principle, with all of the complexities and permutations that may entail. Whether con-sidering the multiple fictions of the diasporic home movies of a Trinidadian/ Scottish family in filmmaker/theorist Elspeth kydd's self-reflexive essay, or the multiple levels of cultural denials unpacked by Sophie Mayer with regard to Michelle Citron's CD-ROM project, *Mixed Greens*, this section examines the complex sets of identifications and dis-identifications inherent in diasporic self-representation. It also looks, via my own contribution, at the uncanny role of the filmic apparatus itself in some recent diasporic first person films, play-ing as it does an active role in the accelerated displacements of contemporary global migration.

Virtual subjectivity, the final section of this volume, looks at the emergence of virtual identities and the implications they have on contemporary self-repre-sentation. Here the disembodiment of traditional cinema and video is further enacted, making questions of 'autobiography' and first person all the more abstract and defamiliarised. Both contributors to this section, Peter Hughes and Alex Juhasz examine the virtual imaginings of politics and communities of YouTubers, yet they do so using very different stylistic and theoretical para-digms. Hughes' rather more sober sociological analysis contrasts nicely with Juhasz's decidedly experimental, yet certainly no less theoretically rigorous and challenging, style. There is the sense in these final essays that the self may have fully come undone, even as its representations proliferate seemingly infi-nitely into cyberspace.

Notes

1   For a much more elaborated discussion of dialogic notions of subjectivity see Nancy (2000); see also Levinas (1998) and Butler (2005).
2   This play on words between complication and co-implication is developed in Renov (2004b).
3   One of the first articles ever written on autobiographical non-fiction film focused on avant-garde films; see Sitney (1978). Two notable, but by no means the only exceptions to which I allude, include Joyce Chopra's *Joyce at 34* (1972, US) and Kazuo Hara's *Extreme Private Eros: Love Song* (1974, Japan). Surely one of the most important prototypes of the first person film is Jean Rouch and Edgar Morin's *Chronique d'un été* (1960), which articulates its address from the start in the grammar of the first person plural 'we'. Some of Agnés Varda's early documentaries, such as her *Uncle Yanco* (1967) and *Daggueréotypes* (1976) also foregrounded the filmmaker's subjective gaze, or as Varda would likely put it, her auteurist vision. There are other early feminist first person films of note, such as Amalie Rothschild's *Nana, Mom and Me* (1974) and Michele Citron's *Daughter Rite* (1978).
4   Renov makes reference to documentary's 'repression of subjectivity' in the introduction to *The Subject of Documentary* (2004a: xviii).
5   Renov makes this argument in his cogent essay on first person films (2008), as do I in the introduction to my book *First Person Jewish* of the same year.
6   The term *ensayo* in Spanish means 'essay' but as in French, it is also the word used for 'trial' as in the phrase 'trial and error', allowing a play on words in Spanish that requires this clumsy explanation in English.

References

Bruzzi, S. (2000) *New Documentary: A Critical Introduction*. London: Routledge.

Butler, J. (2005) *Giving an Account of Oneself*. New York, NY: Fordham University Press.

Cuevas E. and C. Muguiro, eds. (2002) *El hombre sin la cámara: El cine de Alan Berliner/ The Man Without the Movie Camera: The Cinema of Alan Berliner*. Madrid: Ediciones Internacionales Universitarias.

Cuevas E. and A. N. García (2008) *Landscapes of the Self: The Cinema of Ross McElwee/ Paisajes del Yo: El cine de Ross McElwee*. Madrid: Ediciones Internacionales Universitarias.

Dovey, J. (2000) *Freak Show: First Person Media and Factual Television*. London: Pluto Press.

Gabara, R. (2006) *From Split to Screened Selves: French and Francophone Autobiography in the Third Person*. Stanford, CA: Stanford University Press.

Ishizuka, K. and P. Zimmermann (eds) (2007) *Mining the Home Movie: Excavations in Histories and Memories*. Berkeley, CA: University of California Press.

Lane, J. (2002) *The Autobiographical Documentary in America*. Madison, WI: University of Wisconsin Press.

Lebow, A. S. (2008) *First Person Jewish*. Minneapolis, MN: University of Minnesota Press.

Levinas, E. (1998) *Otherwise than Being or Beyond Essence*, trans. A. Lingis. Pittsburgh, PA: Duquesne University Press.

López, J. M. (2008) *Naomi Kawase. El cine en el umbral*. Madrid: T&B editores.

MacDougall, D. (1998) *Transcultural Cinema*. Princeton, NJ: Princeton University Press.

Martín Gutiérrez, G. (2008) *Cineastas frente al espejo*. Madrid: T&B editores.

Metz, C. (1982) *The Imaginary Signifier*. Bloomington, IN: Indiana University Press.

Monaco. J. (1981) *How to Read a Film*. Oxford: Oxford University Press.

Moran, J. (2002) *There's No Place Like Home Video*. Minneapolis, MN: University of Minnesota Press.

Nancy, J. L. (2000) *Being Singular Plural*. Stanford, CA: Stanford University Press.

Nichols, B. (1991) *Representing Reality*. Berkeley, CA: University of California Press.

____ (2001) *Introduction to Documentary*. Bloomington, IN: Indiana University Press.

Rascaroli, L. (2009) *The Personal Cinema: Subjective Cinema and the Essay Film*. London: Wallflower Press.

Renov, M. (2004a) *The Subject of Documentary*. Minneapolis, MN: University of Minnesota Press.

____ (2004b) 'Domestic Ethnography and the Construction of the "Other" Self', in *The Subject of Documentary*. Minneapolis, MN: University of Minnesota Press, 216–29.

____ (2008) 'First Person Film: Some Theses on Self-Inscription', in T. Austin and W. De Jong (eds) *Rethinking Documentary: New Perspectives, New Practices*. Berkshire, UK: McGraw Hill/Open University Press, 39–50.

Ruby, J. (1988) 'The Image Mirrored: Reflexivity in Documentary Film', in A. Rosenthal (ed.) *New Challenges in Documentary*. Berkeley, CA: University of California Press, 64–77.

Russell, C. (1999) *Experimental Ethnography: The Work of Film in the Age of Video*. Durham, NC: Duke University Press.

Sitney, P. A. (1978) 'Autobiography in Avant-Garde Film', in P. A. Sitney (ed.) *The Avant-Garde Film: A Reader of Theory and Criticism*. New York, NY: New York University Press, 199–246.

The Role of History in the Individual: Working Notes for a Film

Michael Chanan

It follows, then, that by virtue of particular traits of their character individuals can influence the fate of society. Sometimes this influence is very considerable; but the possibility of exercising this influence, and its extent, are determined by the form of organisation of society, by the relation of forces within it. The character of an individual is a 'factor' in social development only where, when, and to the extent that social relations permit it to be such.

> Georgi Plekhanov, 'The Role of the Individual in History' (1898/1940: 41)

1

The film archives are full of neglected newsreels and documentaries, fragmentary traces serving as signs of what is mostly forgotten – moments robbed from history, briefly exhibited, and then, except for a few iconic examples, relegated to the shelves and catalogues. This field of the semiosis of the historical trace is the terrain of the film that occasions these notes, which were drafted while the film was being made, and completed after the editing was finished. *The American Who Electrified Russia* is about the role of an individual in history, but also of history in the individual – a biographical investigation of my maternal grandmother's cousin, Solomon Abramovich Trone (1872–1969). Walter Benjamin spoke of 'the enigmatic question of the nature of human existence as such, but also of the biographical historicity of the individual' (1977: 166). To recount this biography, the film constructs a dialogue between family memory and the archive, both public and private, with their photographs and films, documents and mementos, and discovers that there are gaps between them. I guessed this would happen, and from the outset wanted to make a film which

15

Poster based on Soviet original

foregrounded the problems by presenting the process of investigation, and not just the results.

Trone's life was intertwined with History, but in a paradoxical fashion. A participant in the revolutions of 1905 and 1917, he was an electrical engineer who became a director at General Electric (GE), the foremost American corporation of its day, and thus, although unrecorded in the history books, a key figure in the electrification of the Soviet Union. In 1928, when GE became the first American corporation to sign a contract with the Bolsheviks, the signatory on behalf of GE was Trone, who himself was closely involved in the technical design of projects like the Dnepr Dam. Later, after retiring from GE, he worked as an industrial adviser in China, India and Israel. In 1940, he helped to rescue Jewish refugees from Nazism; five years later, he was appointed to the Allied Reparations Commission, which reported to the Potsdam Conference at the end of the war. Ironically I owe my good fortune that he came to live in London when I was growing up to Senator McCarthy and American paranoia about Communism. Trone had gone to live in the USA in 1916, giving up his membership of the Bolshevik Party, and later becoming an American citizen; when they took away his passport in 1953 he found himself on a visit to London, and decided to stay; otherwise I would probably not now be telling his story.

The film will recuperate forgotten history, but the first thing I know I have to accept, because this is a family film, is that in order to make it, I have to be in it. I cannot avoid it becoming a first person film, in which I participate along with my cousin, Trone's daughter Sasha, and other family members, in front of the camera – which is something I have never desired. When I started out in the early 1970s, by making a pair of films on contemporary music for BBC2, I readily adopted the mode of the television arts documentary, or at least that version of the genre that took the form of the filmic essay. Loosely defined, this is a mode of documentary which encourages stylistic experiment, and while the camera focusses on the character and personality of the subject, the filmmaker is present through the 'voice' of the film; it was often introduced by the programme anchor as 'a personal viewpoint'. Within this format, I didn't mind being heard interacting with my subjects on the soundtrack, but preferred not to be seen, and I have pretty much stuck with this since. This time is going to be different: an historical essay and first person family film combined.

2

The filmic essay is loosely defined – because there is no tighter way to define it. The essay film is not a genre in the normal sense, built out of a permutation of a certain repertoire of features. With my theoretical cap on, I have long believed that this is anyway not a very good way to approach the nature of genre, which in practice is always, as Mikhail Bakhtin demonstrated throughout his work, much more fluid and porous than logical definitions seem to suppose. This is especially true in the case of the documentary, of which Joris Ivens somewhere wrote that it constitutes a 'creative no-man's land', like an interloper in the genre system. Even more so in the case of the essay film, which can easily use any of the means and practices employed in any other mode of documentary filming.

Precisely the way the most disparate material gels into a narrative, a tale, or an argument, is the locus of the film's 'voice', which is thus, in part, a structuring absence (one reason it is so difficult to define). The institutional form of documentary, produced by or made for television, is the same, but here (except for zones of greater freedom like arts programming) the director has abdicated the authorial position in favour of the formulaic requirement of the slot, the schedules, the pretence of 'balance', the channel controller's prejudices and whims. The personal point of view of the essay here dissolves into an ideological soup. Nevertheless, if we are going to talk sensibly about the essay film, there is no point in restricting its varieties by arbitrarily limiting its criteria.

Of course, in working for television, I'd accepted that films had to have commentaries – it was part of the deal – but I grew to strongly dislike them. Especially after the experience of a piece of current affairs reportage on human rights in Cuba (*Cuba From Inside*, 'Dispatches', Channel Four, 1988) where the house style not only required a tight journalistic commentary but wall-to-wall speech, with no space for the pictures to breathe. In contrast, in classic documentaries by the likes of Joris Ivens, Georges Franju, Alain Resnais and Chris Marker, the film is visually led, and the spoken voiceover is a vehicle for essayistic and even poetic rumination. But these films rarely turn up in the canons of documentary recognised by the television professionals. (They belong to the art-house, and are only now beginning to come back into circulation on DVD, sometimes as supplementary 'extras' to a feature film.) Marker is a curious exception, because he moved his medium from film to video to multimedia, leaving much of his previous work by the wayside, where sadly it mostly remains (but the titles, including *Letter from Siberia*, 1957, and *Le Joli Mai*, 1963, are legendary). His commentaries for films by others – Resnais, Ivens – are already remarkable for their rich juxtaposition of verbal with visual imagery, or in Bakhtin's word, their dialogical texture. In later films of his own, like *Sans Soleil* (1983), this can no longer be called commentary – it is the very embodiment of the filmmaker speaking through voices, and a paradigm for the whole tradition of expanded cinema, avant-garde or experimental film and video, call it what you will, from the 1960s until today.

Television is exactly the opposite. It turns the use of commentary into a lazy way of making films, with the result that many of them become little more than illustrated radio programmes, nowadays with a dizzying dose of digital graphics. Nevertheless, they are still essay films, but in a mechanical and schematic register. Subject to external requirements like commercial breaks, the commentary keeps going back over the ground after each break before moving on, like a model school essay. Often informative, they remain rather shallow. (This is even nowadays true of science films, which demand a certain rigour, but if one compares the BBC's *Horizon* series today with thirty years ago, there's been some dumbing down.) If this is the result of television's quasi-industrial and increasingly managerialist mode of production, the model is nowadays only broken in individually crafted films by the likes of Adam Curtis, or the poet Tony Harrison, who demonstrate the imaginative use of the medium to develop a much more personal, potent and disturbing essayistic style.

Another mode of the essayistic comes to the fore in one of the dominant forms of television documentary, the presenter-led, which casts a high-profile figure from journalism or academia – such as John Pilger or Simon Schama – in the role of reporter or presenter. The formula here is the illustrated discourse written and delivered by the telegenic talent in ever-changing locations, manoeuvred by a director whose essential function is the technical one of devising the visual treatment. When it comes to sober and serious subjects like civilisation and history, then from Kenneth Clark to Niall Ferguson, what we get is the authoritative version of the mandarin class. The visual style is determined by the producer and director on duty but the personality on screen displaces the director as author of the film, the camera is turned into the talent's inevitable appendage, and generally reduced to an instrument to illustrate the verbal discourse. The image is dominated by the word in a regression to the didactic style of institutional documentary before the arrival of synchronous sound filming around the end of the 1950s.

Nowadays, of course, with the agility of video, there is an alternative, in which the directorial author takes their revenge by stepping into the role of the talent – I refer to names like Marcel Ophuls, Nick Broomfield, Michael Moore – reasserting authorship in a form that is both performative and folds back into the primacy of the camera itself as both witness and *agent provocateur* (capacities originally developed by *cinéma vérité* and direct cinema in the 1960s). Ophuls is the paradigm of the sober but ironic social commentator, in contrast to the buffoonery of Broomfield or Moore. A variant is found in Molly Dineen, who plays an invisible performative role from behind her own camera; as a result, her presence is constantly seen in the return glance of the person she's talking to, ingrained in the picture, but her voice is gentle, intensely inquisitive, and without a trace of the macho confrontation.

Except perhaps for the last, these models were not available to me when I returned to filmmaking ten years ago, after a decade teaching and writing. They were either unappealing, or else demanded more resources than I could lay my hands on within academia. What interested me was taking advantage within the academic arena of the potential of low-budget digital video to make films of ideas. This I proceeded to do in two ways. First, with some short scratch videos, made to be shown at conferences instead of presenting a paper, and thus a maximum of twenty minutes long. These were made entirely from found material, some of it my own, and dealt with topics like 9/11, orchestras and conductors, and film music. Second, long films, where I could explore the theme of a film through dialogue with different interlocutors. The first of these was solitary work, but very fast and mostly intuitive; this was *Human Wrongs* (2001). The second, *Detroit: Ruin of a City* (2005), was extended and planned (although only loosely – we're talking documentary here, which always has to respond to the unforeseen). It also employed a new form of collaboration to replace the dialogue that goes on within the traditional documentary crew.

In *Human Wrongs*, the theme is human rights, and the dialogue is with the writer Ariel Dorfman, as he participates in a series of events in Washington. The subject was his own idea, and he approved the edit but was not involved in it. In *Detroit: Ruin of a City*, about the rise and fall of the Motor City, the main interlocutor is the sociologist George Steinmetz from the nearby University of Michigan, who converses on screen with a range of characters including myself behind the camera. In neither film do I appear in front of camera, since in both cases I am shooting the film myself. The first is a straightforward director/cameraman film, enlivened by Ariel's direct address to the camera. For the second we found a different strategy, that of co-authorship from start to finish. The film is both an historical essay and a city film, but instead of a scripted commentary, we hit on the device of filming our conversation as we were making the film; but still I stayed off camera.

With *The American Who Electrified Russia*, however, I knew from the start that I couldn't remain unseen: if this was to be truly a family film, I had to be located within the family willy-nilly, and it would inevitably become a first person film. (I even in the end allowed myself to include three photographs of me as a boy.) But in order properly to succeed as a family film, it would have to be the first person plural of the family, speaking among ourselves, our own interlocutors. It had to represent the varied memories and various points of view, as well as the ambiguities and the gaps in our individual and collective knowledge, without unduly privileging anyone – except Trone's daughter, my cousin Sasha. (I remember thinking: how to construct this first person plural made up of multiple voices? I decided to film spontaneous conversations among groups of as many as five people, with two cameras, operating the second camera myself. Hopefully, the flow of cutting back and forth between the two would do the rest.)

The other thing which I know from the start: the film is a many-layered quest. To celebrate the memory of the man we all called 'Papa', it must work to recover his biography, which is dispersed among us, as well as consigned to photos and objects and papers but above all, paradoxical: Papa was both a revolutionary, and a director of one of the great corporations of the day. The film therefore needs to get at the gaps in what we know, or think we know, to discover how his biography fits into history. Not simply to present the findings of the investigation, but to include the process of search and discovery within the film, to interrogate the evidence in front of the viewer. Because as everyone says, his story is amazing and fascinating, and makes you rethink what you thought you knew about history but never dared to ask.

3

For years after Trone died, I often recounted something of his story to friends, as a way of keeping his memory alive. In the course of time, I began to think of making a film about him but without the faintest idea of quite how to do it. One friend – a film producer who came up with the title I have now adopted – suggested a low-budget feature film and offered to raise the money, but I said no, I couldn't do that, I couldn't see myself fictionalising his life. Then two things happened which made a documentary film possible.

The first was a discovery I made in a film archive in London. Trone had used his position at International General Electric to provide support for Lenin's plan for the electrification of the Soviet Union, announced in 1920; he himself was the technical designer of the centrepiece of the plan, the hydroelectric dam on the Dnepr known as Dneprostroi, the largest of its type in the world when it was opened in 1932. A few years ago I discovered a film in the ETV archive (now held by the National Film and Television Archive) called *КШЭ* or *KShE*, 'Komsomol Patron of Electrification', by Esfir Shub, which ends with the opening of Dneprostroi. I looked at it eagerly – it is in fact a remarkable film, which I've written about elsewhere (Chanan 2008). But no, he was not in it. Nevertheless, I began to wonder. Might it be possible to recount his life by juxtaposing family memory with archive footage? I did not yet know how complicated this was going to become.

The second element was even more serendipitous. I was contacted by an archivist in Toronto, David Evans, who had found out about Trone by a curious

Dnepr Dam as seen in Shub's *KShE*

Trone (left) in photo by Ilf

route and then discovered my website where I make mention of him. In 1935, when Trone was living in New York, the Russian satirists Ilf and Petrov – best known in the West as the authors of *The Twelve Chairs* (1928), which was filmed by both Mel Brooks in the USA and T. G. Alea in Cuba – visited the USA to undertake an extended piece of photojournalism, which was published both as a series of illustrated texts in the Soviet magazine *Ogonek* in 1936, and as a book, which appeared in English as *Little Golden America* (1944). Evans had read the book, a minor classic of Soviet popular literature, and been fascinated by the figures of Mr and Mrs Adams, who play host to the Russian pair, spending two months driving them across the country from New York to Los Angeles and back. Researching the writing of the book, he discovered that Mr and Mrs Adams were in fact Mr and Mrs Trone – Solomon and his second wife Florence (Sasha's mother). I already knew something about this episode, because Florence had delighted in telling stories about it towards the end of her life, and I'd read the book, but it wasn't until we tracked down *Ogonek* – in the Library of Congress, because there were no copies of editions from those years to be had in any library in the UK – that I discovered several photos in which Trone himself appears (although Florence sadly not).

David became a willing participant in the film when he came to London to find out more – this visit was the first thing that I shot, apart from some previously filmed memories of Papa by close family members – and later he joined Sasha and myself on a visit to Schenectady, and in this way comes to share the narration of Trone's extraordinary life with Sasha. On the editing table, the shape of the film emerged largely through their conversations with family and friends, in which several delightful anecdotes are told. The memories and stories are then interwoven with film archive and family photos, and with a third strand, comprised of interpreters of different moments and aspects of Papa's life: Misha Iampolsky, Tariq Ali and Eric Jacobson, and two historians who knew Trone in different circumstances: Romila Thapar from Delhi, and in London, Eric Hobsbawm. The narrative is thus entirely dialogical in construction; and indeed, on principle, I never considered the use of a commentary. But I always envisaged lots of captions for different types of information, many of them animated (this goes back to my admiration for Santiago Alvarez). The viewer would be invited to read the picture and not just look at it.

4

I start to think more about first person documentary, which has emerged in recent times as one of the major modes of documentary cinema. The term covers a multitude of sins. Some of them are fully autobiographical, many of them inspired by identity politics, but there are also those that choose to speak from a first person position in the role of witness, and sometimes participant observer, without being centred on the autobiographical self; in other words, where the filmmaker is present, on the soundtrack and often in view of the camera, embodying an individual and not an institutional point of view, addressing a piece of the world in front of them. This is what I have decided to opt for.

An early paradigm of this kind of approach is found in Michael Rubbo's reflexive and funny *Waiting for Fidel* (1974), which draws out in front of the camera the tension and dealings, normally unseen, that nonetheless always exist between the filmmaker and the film's funder, who oddly in this case is also present in the film, getting increasingly impatient as they wait for their promised meeting with the great man (which never transpires). I also think of a film by Raúl Ruiz, *Of Great Events and Ordinary People* (1978), where the exiled Chilean filmmaker is commissioned by French television to report on the French presidential elections from the perspective of the Paris *arrondissement* where he lives, and finds the task impossible because people treat him as an outsider; because he cannot vote, the film becomes the view of a non-participant observer. The manner in which special films like these represent the world is individual and stamped with the filmmaker's personality, without quite becoming egotistical. There are certain gradations which depend on where the filmmaker is located culturally, socially and institutionally. Rubbo and Ruiz, as outsiders, adopt an ironic voice. In *The American Who Electrified Russia* my location is not outside looking in (as in my two previous films) but inside looking back. Less ironic.

The first person documentary comes out of the cross-fertilisation of several currents, one of which goes back to the experimental diary film in the style of Jonas Mekas. The documentarist as such first famously stepped out in front of the camera in 1960 in *Chronique d'un été*, when the co-authors of the film, Jean Rouch and Edgar Morin, become active provocateurs of a new kind of self-reflexivity which went by the name of the phrase they attached to the title of the film – *cinéma vérité*. But around the same time, you also had the television reporter first crossing the gap from the voiceover to the talking head in front of the camera, whose speciality is speaking to people on the street and to the camera off the cuff – the former being a trope that in fact Rouch and Morin employ in the opening sequence of their own film. Neither of these modes of filming is autobiographical, but the French film, made under academic auspices by a seasoned ethnographic documentarist and a sociologist, announces a new kind of documentary authorship, or a new self-consciousness of the fact of authorship, which brought into play all the signs of agency that the traditional documentary had always suppressed.

An early paradoxical oddity was a film in which the first person documentary was satirised almost before it properly existed: Jim McBride's *David Holzman's Diary* (1967) is a fake documentary – one of the first of its kind – where the filmmaker, whom only the closing credits reveal as fictional, is an obsessive who places himself bodily in the picture, taking himself and above all his private quest as the very subject of the undertaking. What is prophetically parodied here as an exhibitionist enlargement of the filmmaker's ego is translated over the years into an emphasis on the filmmaker's individual personality, through which the documentary becomes, as it were, an objective representation of the filmmaker's subjective viewpoint. One version of this trend veers towards explicit autobiography, exemplified in more than one film by Ross McElwee that use the diary form as a prop for essayistic reflections. The finest examples of recent years include Nanni Moretti's *Dear Diary* (1993) and Agnès Varda's *The Gleaners and I* (2001), which both, but in quite different ways, combine the modes of self-reflexive video diary and first person *film d'essai*.

Television, meanwhile, being a thoroughly kleptomaniac medium, incorporated every evolving mode of documentary address, subjecting them to its own recombinations. It also, in the process, created new types of personality – or *pace* the sociologist Erving Goffman (1959), new forms of self-presentation in everyday public life – who have populated new genres like the docusoap and reality shows. By the 1990s, television had been transformed, and became one of the favoured locations for first person documentary. Leading the way was the BBC's invention of the 'video diary' – a programme format where the television people gave a camcorder to a volunteer, trained them in how to use it, and helped them edit the results. But television is paradoxical. On one hand it magnifies personality traits and manufactures celebrity; on the other it requires them all to fit the bill. The reporter in first person television reportage would not keep their job if they wandered too far from the required stance — unless, like John Pilger, they are cast as the licensed 'maverick lefty'. But in aesthetic terms, Pilger's films (including the ones he now directs himself) are entirely conventional pieces of reportage which are full of political contestation but do not in any way challenge the dominant modes of representation.

Where the filmmaker goes out to meet a social or political subject in which they take a personal interest, and the film chronicles their experience as they set off to meet their chosen protagonists, then take away the aspects of reflection or analysis which typify the essay, and this mode takes on a more populist and highly performative form. The best-known models are the aforementioned Nick Broomfield and Michael Moore, who both display strong traits of narcissism in performing their chosen and carefully constructed screen personae.

On the surface, the films of Avi Mograbi are similar, but with a crucial difference: like Moretti, the screen characters he creates for himself are split, and in part, openly fictionalised. The fiction, however, is not naturalistic, but anti-illusionist, creating a kind of distanciation, like a return of the Brechtian *Verfremdungseffekt*. Although I find this highly appealing as a viewer, as a documentarist it isn't me, and anyway, in this case, would hardly be appropriate. Exactly what I don't want to do in this film is perform.

5

More thoughts on the essay film. At first sight, the film of ideas lies at the opposite end of the spectrum to the performative first person film. The essay film is likely to be highly individual but without speaking in the grammatical first person. This kind of documentary is not at all new; on the contrary, it is one of documentary's earliest proclivities.

A maverick film producer recently took a column in a leading newspaper to celebrate the re-emergence of the essay film. 'The cinema of ideas has always had a rough ride', wrote Don Boyd (2008), recalling the difficulty he had twenty years earlier raising money from mainstream funders for Derek Jarman's *War Requiem* (1989), 'a production mounted against all the odds, and funded mostly by private artistic patronage'. However, at the 2008 London Film Festival, he said, there were no less than 'four powerful films' which all found funding despite their being highly personal and visual works eschewing conventional narrative. (The films in question: Terence Davies' *Of Time and the City*, Steve McQueen's *Hunger*, Ari Folman's *Waltz With Bashir* and Alex Gibney's *Gonzo: The Life and Work of Dr Hunter S Thompson* – a very curious selection which interestingly ignores conventional genre boundaries.) The reason why this is happening now, he says, is that they not only champion the latest audio-visual technologies but they do so on tiny budgets, thus freeing up their directors 'from the now redundant industrialised processes that have inhibited them for too long'. There is a good deal of truth in this, so I mean no disrespect if I add that it's only half the story. It is clear enough that commercial criteria are generally hostile to a cinema of ideas, yet there has always been this other cinema, working in the margins and interstices, and not only does the essay film have a history that reaches back to the 1920s, but it has never entirely gone away.

As a category of film criticism, the *film d'essai* took paradigmatic shape in France after World War II in shorts like Georges Franju's *Blood of the Beasts* (1949). Here the filmmaker takes on the stance of the literary essay in a tradition going back to Montaigne, and the classic essay film of this kind reveals something of its literary origins in its subtle reflective spoken commentary.

But as a filmic and thus visual form, its beginnings lie in the period of silent cinema. If you were Robert Flaherty, you provided a running commentary through narrative captions, the image thus succumbing to semantic domination. If you belonged to the avant-garde, like Walter Ruttmann or Dziga Vertov, you dispensed with captions altogether, and made your montage do the narration. The effect was given a name in Jean Vigo's concept of the *point de vue documenté*, the documented point of view, with which he introduced *A propos de Nice* in 1929. Vigo here condenses the full scope of the 'city symphony' into twenty minutes of intensely photogenic montage – with attitude. The crucial factor is not the word but the presence of a perceptual logic which is the visual equivalent of the voice. The camera is impersonal, it doesn't say 'I' but 'here is', but neither does the essay as a form of writing need the grammatical first person to be able to speak in an individual voice, style, point of view or attitude.

Jean-Pierre Gorin said somewhere that at the core of the film-essay is an interest so intense that it precludes filming it in a straight line; the essay is rumination in Nietzsche's sense of the word, the meandering of an intelligence (see Gorin cited in Everett 2009). If the essay film is typified by resistance to generic demands, as Michael Renov (2004) has pointed out, this is because it belongs primarily to the idiom of documentary. As noted earlier, an interloper into the genre system, documentary is a highly permissive form. The essay film is documentary at its freest, favouring symbolic and associative thinking over narrative. But it does this, according to Renov, in a double register: a combination of subjectivity and worldliness. It has a commitment to the representation of the historical real, and enlists its powers of expressivity in the service of historical representation. To put it another way, it speaks through the filmmaker's subjectivity even as it reproduces the concreteness of the historical document. If this appears to be paradoxical, it is only because the nature of documentary is misconstrued when objectivity and subjectivity are opposed. Semiotics teaches that it is both, because the photographic image is index and icon at the same time. The voice is individual, even subjective, the film is the objective rendering of what it tells.

The tension between the indexical and iconic dimensions of the archive image – still or moving – is crucial to the problematics which arise with the historical documentary. As a documentarist, I've been using archives almost since the beginning to borrow images for illustrative purposes. But when documentary uses archive in illustrative mode, it is liable to fudge the details by relying too much on accepted conventions. These conventions have a habit of congealing, and all sorts of bad habits and slippages creep in. This is a question I addressed in my book, *The Politics of Documentary* (2008), and is already present in my film, *Detroit: Ruin of a City*, where it arose directly from our archive research. We discovered that Detroit is a city with a particularly rich visual archive due to a special circumstance which has been strangely ignored by film historians, namely the film production activity of the Ford Motor Company which dates back to 1914–15 when Henry Ford set up a film unit in his publicity department – with the result that by the early 1920s, Ford was the largest single documentary producer in the USA (probably the world at that time). All this material is now in the public domain because it was subsequently donated to the National Archives in Washington. Ford continued production until the coming of sound, when instead of technical conversion they contracted out, but ironically, at the same time, Detroit became the subject of films from the workers film movement, so the archives begin to tell another story. We therefore set out to make a film about the rise and fall of Fordism and its relation to the city in which this shift of visual discourse would become evident, and thus help to offer a different narrative of Detroit from the conventional orthodoxy. The richness of the Detroit film archives – albeit with crucial gaps – provided an opportunity to counter the conventional mode of usage, with its hidden slippages; but to do this properly meant reducing the illustrative mode as much as possible, and using different strategies. For example, something very simple: using captions to signal the provenance of archive images, which orthodox documentary does not normally do with actuality footage, only with movie clips and scenes that have to carry a special label, like 'reconstruction'. By this act of naming, we wanted to draw attention to the way the representation is shaped by whoever took it and for what purpose, to warn the viewer about making assumptions (the assumptions upon which the conventions depend). Sometimes we did this by looking at archive footage on the viewing table and recording our conversation about what it might be as we viewed it for the first time. We also constructed montage sequences of images already seen (and identified) mixed in with new ones, to provide an iconic portrayal of the unfolding history and culture of the automobile (to the accompaniment of the score contributed by Michael Nyman, our third collaborator). These issues now come back to me from another angle in the new project which has prompted the present reflections.

6

The filmmaker who takes their own family as the subject is inevitably drawn in to the picture themselves, although they can adopt this position without the film necessarily becoming autobiographical, or only minimally so. But inevitably, if I make a film about my family, even if I am trying to focus on the others, it will say something about myself, and the result will be a first person film, however subdued. Annie Griffin played on this inevitability in her brilliant short *Out of Reach* (1994), where she interviews the members of her family from behind the camera about herself, thus turning out both a portrait of an American family and a self-portrait in which the portraitist is never seen but only heard.

A particularly interesting example for me is Andrés Di Tella's *La televisión y yo* (*Television and Me*, 2003), which presents a dialectic between the private sphere of family history and the public domain of national history in Argentina. The film derives its title from Di Tella's fascination with his early memories of watching television plus the fact that his grandfather manufactured television sets. Indeed, as one of the country's foremost entrepreneurs, his grandfather crossed paths with General Perón, and his family history is thereby interpolated into the country's political history. By pointing to the gaps in the various stories it tells – the family secrets, the mysteries about exactly what happened and how – Di Tella shows that official history can be prised open a little, and the lacunae of forgetfulness begin to give up something of what lies hidden. But as he begins to investigate his grandfather's life, he enters into a dialogue with his father – a sociologist who has written the grandfather's biography – about what it means to write family history. Can a son know his father? Can a family recount anything other than family legend? It is because of the intersection of the public and private that this film was particularly fascinating to me as I embarked on *The American Who Electrified Russia*?

The family filmmaker is inevitably drawn in to the fray. I discovered that I was not alone in finding the details of Papa's comings and goings confusing, and I learned that family memory does not escape the general rule of memory: it is always fragmentary, full of gaps, associative, abbreviated, disorderly, and has no respect for chronology. History, by contrast, is the orderly narration of the past. It celebrates chronology, discards the associative, and seeks to root its narrative in solid, concrete documentation – although of course it is always already selective, according to the interpretive scheme of the historian, which generally means it elides the gaps so you don't notice them. Historical documentaries on television do the same. The conventional approach when faced with inconsistent evidence is usually the 'best guess' – do the research, then present what seems the most likely version; but this now seems to me tendentious, because it suppresses uncertainties which are themselves of interest and significance. (What are the words blacked out on the copies of FBI correspondence?) I notice, as I begin to edit the first conversations I filmed with two brothers and a cousin, that their reminiscences were punctuated by pauses where they wonder if they are remembering correctly. For my purposes this is good, so I include them. But how to make the unself-doubting images which come from the archives do the same?

Family memory is a paradoxical and fluid space, far from homogenous. Each member of the family has their own memories, variously shared with other family members but not necessarily by all. The stories remembered individually are not always the same, and often come in slightly different versions. They enter circulation as family memories through oral telling and retelling. They often become attached (or attach themselves) to photographs and home movies. We have learned, however, to be suspicious of those family albums because, among other things, they often turn out to represent screen memories in the Freudian sense – images which screen out other memories, less celebratory, less happy, and sometimes repressed. Nevertheless, a critical question arises: since photographs and films are real documents, why are they seldom regarded by historians as primary sources? What do they lack? Why are they only seen as illustrations? Because the evidence they represent is seen as full of uncertainty? But don't all images call to be interrogated – where is this? and when? what is going on? who took it? Indeed a little deduction goes a long way, and they begin to give up their secrets, no longer markers of social forgetting, but definite indications of bits of histories and biographies that have been erased.

As each element in the film took shape, it also generated problems and puzzles which prompted new questions – for which answers were not always forthcoming. Often what is missing is semantic knowledge, of the kind that if you're lucky is recorded in notes on the back of the photo (date, place). But even where this exists, there remain whole areas of knowledge always absent from the image – like what had just taken place a moment before the photo was taken. And perhaps above all, what exactly Papa himself was thinking and feeling at the moment of the photo. I am not saying anything new here about the problems of working with photos – merely registering the fact that family photos give you access to aspects of both individual and socio-historical reality that remain hidden from the purview provided by public archives, but these are only tantalising glimpses of the private life which is otherwise only preserved in other fragmentary mementoes. The temptation, the pull of the well-crafted narrative which elides the gaps, must be avoided if you don't want to idealise.

Once you've opened this Pandora's box of uncertainty, the first idea – using archive footage to juxtapose history and family memory – rapidly appears too simple. The archive is no longer a question of illustration, but of evidence, and not in any simple way, but often only indirect or incomplete. For example, there is an archive of historical events at which Trone was present – like the Potsdam Conference – but in which he is not to be seen. (Of course not: the newsreel format concentrates entirely on the star players and their immediate entourage.) The newsreel registers the historical real, but is only a surrogate for biographical experience. There are innumerable documentaries which use the archives in this way without questioning the nature of this surrogacy. Here it is necessary to interrogate the illustration for the unknown histories behind it. Especially because of another problematic that our research has turned up, when we realised that the facts of Trone's biography rehearse a history that remains unknown to History in both the USA and Russia itself.

If you look in the history books, you won't find Trone's name. There's nothing about him, for example, in *The Generation of Power: The History of Dneprostroi*, by Anne Rassweiler (1988), nor in *The Electrification of Russia 1880–1926* by Jonathan Coopersmith (1992). But even more puzzling, neither is there practically any mention in these monographs of General Electric, despite the fact that in 1928, GE was the first American corporation to sign a contract with the USSR. GE provided the design for the giant turbines which drove Dneprostroi; the turbine we see being constructed in Shub's film is being built in Russia by a Komsomol brigade under GE's technical supervision, like the Dneprostroi installation itself. Knowledge of this association was not suppressed at the time, in either country, but by the time Shub made her film celebrating electrification in 1932, it was no longer convenient in Russia to mention General Electric by name. Nevertheless she does not suppress the filmic evidence of the Americans' presence, who are pictured several times: an adviser on the shop floor, others relaxing on the beach below the dam, and one of them contributing a speech at the official opening ceremony. Here, Shub's film transcends the illustrative mode entirely, and becomes a primary historical source, a piece of evidence about forgotten facts.

7

Perhaps the lesson is that history is not something fixed in the past, but a palimpsest where any one version is liable to be overwritten by another, although sometimes in such a way that the layers can be recovered. This idea lies at the heart of the film, in the scene where David brings out the book which Dimitri has sent to his father after annotating it and enclosing some of his own photos with their own annotations on the back. The book is an account of the rise of Stalinism by an employee of GE working in Russia on their behalf, who was one of those arrested in the xenophobic first wave of Stalinist terror. Some of Dimitri's photos correspond to scenes of the official inauguration of Dneprostroi which come at the end of the film by Shub. I saw these photographs for the first time through the camera lens as David takes them out of their envelop and shows them. It was obvious to me almost immediately that they could be edited into Shub's films like reverse shots. When I started editing, this was one of the first sequences I tried out. But this example also speaks to me of the limits of documentary representation, because what these images do not convey is my own astonishment at what I was being shown and told.

What do I learn from this? That what is captured by the camera is always already external to the person filming, and what the first person filmmaker feels about what they're filming at the moment they feel it is irrelevant. It's not imaginary, like fiction.

The fiction film is full of formulae for generating feelings in the viewer, coded in advance according to the dominant genre in question; indeed these associations are difficult to avoid, although every now and again a director comes along who changes the rules. To the extent that documentary remains true, however, to Ivens' idea of a 'creative no-man's land', when the filmmaker sits down to edit, they must confront their material without any preconceptions, but listening and watching, attentive to what it brings. You isolate and concatenate the most telling and pregnant moments, construct a storyline or an argument (but not a plot: then it would become fiction), and what these scenes feel like is liable to change as the editing proceeds. But unless you fall back on formulae dictated by convention and laziness, this is not so much about instructing your viewer what to feel, more about mobilising their attentiveness, intelligence and curiosity about the world.

This, at least, has been my working hypothesis in making this film, although I readily admit that writing this up afterwards, I'm conscious that I've rationalised the thought processes that contribute to the end result, which as I finish writing, remains to be judged.

References

Boyd, D. (2008) 'Certificate: Thoughtful', *The Guardian*, 12 November, www.guardian.co.uk/film/2008/nov/12/war-requiem-film.

Benjamin, W. (1977) *The Origin of German Tragic Drama*, trans. J. Osborne. London: Verso.

Coopersmith, J. (1992) *The Electrification of Russia 1880–1926*. Ithaca, NY: Cornell University Press.

Chanan, M. (2008) *The Politics of Documentary*. London: British Film Institute.

Everett, K. (2009) 'Crafting an Elegant Essay Documentary', www.sf360.org/features/crafting-an-elegant-essay-doc.

Goffman, I. (1959) *The Presentation of Self in Everyday Life*. Garden City, NY: Doubleday.

Plekhanov, G. (1940) *Essays in Historical Materialism*. New York, NY: International Publishers.

Rassweiler, A. (1988) *The Generation of Power, The History of Dneprostroi*. Oxford: Oxford University Press.

Renov, M. (2004) *The Subject of Documentary*. Minneapolis, MN: University of Minnesota Press.

The Curious Incident of
the Dog in the Nightime

Andrés Di Tella

1

I want to talk here about my experience making a documentary, *Fotografías*
(2007). Describing some of the problems I have been faced with and keeping
to the specifics of my work may, however, allow me to explore wider questions

that are probably of concern to all filmmakers working in first person narratives. The film is hard to describe for me at this stage, but it could be said to be about my relationship with India, where my mother was born. My father is Argentinean of Italian origin, which is very common in Argentina, as you may be aware. But there are virtually no Indians in our country so, in my *family romance*, my mother was always 'the only Indian in Argentina' (that was until I found the 'other' Indian in Argentina: but I don't want to give away the whole story). In the film, that relationship is narrated in the first person, starting from a series of photographs that my father gave me and which evoke the story of my mother's life. It is also narrated through recollections and images related to India and to an Indian identity that I never wanted (or was never able) to assume as my own. Partly, because my mother didn't want to – or wasn't able to – convey to me anything of her original culture. And in part, due to a traumatic experience from my childhood spent in London, where to be identified as an Indian was to belong to an undesirable category. This entire problem takes on immediacy, in the documentary, through a trip to India, with my wife and my son: my first trip to India since a single previous trip when I was a child.

2

Faced with the prospect of the trip to India, I started reading other voyagers' accounts, for instance that of my filmmaker colleague Louis Malle, who in 1970 made a legendary series of nine documentaries on India, *L'Inde fantome*. A notebook Malle kept during that experience has been recently published in France (Malle 2005). I copy out some of the entries, which could reflect my own perspective: 'January 19. The risk in this enterprise is to lose the subjective aspect, working as I am with such a complicated and absorbing reality'. I can go as far as understanding the sensation expressed by an (archetypically French) sentence such as '*L'Inde, ça n'existe pas*.' But what I can't share – however much I would like to – is the permanent feeling of alienation that surfaces in the notebooks and in Malle's voiceover narration in the film, with the inevitability of a refrain. Near the end of the trip, Malle writes:

How to be an Indian? The great question, with the strangeness, the difference, the exoticism, the folklore, returning once and again. Those disturbing, incomprehensible looks, that questioning that goes back and forth, from us filming them, without understanding them, from them looking at us filming them, as if we were Martians. Two worlds touching, without ever penetrating one another: that's all there is, between camera and subject. (2004: 204)

Unlike Malle and so many European or 'Western' travelers to India, although I can share a certain sense of exoticism or even alienation, I cannot help feeling implicated. My 'Western side' – 'If you could only see my Western side...' to quote from the refrain of a song by the Afro-Brazilian singer Milton Nascimento, addressed *To Lennon and McCartney* (*Clube da esquina*, 1972) – can identify with the perplexity of those voyagers faced with the 'otherness' of India. But all the same, I know that if those travellers came upon me, I would also be 'the other'. The uncomfortable feeling that all these texts give me is that they are talking about 'the other' but they are talking about me.

3

What is interesting about the autobiographical mechanism is, precisely, that it allows you to see yourself as *other*: the one who tells the life is telling the story of the one who lived it. And in contemporary autobiography, of course, the identity of the author is no longer the point of departure, but rather, the autobiography becomes an experience that allows you to sketch an identity, joining the dots. Identity, therefore, as something contingent, necessarily incomplete, permanently mutating inasmuch as experience confronts it with different possibilities.[1] The autobiographical narrative elaborated in *Fotografías* reflects an identity under construction, alternatively based, now on memories, now on cultural references and, finally, on the encounter with India, which re-signifies all of the previous elements. By the same token, *Fotografías* may finally be said to be less about a given reality documented by the camera in India than about its own documentary process. In the context of the film, the events and encounters documented in India have to be at the service of telling the story of what happened to 'me' (the figure of the documentarist documented) in that experience of constructing an identity.

And who cares about that identity or about what happens or fails to happen to *me*? Answer: only the audience. There is a kind of complaint directed at authors of personal or autobiographical documentaries, as if we were egotists or victims of extreme narcissism. (There is surely narcissism at work. How could there not be? But curiously nobody talks about a worrying lack of self-esteem or a negation of intimacy when a filmmaker makes one of the more 'objective' or 'social' kind of documentaries). I really think it is the other way round. To put into a film autobiographical substance, to sacrifice one's own family, to expose intimacies of experience, all of that is ultimately a kind of public offering. An autobiographical documentary is a curious act of *responsibility*. I assume responsibility for this story. I answer for it with my life. I answer for my ideas about film and art (and life) with my own life. I lay down my own body there, with no surrogates. And of course, in so doing, I confess my limitations. And in this case as a spectator I can bear witness to having benefitted from the generosity of so many autobiographical projects, so much so that they pushed me towards my own project. Marcel Proust (1954) says the writer offers the reader a sort of optical instrument that allows him to see that which, without the book, he would not be able to see for himself. That the reader recognises in himself what the book says is proof of the truth of the book. Proust wrote an evidently autobiographical work, but one could say that he did not write it in order to tell us the story of his life, but rather that he told the story of his life in order to illuminate in his readers their own lives. And of course you do not have to have an Indian mother.

4

In autobiography, of course, there's always an element of fiction, inevitable when you are telling 'your story' (*cuando uno se cuenta a sí mismo*). You have to at the very least make up that character, the I of the story, the narrator of the autobiography and the protagonist of the documentary. I will not deny there is a discrete fictional operation at work there. But it is not a fictional construct of any kind whatever. It is a construct that reveals a kind of truth. You are not free to make an autobiographical construct of any kind, you are just not. You will make a kind of construct that will inevitably talk about who you are. Whatever you say, you will end up by confessing who you are. In a sense, it is exactly Freud's notion, which is somewhat paradoxical: the idea of the family romance as a way of creating a myth, of fabricating memories, but whatever you do fabricate or construct ends up revealing who you are. There is nowhere to hide.

All the same, I would not like to fall into the trap of discussing the question of 'fiction vs documentary'. It seems to me important that there should be a certain degree of belief, in both the maker and the viewer of documentaries, that we are dealing with something that is true, that in this story we are telling there is a very direct relationship to the real, that it is not just something someone made up. And I think it is precisely that ingredient, specific to the documentary, that sparks in the viewer an association or a reflection on his own life. There is also the question of whether the documentary conveys a certain kind of knowledge, which in a way is what the documentary tradition is predicated upon. It is believed by some that there is such a thing as 'epistephilia', or the desire to know, or the desire for knowledge, as a species of motivation for the documentary viewer. This may be so, and I am not dispensing with the possibility that this may be happening with my own films. But I am certain that there is something else at work, a phantasmatic dimension usually assigned to fiction that I find much more appealing to operate with in my films, without leaving documentary territory.

There's a scene at the beginning of the film where I am with my little son Rocco in a pitch-black basement, only illuminated by torchlight, opening a trunk that belonged to my mother. It's a good example of how the simple process of narrative takes you to the edge of fiction and the phantasmatic. I can simply show Rocco rumagging in his grandmother's trunk and finding a series of slides of Freud's house in London, statuettes and portraits of Indian gods and a variety of objects that belonged to my mother and that tell us something about who she was. Finally, Rocco finds these huge Indian puppets, whose strangeness he finds intimidating. 'Better put them away!' he says, quite earnestly. There's a little story there, as it is, without adding anything else. Of course I knew these things were there, although not all of them. I certainly had not hoped for the Freud slides! But I did not know which things Rocco would pick out or in which order and least of all could I have imagined Rocco's reaction. Nor could I anticipate that the discovery of the big puppets and my son's fright would provide a kind of natural dramatic conclusion to the scene. There is a premeditated kind of storytelling at work there, though, dramaturgy or fiction in other words.

Now, if I add to that the story that my mother told me, that someone once

said to her that those puppets were possessed by evil spirits and that they had to be burned, I would be taking a decisive step in the direction of fiction, even if it is something that 'actually happened' (the *story*, at least, was real). I have to begin to deal with the issue of plausibility and at the same time with the question of what the narrator himself believes to be the case. And, simultaneously, I am generating in the viewer the expectation that this narrative element that I am putting on the table now will take on narrative significance *later*. And there, you are caught up in the logic of fiction. It is in the line of what Jorge Luis Borges was getting at in 'Narrative Art and Magic' (1981). As in magic, nothing is casual, there is no such thing as chance, everything is heavy with significance. Once someone puts a pistol away in a drawer, something will have to happen with that pistol. I finally decided not to tell the story of the evil spirits, however much I found it attractive and resonant, because of all these implications. In weighing all the elements at play in such a simple scene as this, you are already some distance away from the myth of the pure documentary record.

5

What happened is that I returned to Buenos Aires with the material I had recorded on my trip to India and began to tell my friends, my editor, my producer, like one does, all the things that had happened to me there. And I realised that none of what I was talking about was in the material. I had gone there with a difficult idea to put in practice: to defy all my fears, the fear of facing the reality of India, the fear of not being able to understand anyone, the fear of losing my son Rocco in the crowd. To have all this in mind, to juggle everything, hoping Rocco would not get sick and that my wife would not feel ill at ease, concerned that the camera crew not get into any trouble, wondering what would happen when I met my mother's family – my family – which was quite unknown to me... It was all rather difficult to deal with. And at the same time, I was trying to make a film out of all this. It was too much. And to all that, of course, you have to add what was happening to *me*. During the entire first week of our stay in India I was unable to sleep, I was in a kind of feverish state. And every day I had to make decisions as to what we were going to shoot. And often I did not have a clue. But I tried to hold on to a plan, which of course did not respond to what was 'happening' but rather to what I had imagined or assumed.

The first day, we went out to shoot in a poor neighborhood in Madras. I was afraid we would get mugged, our equipment stolen, all kinds of fears again. Of course, coming from Argentina... None of that happened in the end, quite the opposite. I had a surprisingly fluid rapport with my family – and with India.

Lots of things happened which I can really say changed my life, or better still, changed my sense of place in life, which is another way of saying 'identity'. Identity is what places you in a territory that is your 'own', in contrast to another territory, which is 'foreign' or 'alien'. The definition of the latter, the territory of the 'alien', is as important as – if not more important than — the territory defined as your own (that is how so-called 'Orientalism' works, describing the Orient to better assert the identity of the West).[2] It is as if a door had been opened onto a whole other possible dimension to my identity which, until the trip, had remained placed in the 'alien' territory. And suddenly it turned out to be part of my own.

But *that* was not in the material I had brought back. At least, not in any self-evident way. It was not easy to realise *where* that process was to be found. I had the constant feeling that, in any event, whatever was happening was happening *off camera*. All the same, the problem was I could never anticipate it. If one day 'something' happened during a family dinner, the next day I would ask the crew to attempt to shoot during dinner (which was also, inconveniently, their own dinner) to see if we could catch something. As you can imagine, that evening nothing happened. And so on. It is like the impossible challenge of the documentary: how to record people's so-called 'interior' processes through an exterior record such as that provided by camera and microphone?

The challenge therefore passed from the shoot to the editing room. How can you show, in a documentary, what you *did not* shoot? Or rather – and the distinction is perhaps significant – how does what you shot end up reflecting the experience that you did not shoot? And so: the job was to go back to reviewing the raw footage to see where I could find an echo of the experience, even in my mistakes, in the stuff that at first sight seemed to be of no use.

6

This is also related to my discovery of a strand within the documentary that one could associate with the essay, *ensayo* in Spanish, which I understand in the sense of the Spanish expression *ensayo y error* ('trial and error'). If there is no trial and error, all we hear is the voice of authority. To talk with authority about a subject: there's something disagreeable in that. To start with myself: my first film, *Montoneros, una historia* (1994), is a rather unorthodox version of the Montoneros guerrilla movement in Argentina and that entire political experience of the 1970s. But, formally, I have to acknowledge that there is something authoritative about it. It is as if I said: this is *the* version; even if the title, 'Montoneros, *una* historia', suggests it is just *one* story, out of many other possible stories. But there is nonetheless something quite emphatic about the film. And nowhere can you see the many doubts I entertained, or the wrong turns, or how my vision changed regarding the phenomenon being documented (by the fact that I was making a documentary).

In my more recent work, however, probably as a result of all my previous experiences playing within the conventional limits of the documentary genre, there appears this idea of the essay, or *ensayo*, as the possibility of *error*. And error begins at home, right? I am increasingly a believer in the eloquence of mistakes and failure. I am currently grappling with the ways in which the failure of a project, or the mistake of an idea crashing against reality, can express the truth of that idea or the meaning of that project. And I am always looking for ways of somehow reflecting that failure in the film. (It is not as easy as it seems!) For example, in this film about India, there's a moment when the cameraman left the camera on, unawares, while I was somewhere else. And he starts complaining about the lack of a plan, that I had arrived late at the shoot and that was intolerable, that we were in India and the director has us waiting somewhere for two hours... That moment reflects better than most of the 'successful' material – where we did *get* what we set out to shoot – the attempt to capture an experience that slips away from my control, the whole idea of trying to understand my mother's story, why she left her family and never talked to us about it, all these questions without possible answers. And this unpredictable

error, this moment with the cameraman, is where we are perhaps closest to the reality of the experience of making this documentary in India. Which of course was a spectacular failure, in accordance with the impossible ambition behind its making. But failure, as a rule, tends to be more interesting than success. Failure can also be quite funny, which is never unwelcome within a documentary context. And making a fool of yourself is always commendable in an autobiographical project. The art of the documentary essay, as I understand it, lies in finding something in this moment with the cameraman, for instance, which is a typical moment to be thrown away: the camera was left on by mistake, everything moves as if out of control, all you hear is a voice complaining about the director. That scene should go in the trash. But maybe something is being told there that cannot be told by the things I set out to shoot.

The difficulty in the editing room, where I am finishing the film as I write these notes, is to construct a story that tells the tale I wanted to tell – the story of my mother, my reflections about identity, the idea of India – but also *that something else*, i.e. what happened during the whole process. I have to construct a narrative in relation to all such moments, the ones that did not work according to plan, which on the other hand are the ones that have the most life. I think a documentary must at least convey the feeling that what we are witnessing was not planned. Like my Italian friends say: 'Make it look like an accident'. There's one of the key differences with fiction, as Borges would have understood. And of course documentaries *are* planned! But luckily there are always enough moments that defy any plan. And the fun of the genre lies in respecting that spirit of unpredictability. The worst thing in a documentary is to plan too much, or in any event to believe too much in the plan. I think that's what the great documentary photographer Alfred Stieglitz was talking about when, interviewed about his working methods, he said: 'The only thing in which I have been actually thorough has been in being thoroughly unprepared' (quoted in Dyer 2005: xiii).

I, for one, had to write a project, to obtain funds, and even a highly detailed script that I handed over to our National Film Institute, which classifies projects as with or without 'interest', based on 'documentary' criteria quite distant from the working practice of most documentary filmmakers. Since the idea was to record the experience of my encounter with that Indian universe, which was both my own and altogether alien at the same time, everything related to the trip was just something I could only imagine. All the same I had to make plans. The documentary filmmaker, as everybody is aware, does not just record whatever happens in front of the camera. The documentary filmmaker always imagines first what might happen. And then makes a plan in order to attempt to capture it in pictures and sounds. Sometimes, based on what you have observed, you film what you already know is going to happen. Many other times, you expect things to happen which do not. And again, as a rule, what does not happen according to plan is what is most revealing. But you have to be alert. It's like the well-known case of Sherlock Holmes ('Silver Blaze', in *The Memoirs of Sherlock Holmes*, Conan Doyle, 2008) in which the policeman asks Holmes if anything that he had observed had struck him as worthy of attention. Holmes answers: 'The curious incident of the dog in the nighttime.' The policeman objects: 'But the dog didn't do anything in the nighttime.' To which Holmes of course retorts: '*That* was the curious incident.' The fact that the dog did not bark when someone went into the house was proof that the criminal was someone the dog was familiar with. In similar fashion, the documentary filmmaker has to be alert to what fails to happen, what is left unsaid or what cannot be seen. And then, like Holmes, he must learn to draw his conclusions from the case and tell the story.

Notes

1   *Autobiography*, by Barbara Steiner and Jung Yang (2004) provides a panorama of auto-biographical practice in contemporary art.

2   *Indika* by Agustín Paniker (2005) provides an excellent historical account of 'Orientalism', in

particular as referred to India, updating concepts put forward by Edward Said in his classic *Orientalism* (1979).

References

Borges, J. L. (1981) 'Narrative Art and Magic', in *Borges – a Reader: A Selection from the Writings of Jorge Luis Borges*, eds E. Rodriguez Monegal and A. Reid. New York: E. P. Dutton, 34–8.

Conan Doyle, A. (2008) *The Memoirs of Sherlock Holmes*. London: Penguin Classics.

Dyer, G. (2005) *The Ongoing Moment*. New York, NY: Pantheon Books.

Malle, L. (2005) *L'inde fantome: carnet de voyage*. Paris: Editions Gallimard.

Paniker, A. (2005) *Indika*. Barcelona: Editorial Kairós.

Proust, M. (1954) *Contre Saint-Beuve*. Paris: Editions Gallimard.

Said, E. (1979) *Orientalism*. New York, NY: Vintage Books.

Steiner, B. and J. Yang, J. (2004) *Autobiography*. London: Thames & Hudson.

Impersonations of Glauber Rocha by Glauber Rocha

José Gatti

Glauber Rocha is the winged Prophet. It should also be said that a Prophet has no obligation to be reliable; all he must do is prophesy. Through film, writing, speech and life, Rocha became a magical personage, with whom it is not easy to share country and time. He is one of our strengths and we, Brazil, we are his frailty.

Paulo Emílio Salles Gomes (1975/1986: 212)

In 1999 I was hired by the Brazilian Ministry of Education to survey the work of an academic department at the Southeastern University of Bahia, in Vitória da Conquista, a prosperous city of over 300,000 inhabitants. I was accompanied by my dear colleague Antonio Eduardo Oliveira, who shared my surprises during that visit. As a segue to the usual warm welcome, we were constantly reminded by faculty, students and clerks that Conquista, as the city is nicknamed by its inhabitants, was 'Glauber Rocha's native town'. Not surprising: after all, Glauber Rocha, who died in 1981 at age 42, is historically acknowledged as Brazil's foremost filmmaker and that would certainly not go unnoticed by the locals. But whenever I dared ask my interlocutors if they had seen any of his films, their usually timid reply was 'No'. (I should inform the reader that in 1999 screenings of Rocha's films were scarce and none of them had yet been remixed and released on DVD). One literature professor, after having answered 'Yes', was surprised when I asked 'Which film?' He said: 'That one in which the peasant ends up running from the desert towards the sea... *Land in Anguish* [1967], isn't it?' It was a forgivable confusion with *Black God, White Devil* (1964); both films rank among Rocha's most famous works.

During that visit, I never disclosed that I had written a dissertation and published one book and several essays about Rocha's films; I did not want to confront the sense of ownership and pride of Conquista's citizens. No matter what Rocha had done to deserve fame, he belonged to them. But something else was yet to come. I was driven to the airport by a young man, a careful chauffeur, who took his time to show me part of the downtown area. The unavoidable reminder had to come up; he even showed me the house where Rocha had been born, in 1939. When asked about his films, his answer was prompt and straightforward: 'No, but I saw him when he made a film here, a couple of years ago.' 'Is that so? What film was that?', I couldn't help but ask. He answered, 'It was that film – what's the title? – with the lady who almost won the Oscar, remember?'

Indeed, the last sequence of *Central Station* was shot in Vitória da Conquista in 1997, and my driver had witnessed filmmaker Walter Salles in action. And the lady in question was Fernanda Montenegro, star of Salles' film and one of Brazil's most prestigious actors.[1] I am sure Salles would have been proud to be confused with Glauber Rocha. But the incident showed me how much Rocha's persona impregnated every successful Brazilian filmmaker; that even though his films are often seen as hermetic and cryptic, his biography transcended his work; that despite the fact that his films have become, more than ever, fodder for academic research, his name, more than his films, has also seeped through different social classes and cultural environments.

Towards the end of his career, Rocha's own life became more and more identified with his work. For Rocha, that meant much more than just presenting his presence as an auteur – that meant exposing his own burden of representation as the foremost Brazilian film director, the *Cinema Novo* leader, the cultural rogue, the enemy of censorship, the once opponent and then supporter of the right-wing military, the enfant terrible of many a film festival. He was the same man who could author *Land in Anguish* (considered by many critics as the foremost creation of Brazilian cinema), win the Critics' Prize at Cannes and behave like a real pig at social events. At the Cannes film festival, he was once invited by Elizabeth Taylor for a dinner where he reportedly made little dumplings out of his food throughout the night, throwing them at the star's cleavage, all the while claiming that in his part of the world people did not use silverware.[2]

But he was far from being a tabloid celebrity and his presence as an auteur marked different media. He wrote screenplays, poems, a stageplay and a novel;[3] several books on theory, film history and criticism; innumerable newspaper articles, most of them with his own spelling and house style (often turning his texts into a reading test). Indeed, he never made any efforts to make his films easy to watch, his texts easy to read, his ideas easy to understand. Not unlike Carlos Drummond de Andrade's verses, 'In the middle of the road there was a stone/there was a stone in the middle of the road', Glauber Rocha posed a challenge to anybody who dared tread down his road.[4]

But instead of delving into anecdotal episodes of Rocha's biography, the aim of this chapter is to examine his appearances on the screen. From that perspective, I believe *Claro*, a feature film he both starred in and directed in Rome, in 1975, marks a turning point in his career, one in which the filmmaker clearly presents himself in his film, as a visible and audible part of the narrative. I also claim here that his presence, whenever evident in that film, sets the tone for possible readings of the scenes. In other words, his persona provides new inflections for what has just been shown; be it an indoor performance by a cast of actors or the recording of a political rally on the sunlit streets of the city. Persona or impersonation, the sole certainty that emerges from that film is that Glauber Rocha plays Glauber Rocha. And as in *chiaroscuro* painting, in *Claro* his presence functions as the incidence of light that produces a tridimensional grasp of the scene, of the film, of cinema and its possibilities as a means to (re) present reality. My contention here is that Rocha's screen persona can provide new possibilities of answers to the questions faced by the viewers. Moreover, in *Claro* these questions are eventually posed directly to the audience, as one of its characters, a bearded, long-haired young man looks directly into the camera lens and shouts: 'Silence! Silence! What are you looking at? What is the matter? What are you hearing? What are you saying? Where are you going?'

These basic questions – which ultimately could be addressed to any audience at any film screening – are at the core of the narrative of that film. They seem to demand that the audience define the status of their own spectatorship. Moreover, these questions may shed doubt on the film itself, but more than that, they shed doubt, as we will see, on the possibilities of cinema itself. Thus *Claro* interpellates its public in an unabashed, candid way.

When Glauber Rocha made *Claro* he was at the end of an odyssey which was often defined as his period of exile. Brazil was under the tight grip of a military dictatorship that arrested, tortured and scattered many of his friends into exile throughout the world. Rocha, in his turn, had been arrested and often threatened by the military, but was never officially exiled from Brazil. No wonder that the period is often described as Rocha's self-exile, something that was sometimes interpreted as an act of self-defence (yes, he could be arrested again), but often seen as a virtual dropping out. Rocha, however, insisted on his need to go abroad, claiming the lack of conditions to film in Brazil (despite the fact that many of his colleagues decided to stay and managed to work in the country).

He was to make three feature-length films outside Brazil: *Der Leone Have Sept Cabeças* in the Congo in 1969; *Cabezas Cortadas* in Spain in 1970; and finally *Claro* in Italy. These other films, not unlike *Claro*, can hardly be classi-fied as works of fiction or documentary, often blending techniques and genres, making it difficult for critics and historians to define them.

In his African film, religious rituals are portrayed side by side with Brechtian sketches shot in sequence that include different characters: German soldiers of fortune, a priest of liberation theology, a voluptuous blond seductress, a CIA agent and a Portuguese swindler. In Spain, Rocha researched the roots of European pre-Christian traditions and assembled a parodic portrayal of a Latin American dictator in exile. Rocha's dictator talks on the phone about the death of his wife and its impact on the people – a clear reference to Argentinian leader Juan Perón and his wife Evita. (Perón's exile in Spain, from 1955 to 1973, did not keep him from commanding the Argentinian political scene, literally over the telephone). Each of these films highlight the themes that are at the core of his work: the politics of colonialism, the politics of mysticism and the politics of sex.[5]

We can sense, in this scenario, elements that evolve from the (cultural and political) context in which Rocha situated himself in Brazil as well as the ele-ments that helped forge his complex public persona and the tragic burden of this persona in his own private life. If, as Michael Renov reminds us, the essen-tial ingredients of an autobiography as a form of representation are the self, a life and a writing practice (2005: 237), in *Claro* the filmmaker shows a little of himself, some fragments of his life and a great deal of his filming practice. Rocha is set here to build a character, a persona based on himself but invested with responsibilities that a politically conscious filmmaker cannot minimise. From this perspective, *Claro* can be seen as an arena in which Rocha also plays the role of Filmmaker, rather than what could be seen as an autobiographi-cal documentary. I believe Rocha's appearance before the camera can serve as a statement of his own role as a Brazilian filmmaker (one who represented the leader of a cultural movement of international projection such as *Cinema Novo*), but also the intricacies of his politics (which could swing from a clear leftist alignment to a rather conservative understanding of the acts of Brazil's military leaders).

The filmmaker had already hinted at his own presence in some of his earlier films, albeit in indirect or allegorical ways. For example, Rocha's personal expe-riences helped create the character Antonio das Mortes, who appears in both *Black God, White Devil* and in *Antonio das Mortes* (1968). He claimed to have met the hitman José Rufino, who was famous in Vitória da Conquista, and who inspired the creation of the character (Fusco 1987: 31).[6]

In *Land in Anguish*, for instance, Paulo Martins, the main character played by Jardel Filho, is a journalist who faces his need for poetry and his duty as an intellectual involved in politics. The film is set in an imaginary Latin American country, Eldorado, which undergoes a fascist *coup d'état*. The country has strong resemblances to Brazil in that same period, with added references to other Latin American countries – no wonder the film is spoken in Portuguese but Spanish words burst without warning into the midst of the dialogue or in the names of the characters, making clear the transnational metaphor of Eldorado. Many critics have seen in the character Paulo Martins allegories of this or that Brazilian journalist but, as Rocha once confided to American scholar Robert Stam, Paulo Martins was *also* a metaphor for himself.[7]

Rocha worked many years as a journalist in his native Bahia and, as mentioned above, wrote editorials for Brazilian newspapers throughout his career. Brazilian writer Carlos Heitor Cony remembers being imprisoned in the same cell with Rocha and other intellectuals back in 1965, after a protest against the censorship imposed by the military regime. He says that while in prison Rocha spent his time writing the first treatment of the screenplay of *Land in Anguish*, in the very heat of the moment, which can be seen as an indication of how much his personal experience became part of his work.

In 1968 he was to make another experiment in which author and film converge: *Cancer*, which was edited only in 1972 and never shown on a regular circuit of exhibition. Rocha defined it as a film that is 'linked to the cultural, existential and human experience of the author [...] It is a work that I made to have fun with my friends [...] The film has no plot. Just three characters within a violent action. What I sought was a technical experiment, about the problematic of the resistance of the duration of the shot (in order to) study the quasi-elimination of editing whenever there is a constant, verbal and psychological action within the same shot [...] 27 sequence shots and three actors improvising situations of psychological, sexual and racial violence' (1985a: 33).

Racial violence in Brazil had been addressed in his first feature film, *Barravento*, completed in 1962 (and which won the main prize at the Karlovy Vary film festival, in Czechoslovakia). But in his early feature films one can already detect many of the problems Rocha experienced in his youth concerning sexuality. In *Pátio* (1959) a man and a woman, lying on a checkered tile floor, are unable to touch each other's hands. The woman was played by Rocha's first wife, Helena Ignez.[8] In his second film, *The Cross on the Square* (1959), two men roam Bahia's colonial quarters until one of them grabs the other's testicles and makes him scream in pain. Actor Luiz Carlos Maciel recalls that that scene was not in the screenplay, having been improvised by Rocha on the spot (1996: 57). Rocha claimed the film – possibly the first dealing with homosexuality in Brazil – was still immature and was not ready to be shown. This film is now lost, having been seen by a small audience at the few screenings it had in Bahia.

Nevertheless, a delicate matter such as homosexuality was not at all easy to deal with in the left-leaning though moralist 1960s; one can but imagine the pressure felt by Rocha at the time.[9]

In *Claro*, however, it is Rocha's own presence that is seen and heard throughout most of the film. If Rocha's subjectivity was reasonably evident in his early works, in *Claro* the *mise-en-scène* points to a practice he would further develop in his last films, such as *Di-Glauber* (1977) and *The Age of the Earth* (1980). In both of these films his presence is also made evident, either as voiceover narration or plainly directing the scene, giving instructions to the cast before the camera.

This practice was to reach its apex in his contribution to the television programme *Abertura*, in the late 1970s, which was a weekly news show that gathered journalists who had defied the military censorship of the press. In *Abertura*, Rocha 'pretended' to interview artists and intellectuals in order to debate Brazilian cinema or politics. At times he would invite unexpected guests – such as the parking valet from across the street, in order to discuss the political situation of Brazil on the eve of the demise of the military dictatorship. Most of the time his gesturing would take over the screen, keeping the interviewee out of the focus, and his voice would take over the soundtrack – thus making obvious the *mise-en-scène* that usually levels and homogenises all interviews in regular talk shows (see Mota 2001: 93).

Rocha would go much further on this trajectory that mixed author and work: in 1980, at the Venice Film Festival, he did not accept the fact that Louis Malle's (rather conventional) *Atlantic City* won first prize, to the detriment of his own (highly experimental) *The Age of the Earth*. His voice was heard all over the Lido and he even tried to physically attack Malle (see Del Picchia and Murano 1982: 5). That was the last phase of his career (as well as of his life). Disappointed in the way Brazilians received his work, he would move to Portugal, when his health was already failing.

Claro was his first feature film after a period of five years during which the Brazilian director travelled extensively, wrote for the screen and stage and produced his (semi-)autobiographical novel. In this period, as author Sylvie Pierre puts it, Rocha 'always kept Brazil in the soles of his windshoes' (1996: 70). Despite all the difficulties he might have to face in order to continue his work in Brazil, Rocha aligned himself with the exiled, tracking the (albeit romantic) path of the Third World artist (or Tricontinental, as he and Jean-Luc Godard once dreamed of being), one who can fit himself in the struggles spread throughout the world.[10]

The film opens with handwritten credits and the face of the Woman, a character played by French actress Juliet Berto, who will puncutate the entire narrative with her presence.[11] A howling male voice is heard – he seems to prattle in some unknown language, made up of long, wailing vowels. The Woman howls back, walks, hops and dances among ancient Roman ruins, watched by groups of tourists who seem baffled by the performance. Little by little, the voices of the Man and the Woman seem to engage in a bizarre dialogue of primal screams. The foreignness of the Woman is stressed by the garment she wears – a poncho, or blanket such as those worn by traditional Latin American peasants. The gap produced by her presence amid the Roman ruins seems obvious: that 'classical' environment, the very hub of the civili-sation that entailed the process of colonisation is suddenly invaded by the disturbing presence of the primal voices of the colonised. As Rocha would put it, the film 'is a Brazilian view of Rome, or a statement of the colonised about the land of colonisation' (in Rezende 1986: 212).

After a few minutes, a new sound interrupts the supposed dialogue of Man and Woman – we hear the second movement of Villa-Lobos's *Bachianas Brasileiras No. 5*, a piece composed for eight cellos and a soprano voice. That is perhaps the most celebrated erudite piece of music ever composed by Brazilian composer Villa-Lobos, who attempted to find a syncretic link between the popular music of Brazil and the European baroque tradition as represented by J. S. Bach. This piece features the operatic voice of the Spanish soprano Victoria de Los Angeles – a voice which sings about the birds of the Brazilian hinterland, as if it were that of a rural dweller who walks in the bush and speaks with different birds. The soundtrack produces an inevitable differential, one that reframes the impression the 'primitive' voices of the Man and the Woman might have caused. For the operatic, high-pitched voice of Victoria de Los Angeles is here summoned to engage in a three-way conversation piece, one which attempts to articulate primal utterances with the highly-trained vocal apparatus, thus producing an effect of strangeness.[12]

The atmosphere changes again in the sequence that follows, when the *Bachiana* is replaced by another string concerto by Villa-Lobos, turning what was to be a somewhat joyful scene into an *opera buffa*, in which the Man (finally) appears on the screen and pretends to torture the Woman. With fake moves, he kicks the Woman and makes her roll on the asphalt, with the Roman Coliseum in the background. She hardly reacts, he keeps 'beating' her, at the same time the Man – Glauber Rocha himself, we now see – directs the move-ment of Mario Gianni's camera. Asian tourists who happen to pass by eagerly photograph the performance, in a scene that blends hints of tragedy, traces of comedy and straight direct cinema.

Whatever considerations one could make about these two sequences – whatever obvious allegories one can find in the Woman or the Man, the

oppressed and the oppressor, the colonised and the coloniser – all these categories undergo a process of complication and even confusion. Is that a parody
of oppression? Whose voices do we hear? What is the role of the landscape in
the definition of the characters? Once again, as in many of Rocha's films, more
questions than answers arise from the visual and aural images that surround
the spectators.

As noted earlier, *Claro* unfolds different types of *mise-en-scène* and filmic
practices. Sequences of tongue-in-cheek performances are clearly not to be
taken seriously. One example: an American couple argue in despair – he is a
repentant white Vietnam veteran and she is a black woman who clearly sym-
pathises with the Vietnamese he killed in action: 'You murdered my people!'
The sketch is followed by images of newspapers announcing the Vietnamese
victory over the United States, thus reframing – or rekeying – what seemed a
laughable parody of melodrama into a fragment of true conflict.

In another scene, an elegant European lady, donning a fancy evening gown,
addresses the camera and tells her story, over and over: she is a Turkish prin-
cess who was brought up in a harem, and so on. Her presence suggests the
decadence of a ruined Europe, blending her character with the surrounding
landscape. *Claro* turns the city of Rome, in this sense, into an active element
of the narrative. The motifs of colonialism and imperialism are indelibly connected to the imagery of the city and the film thus manages to link different
forms of oppression to different historical contexts, suggesting wide Braudelian
bridges in time.

Two scenes are dedicated to episodes of the history of the Roman Empire
proper. The story of Julius Caesar, Mark Anthony, Cleopatra and Octavius
is told by a bearded young man wearing a flowered shirt and loose tie, who
appears next to the Woman in a close up shot. His speech seems to falter – has
he forgotten his lines or is he a bit altered? The Woman listens and patiently
fills some of the gaps in his speech. The story of the Roman Empire goes on,
but now the setting is quite different: in one of the lengthiest sequences,
the Woman is now in a lavish living room, still wearing the Latin American
poncho, playing with biscuit figurines and other decorative objects, while a
conservative middle-aged lady recites another fragment of the history of the
Roman Empire, moving around in the heavily furnished living room. She looks
like an aristocratic lady, with a flowered dress and hat that evoke 1930s fashion. She also falters, drinks, stumbles and falls throughout her performance.
Thus fragments of the history of Rome can be told in different tones, in different settings, by different characters, even though the text seems to have come
from the same written source, with the same literary style, thus producing an
uncanny continuum of a narration in ruins. But spectators soon realise that,

despite the seriousness of the recitation, the lady is played by a man: Italian actor Carmelo Bene. The sequence could be seen as one more provocation, were it not for one detail: the striking resemblance of Bene with Rocha himself. At a first glance, it would not be surprising if some spectators took one for the other. The same complexion, similar facial features, apparently the same build. From this perspective, Bene seems to act, in some tortuous way, as Rocha's transgender double on the screen.

However, *Claro* is not just a collection of funny or repetitious sketches. The film also features documentary fragments of Italian political life of the 1970s. Demonstrations and rallies are shown, people come up and tell their story to the camera. The Woman sits in a balcony facing a square and talks to another woman, a resident who describes the working-class neighbourhood and the demonstrations and denounces the police brutality. Juliet Berto plays, here, the role of a politically engaged documentary interviewer, one who channels the voice of the ordinary citizen.

In one of the political rallies, during a screening for workers in an open plaza, the Woman asks the projectionist: 'Do you have any filmmanifesto (sic)?' The young man says 'Yes, we have one, by Eisenstein' and she teases him: 'Oh, His Majesty Eisenstein!' The man seems not to notice the mocking and goes on, 'Yes, and by Jean-Marie Straub, Jean-Luc Godard, and...' She interrupts him: 'And what about Andy Warhol?' 'No, he is too far right for us.' Berto asks: 'And what about Visconti?' 'Yes, Visconti, Fellini, Antonioni and also *il maestro* Rosselini', to which the Woman, with a naughty smirk on her face, makes the sign of the cross and sighs: 'Oh! Yes!' Rocha and Berto seem to use the opportunity to fathom – and overtly criticise – the aesthetic preferences of the partisan left. No, *Claro* is not easily accepted, for it shoots in every direction.

Towards the end of the film, the Woman and the Man visit one of Rome's poorest neghborhoods. This is perhaps one of the most intimate and candid appearances of Glauber Rocha on the screen. It is here, for the first time, that Rocha presents himself as a fully-fledged performer, one who plays his own role, the Filmmaker. If, in the opening sequences of *Claro* he interacted with Berto, in this fragment of the film Rocha takes over the scene, relegating Berto to a supporting role.

The excerpt I want to approach begins with the Man and the Woman running along a railroad station platform. They seem to have disembarked and are leaving the station – even though there is not a single train in sight. The soundtrack features Villa-Lobos's piece *The Little Train of the Caipira*, which is part of *Bachiana No. 2*. 'Caipira' is a Brazilian word which means peasant, or person who lives in the backwoods. In this piece the orchestra emulates the sounds of a steam engine, a device that provides the scene with a bizarre

Rocha, Berto and the People. Courtesy of Tempo Glauber.

atmosphere, since no trains can be seen – and the only train featured sounds like an orchestra. As a result, the 'train' is represented (on the soundtrack) but not 'realistically' seen (on the screen).

The couple crosses the street and enters a Roman shantytown. Once there, Man and Woman talk to the dwellers, as if they were collecting their complaints for a documentary. Rocha oftens turns people around, in order to position them before the camera, which adds to the veracity of the 'filmmaking'. However, the audience does not hear what they say. It is as if the very act of filmmaking were the object of the scene; not the 'reality' of the shantytown. Here, in contrast to the train, they are seen without, in some sense, being represented.

The sequence that follows shows Rocha leisurely rocking in a chair, apparently listening to a record player. (Would the Filmmaker be resting, after having accomplished his mission?) After a few seconds he gestures as if to tell someone to change the record – and then we hear Carmen Miranda's voice, singing *Primavera no Rio*, an old standard of the 1930s that tells of springtime in Rio, with its colourful flowers and frolicking, beautiful women. The rather nostalgic atmosphere that settles in is emphasised by the ceaseless rocking of the chair. (In a certain sense, the scene seems to evoke the filmmaker's self-imposed exile and endless expectation). Nevertheless, the scene is disrupted by a peculiar gadget that Rocha brings into the scene: a telephone. He smokes a cigarette and utters scattered phrases to the mouthpiece: 'The minority of the masses. Half of the people are revolutionary. The labour of the masses. Yes. Day after day. Of course, of course, of course. Everyday. House, road. It can also be rhetorical or dialectical.' The sequence ends with Rocha's lively singing along with Carmen Miranda: 'Springtime is the season of love!'

Could these phrases be excerpts of what had been spoken at the shantytown in the previous sequence? Are they simply fragments of the speeches heard at the political rallies depicted in the film? Are they perhaps verses of a poetic performance that picks up its words from the experience of life outside the scope of the camera? These are probably unanswerable questions – no wonder one of the lines refers to the title of the film: 'Of course, of course, of course' – or, in Portuguese, 'Claro, claro, claro', which can also mean 'clear'. But of course, nothing is clear, except for the presence of the filmmaker, his own experience, his own sentiment. The complex articulation of Miranda's joyful, carnivalesque singing, the rocking chair and, most of all, the quasi-parodic casualness attached to his voice empties the words of their original signification, portraying the uselessness of a certain political cinema based on the repetition of empty directives. What is the use of repeating, in documentary mode, the same slogans that were used to pep up the crowds at a rally? What can be more political than showing the limits of political cinema itself? Rocha's strategy, in a way, renders a gesture of utmost courage, one that runs the risk of throwing his own film onto a burning pyre – and of turning the filmmaker into a sacrificial lamb. The presence of the author, in this scene, casts a totally different light, a different understanding of the film. The scenes of the political meetings, the poignant story told by the lady about the police brutality, even the fake, theatrical sketches depicting runaway Turkish princesses, repentant Vietnam veterans or old ladies nostalgic for the Roman Empire – all that seems to be levelled by the filmmaker, who smokes and rocks on a chair, listens to old songs by Carmen Miranda and pretends to speak on the phone.

Very little is left over after that.

In the last scenes of *Claro* we see Rocha sharing a joint with Berto, a candle in the foreground; he feeds her rose petals, straight from his hands. It is as if *Claro* had to end with a delicate homage in honour of his star – here, we are far from the opening scenes, in which Berto was continuously 'kicked' by Rocha. These now are images of love and affection. *Claro* is thus the screen record of a love affair, for Berto was indeed Rocha's partner during his Roman exile.

The film ends with a collage that sums up many of the issues of sex and politics previously brought up: juxtaposed images, such as the portrait of Ho Chi Minh described as 'The Victor' on the cover of *Time* magazine; *Playboy* centrefolds; glimpses of Italian newspapers headlining one more terrorist attack by the Red Brigades; Berto being made up for a scene that was never included in the final edit; fragments of paintings depicting scenes of love and sex. These images refer directly to the world of the 1970s, a world off-screen – where the struggle goes on. And if cinema is capable of (re)presenting the reality that lays there, beyond the boundaries of the screen, Rocha seems to remind us that he will only be able to accomplish that task by exploring the boundaries of his own self, exposing either the vulnerability of his politics or yet declaring the certainties of his love.

Notes

1 Montenegro eventually 'lost' the Academy Award for Best Actress to Gwyneth Paltrow, who had starred *Shakespeare in Love*.
2 When I asked Dona Lúcia Rocha, the filmmaker's mother, about this incident, she told me she had met Taylor many years later, at a film festival in New York City, and that the star had the fondest memories of her son.
3 That is *Riverão Sussuarana*, a book in which Rocha himself is one of the main characters, one who interacts with other authors and personages of Brazilian literature and history. Halfway through the novel, however, he turns his text into an investigation of the death of his sister, actress Anecy Rocha, which he defined as a 'cultural murder'. Anecy Rocha fell into an empty elevator shaft, after having fought with her husband.
4 My translation. The original verses are 'No meio do caminho, tinha uma pedra/tinha uma pedra no meio do caminho' (Drummond 1973: 12).
5 Sex, however, was then considered a minor theme by many of his contemporary admirers, as compared to the more 'noble' ones (say, class struggle?), which placed Glauber Rocha, the Third World filmmaker, in the roster of the revolutionary artists.
6 José Rufino, as the cowmen and rural workers of the surrounding area, often wore the same heavy outfit Antonio das Mortes dons on-screen. Even though Vitória da Conquista is located in a tropical latitude, it is nearly 1,000 metres above sea level and temperatures can drop to 5°C.
7 In *Land in Anguish*, Paulo Martins is constantly fractured between his calling as a poet and his duties as an engaged journalist. The poems the character recites on screen were written by Rocha, except for *Martín Fierro* (José Hernández, 1872), whose title is mentioned by Martins.
8 Helena Ignez was a well-known beauty queen in Bahia in the late 1950s. She became a praised film actor and, after having separated from Rocha, married another avant-garde filmmaker, Rogério Sganzerla. She would star Sganzerla's key film, *The Red Light Bandit* (1968).
9 Rocha's private struggles with either his sexuality or drugs will certainly be relevant, as far as a reading of his work is intended as an approach to his subjectivity on film; however, some of these issues will only be made clear when his diaries are published. Lúcia Rocha, his mother, once told me that the only copy of that film was kept by 'a Dominican priest in a monastery outside Paris'.
10 Rocha appeared in Godard's *East Wind*, shot in 1969 in Italy, portraying himself as a Third World filmmaker standing at a crossroads with his arms spread (in a rather Christlike figure) and pointing to the possible ways of political cinema.
11 Berto (1947–1990) was quite well-known in the political and art film circuit at the time of the film's production, having worked as one of the protagonists of Godard's *La Chinoise*. Rocha and Berto were lovers for three years, from 1973 to 1975. In the authorized transcription of the film, her character is named *Moça*, which is better translated as Youngwoman, whereas the Man is named *Glauber Rocha*, which can be seen as one more indication that Rocha wanted to make sure it was understood he was representing himself (see Senna 1985: 403).

12 That strangeness was probably already in the *Bachiana* itself, even though the etiquette of a proper audience would not allow for that acknowledgement — but who would believe in the operatic, highly educated voice of a rural worker in the backlands of Brazil?

References

Del Picchia, P. and V. Murano (1982), *Glauber, o Leão de Veneza*. São Paulo: Escrita.

Drummond de Andrade, C. (1973) *Reunião*. Rio de Janeiro: José Olympio.

Fusco, C. (1987) *Reviewing Histories: Selections from New Latin American Cinema*. Buffalo, NY: Hallwalls.

Gatti, J. (2005) 'Der Glauber Have Sept Cabeças', in G. Mosquera and J. Fischer (eds) *Over Here: International Perspectives on Art and Culture*. Cambridge, Mass.: MIT Press: 364-383.

Maciel, L. C. (1996) *Geração em Transe: Memórias do Tempo do Tropicalismo*. Rio de Janeiro: Nova Fronteira.

Mota, R. (2001) *A Épica Eletrônica de Glauber*. Belo Horizonte: EDUFMG.

Pierre, S. (1996) *Glauber Rocha*. Campinas: Papirus.

Renov, M. (2005) 'Investigando o sujeito: uma introdução', in M. D. Mourão and A. Labaki (eds) *O cinema do real*. São Paulo: Cosac Naify: 234–57.

Rezende, S. (1986) *Ideário de Glauber Rocha*. Rio: Philobiblion.

Rocha, G. (1976) *Riverão Sussuarana*. Rio: Record.

____ (1985a) *Glauber por Glauber*. Rio de Janeiro: Embrafilme.

____ (1985b) *Roteiros do Terceyro Mundo*, org. Orlando Senna. Rio: Alhambra/Embrafilme.

Salles Gomes, P. E. (1986) 'Glauber', in C. A. Calil and M. T. Machado (eds) *Paulo Emílio: Um Intelectual na Linha de Frente*. São Paulo: Brasiliense/Embrafilme, 212–13.

The Self-portrait Film: Michelangelo's Last Gaze

Laura Rascaroli

'A director does nothing other than seek himself in his films – which are documents not of a finished thought but rather of thought in the making.'

(Antonioni 1994: 57; author's translation)

Though it can be traced far back, the self-portrait as an artistic genre in Europe coalesces in the sixteenth century – even if the term itself is more recent, and reflects the notion of the self that prevails in Western societies in the late eighteenth century, with Romanticism and its 'invention' of the self as a self-contained object of awareness.[1] The sixteenth century, however, is the period that sees a clear rise in both literary autobiography and the painted self-portrait, probably as a result of increased social mobility and ensuing changes in people's awareness of their individuality (see Trilling 1972) – and as a consequence and a reflection of the new position held by the artist in society (see West 2004: 163–4).

The term has also been borrowed to describe literary texts. Written self-portraits can be seen as a form of autobiography, but one that does not depend on narrative construction. For this characteristic, they have much in common with the essay. Indeed, Phillipe Lejeune has thus defined Montaigne's *Essays*: 'One sees that the text of the *Essays* has no connection with, as we define it, autobiography; there is no continuous narrative nor any systematic history of the personality. Self-portrait rather than autobiography' (in Beaujour 1991: 2).

For Michel Beaujour, author of a seminal text on the genre, the lack of continuous narrative is, indeed, a defining characteristic of the literary self-portrait:

This genre attempts to create coherence through a system of cross-references, anaphoras, superimpositions, or correspondences among homologous and sub-stitutable elements, in such a way as to give the appearance of discontinuity, of anachronistic juxtaposition, or montage, as opposed to the syntagmatics of a narration, no matter how scrambled, since the scrambling of a narrative always tempts the reader to 'reconstruct' its chronology. The totalization of the self-portrait is not *given* beforehand: new homologous elements can be added to the paradigm, whereas the temporal closure of autobiography already is implicit in the initial choice of a curriculum vitae. (1991: 3)

The above quotation introduces a description of the self-portrait that closely evokes filmic language. The temptation to borrow such description and use it to illustrate the features of audiovisual self-portraiture is too much to resist. Indeed, Raymond Bellour was prompted to write that the self-portrait is perhaps the only form of autobiography truly achievable in film; defying the shortcomings of the cinematic apparatus and language in terms of respecting the autobiographical pact,[2] the self-portrait 'is distinguished from autobiogra-phy by the absence of a story one is obliged to follow' (1989: 8):

The self-portrait clings to the analogical, the metaphorical, the poetic, far more than to the narrative. Its coherence lies in a system of remembrances, afterthoughts, superimpositions, correspondences. It thus takes on the appearance of discontinu-ity, of anachronistic juxtaposition, of montage. Where autobiography closes in on the life it recounts, the self-portrait opens itself up to a limitless totality. (1989: 8–9)

If the pact of the self-portrait is 'I won't tell you what I've done, but I shall tell you *who I am*' (Beaujour 1991: 3), its rhetorical structure, as in the diary and related forms (travelogue, notebook) is that of an 'I' talking to him- or herself, and addressing 'the putative reader only insofar as he is placed in the posi-tion of an overhearing third person' (1991: 9). For Beaujour this is why, in his *Roland Barthes par Roland Barthes* (1975), for instance, Barthes sometimes refers to himself as 'he', in order to preserve the I-You relationship, 'despite the resistance of the discourse adopted, and to reserve in his text a fictional place for the reader' (ibid.). Other self-portraits are instead more solipsistic, as Augustine's soliloquy destined for God, or Montaigne's dismissal of readership in the foreword to his *Essays*. For Beaujour, the reader thus positions himself as *addresser*, which is why 'each reader *knows* himself' in the self-portrait, and 'can become, in turn, the one who writes them' (ibid.).

Filmmaking, needless to say, is not literature – while a comparison with the written self-portrait may (partly) elucidate its narrative and verbal components, the film's visual and aural constituents must also be accounted for. It is not by accident, for instance, that in her *Les Glaneurs et la glaneuse* (*The Gleaners and I*, 2000), when she clarifies that her film is also an act of self-portraiture,[3] Agnès Varda films one of her hands with the other hand, which holds her DV camera, and is driven to compare the activity of filming herself to a self-portrait by Rembrandt, a postcard of which she brought back from a trip to Japan. A filmic self-portrait will unavoidably be indebted to painting – while being yet another, different form. And the self-portrait has also, of course, a long and (for the cinema) relevant tradition in photography and, more recently, in video art. Artistic visual practices have started, since the 1960s at least, to challenge long-established conventions, so much so that today one no longer needs to think of the self-portrait as a traditional artistic genre:

> Contemporary technologies have broadened the definition of what self-portraiture can be. In the 1960s, the American artist Robert Morris … was working on ideas based on conceptual portraiture, using bottled body fluids and medical scans. Mona Hatoum produced *Corps Etranger* in 1994, a video installation of an endoscopic journey through the landscape of her own body, and Mac Quinn's cryogenic sculpture *Self* (1997) contains nine pints of his own blood. (Rideal 2005: 10)

Bellour considers the medium of video particularly suitable for audiovisual self-portraiture. He recognises that the tradition can be traced 'in certain obscure corners of the modern cinema' (1989: 9), but then focuses on video art, first (from the early 1970s) American, and then European. His examples range from Vito Acconci's *The Red Tapes* (1976) to *Scénario du film 'Passion'* (1982) by Godard, from Peter Campus's *Three Transitions* (1973) to Bill Viola's *The Space Between the Teeth* (1976). For Bellour, there are four reasons why 'video seems to lend itself more particularly, and certainly more exclusively than cinema, to the pursuit of the self-portrait' (ibid.): the instant feedback provided by video; the possibility for the author to more naturally include his or her body; the ease of postproduction intervention on the image; and the role of mass communication (the TV screen to which video is bound) to perform the role fulfilled by rhetoric. Video is indeed, as Rosalind Krauss proposed, an inherently narcissistic medium, in which the body is sited in-between two machines: 'The first of these is the camera; the second is the monitor, which re-projects the performer's image with the immediacy of a mirror' (1976: 52). It is certainly true that video, thanks to its inexpensiveness, immediacy, wide availability and versatility, facilitates experimentation more easily than the cinema; this is the reason why pure cinematographic self-portraiture is rare, and few are the declared 35mm self-portrait films.

While the literary self-portrait is a monologue, with the reader in the paradoxical position of addresser, the visual self-portrait's tradition is one of direct
interpellation, owing to the gaze that the image of the artist/author in the portrait very frequently exchanges with the spectator standing before it. We find
a confirmation that this form of 'I-You' relationship continues in video self-
portraits in Vito Acconci's description of his own *One Minute Memories* (filmed
between 1971 and 1974): 'I was thinking in terms of video as close-up, video
as place where my face on-screen faces a viewer's face off-screen – a place for
talk, me talking to you, the viewer' (in Bellour 1989: 23). It is interesting that,
in Acconci's description, the gaze of the face in close-up is first posed as pure
interpellation, but quickly transforms into dialogue.[4]

And yet, similarly to the literary self-portrait, the audiovisual one has much
to do with the monologue, in which the spectator is in the position of an
overseeing/overhearing third person. First of all, the self-portrait's gaze is a
mise-en-abyme – the spectator looks, through the eyes of the author, at the
author: 'The viewer of a self-portrait also occupies a strange position of looking
at a metaphorical mirror that reflects back not themselves but the artist who
produced the portrait' (West 2004: 165). The identification of the spectator is,
therefore, with the author; the spectator becomes the addresser.

Unsurprisingly, the self-portrait is often described as a diary: 'Because
self-portraits merge the artist and the sitter into one, they have the allure of
a private diary, in that they seem to give us an artist's insight into his or her
own personality' (West 2004: 163). As a private,[5] diaristic gesture, self-portraiture implies a paradoxical spectatorship: 'The self-portrait can be compared
to a diary: a personal and exclusive viewpoint rarely produced with publication in mind, within which relationships and emotions may be explained and
analysed' (Rideal 2005: 43). Hence, the self-portrait (precisely as a diary) is
addressed primarily to the Self as other. The reader or spectator is let into the
privacy of the addresser's dialogue with his or her Self; he/she is invited to set
up a paradoxical identification with the author as addresser. At the same time,
it is easy to argue that the self-portrait, with its aim of self-presentation and
its ambition to be a bid for eternity, is also always meant for a public; or, more
specifically, for that special audience that is posterity.

CELLULOID AND BEYOND: AUDIOVISUAL SELF-PORTRAITS

A broad and flexible approach to the genre would suggest considering all first
person, autobiographical films which involve self-representation (diaries,
travelogues, notebooks, letters, poems and autobiographical documentaries)
as instances of self-portraiture.[6] Indeed, critics have, with various degrees of

persuasiveness, called films self-portraits, ranging from the radically experimental to fiction to documentary. Examples include the avant-garde piece *Emak Bakia* by Man Ray (1926), on the basis that 'it represents a constellation of Man Ray's formal and iconographic interests and achievements' (Aiken 1983: 240; see also Gambill 1980: 34); *Intervista* (*Federico Fellini's Intervista*, 1988) by Federico Fellini, which was described as a 'self-portrait of the artist as a mature man' (Degli-Esposti 1996: 167); *Manhatta* (1921) by Strand and Sheeler, which was seen by one critic as a 'national self-portrait', because it 'draws together a set of cinematic images to project the American artist's embodied experience' (Gerstner 2006: 158); and Dominique Cabrera's *Demain et encore demain* (*Tomorrow and Tomorrow – Diary 1995*, 1997), on the basis that Cabrera exposes herself on screen under her various identities of woman, daughter, sister, mother, lover, citizen and filmmaker (see Calatayud 2001).

Within his study of the autobiographical documentary in America, Jim Lane (2002) studied a specific form of US nonfiction cinema as 'autobiographical portraiture'. These films use 'voiceover narration, formal interviews, home-movie footage, and still photographs as well as interactive modes of shooting to establish a less plot-driven and more synchronically organised representation', in this differing from the journal entry fashion of the autobiographical documentary (2002: 94). This set of films, which developed since the early 1970s, can be divided for Lane into family portraits (with such early examples as Martin Scorsese's *Italianamerican*, 1974, and Alfred Guzzetti's *Family Portrait Sittings*, 1975) and self-portraits. The latter category 'replaces the family with a number of external forces that have connections to the way the portraitists see themselves. Thus the self is constructed in relation to art, film, politics, unemployment, hometown, infertility, and many other places, traditions, and ideas' (2002: 120). Among Lane's examples of self-portraits are Jon Jost's *Speaking Directly: Some American Notes* (1972), Jerome Hill's *Film Portrait* (1972) and Michael Moore's *Roger and Me* (1989).

While it is easy, and indeed unavoidable, to find elements of the representation of the self in all subjective, first person films, be they experimental or mainstream, fictional or documentary, one has to wonder when this approach ceases to be sound and viable. It is very difficult, indeed, to determine where self-portraiture ends and autobiography begins, or vice-versa. The above-described critical practice poses the question of generic boundaries – how elastic is the self-portrait as a genre? When should we stop talking of self-portrait, given that most art is, to a certain extent, autobiographical?

Take the case of Manoel de Oliveira's *Porto Da Minha Infância* (*Porto of My Childhood*, 2001), an overtly autobiographical account of the director's time in Porto as a child and then as a young man. The film, part documentary part fiction, mixes reconstructed sequences, with an actor playing de Oliveira, and archival images of the times and events which the director himself describes in voiceover. *Porto of My Childhood* is an autobiographical account of de Oliveira's youth, an account whose authenticity is endorsed by the director's own voice-over. However, the indexicality of the cinematic apparatus means that the artist as a young man is present in absence (he is either evoked/described by the voiceover, or replaced by a stand-in). The film could, however, also be read as the self-portrait of the artist as an old man, of the contemporary de Oliveira, while he reminisces about the past and evokes autobiographical data. The film is also, of course, a documentary on the city of Porto.

I suggest that specific films can be grouped together as more explicit and accomplished representatives of the genre. Thus I advocate here a selective approach, based on an evaluation of the self-consciousness of the director's gesture – as testified, for instance, by the film's title, by its textual commitments and characteristics, or by the author's comments in interviews and other paratexts.

Three examples of declared self-portraits by well-known film directors are Jonas Mekas's *Self-Portrait* (1990, video printed in 35mm); *JLG/JLG: autoportrait de décembre* (*JLG/JLG: Self-Portrait in December*, 1995, 35mm); and *Cinéma, de notre temps: Chantal Akerman par Chantal Akerman* (1997, TV), by Chantal Akerman.[7] Two films that their authors have described extra-textually in terms of self-portrait are Jean Cocteau's *Le testament d'Orphée* (*The Testament of Orpheus*, 1960) and Agnès Varda's *The Gleaners and I*. About the first, Cocteau remarked: 'My film is nothing other than a strip-tease show, consisting of removing my body bit by bit and revealing my soul quite naked' (in Williams 2006: 98); and again: '*Le Testament* is nothing other than an attempt at a self-portrait, a self-portrait concerned with profound likeness' (ibid.). As for the second, Varda has frequently described it in interviews as a self-portrait (see, for instance, Meyer 2001).

An incomplete list of declared self-portrait films includes: Jerome Hill's *Film Portrait* (1972, 35mm), Chuck Hudina's *Self Portrait* (1972, 16mm), Andris Grinbergs' *Pashportrets* (*Self-Portrait* 1972, 35mm) and his *Pashportrets. Testaments* (*Self-Portrait. Testament*, 2003, 35mm), Maria Lassnig, *Self Portrait* (1973, 16mm), Daniel Singelenberg's *Another Shot* (1973, 16mm), James Broughton's *Testament* (1974, 16mm), Diana Barrie's *Night Movie #1: Self-Portrait* (1974, Super 8), Gail Camhi's *Coffee Break* (1976, 16mm), Unglee's *Forget Me Not* (1979, 16 mm), Marcel Hanoun's *Un film, autoportrait* (1985, 16mm), Vilgot Sjöman's *Self Portrait '92* (1992, TV), Robert Kramer's *Berlin 10/90* (1993, Beta SP), Anja Czioska's *Roof – Shower – Underwater 3 BandW Hand Developed Film Prints* (1994, 16mm), Olivier Fouchard's *Autoportrait*

(1997, Super 8) and *Autoportrait refilmé* (1998, Super 8), Brian Frye's *Self-Portrait as Kaspar Hauser* (2000, 16mm), Louise Bourque's *Self Portrait Post Mortem* (2002, 35mm) and Lin Qiu's *Self Portrait 2* (2006, miniDV). Even this eclectic list demonstrates that the audiovisual self-portrait is not confined to video but uses all formats, from Super 8 to 35mm; while at the same time being a decidedly experimental form, due to the high level of personal content and the affinity for research that self-portraiture has always displayed. Indeed, these films are extremely diverse in style, format, length (they range from two to 105 minutes) and technical specifications, and interpret self-portraiture in totally dissimilar and idiosyncratic ways. This is, somehow, unsurprising. Self-portraiture, in fact, for obvious reasons is necessarily original – hence unique, avant-garde and modern. As Beaujour noted of the written form, 'Self-portraitists make self-portraits without knowing what they are doing. This "genre" proffers no "horizon of expectation." Each self-portrait is written as though it were the only text of its kind' (1991: 3).

And yet, while being necessarily unique, many self-portraits feed on analogous themes, ideas and obsessions. All art historians who have studied self-portraiture in painting, for instance, point to the fact that it is an eminently narcissistic genre, as well as the epitome of self-analysis and intimate dissection. At the same time, the self-portrait was traditionally used as a tool to present and to demonstrate one's skills to potential patrons; to ensure one's artistic survival and recognition; and to indicate one's perception of his or her position in society. Hence, the self-portrait is a contradictory genre, which merges the most intimate artistic gesture with the most public display of image-management: 'The self-portrait is the artist's most personal form of expression. It is the ultimate means of self-analysis, presenting an opportunity for self-reflection, self-expression and self-promotion; a bid for eternity' (Rideal 2005: 7). Self-portraits are usually statements simultaneously about the artist's personality and her status in society. Frequently, they include the tools of their author's art, as well as objects situating her in space and in time. While being a narcissistic mirror of the self, and a locus for the expression of the artist's most intimate self-concerns and personal legacy, in fact, the self-portrait is never isolated from other discourses, and also always engages with the external world, even just by including the markers of one's time and society: 'Self-portraiture records not only what the artist looks like but also how they interpret themselves and the world around them' (Rideal 2005: 8).

All-important themes of the genre are death and *vanitas*. Each self-portrait freezes a moment in time, hence capturing the work of death; and each is, potentially, the last one; and, therefore, a *memento mori* – the reminder of the transient nature of vanity, and the meaninglessness of earthly life. Furthermore, despite its promise 'to deliver the artist in some capacity to the viewer' (Jones 2002: 951), the self-portrait also poses the problem of whether we can ever 'know' the subject behind the image. This is evidently because 'The subject is neither identical with itself nor with the portrait each one of us paints of ourselves, that consoling fiction of an autonomous ego invested with "attributes of permanence, identity, and substantiality"' (Lomas 2000: 187). Indeed, irrespective of the medium through which they are accomplished, all self-portraits are deeply concerned with the relationship and negotiation between the portrayed self and the original self; so much so that the self-portrait can be seen as a 'transaction', a 'dialectic of self and other' (ibid.). This question entails a corollary of issues and discourses, many of which will be of clear interest for my case study, and which I list here: the contrast between the ideal body and the natural body; the double and the divided self; the mirror image and the processes of recognition and misrecognition; the name and the signature; the act of revealing and the act of concealing.

It is opportune to begin to note here that some of these themes (and at least those of the split self and the double, of misrecognition and concealment) are not only relevant to Antonioni's final filmic self-portrait, but in many ways to his entire oeuvre.

ANTONIONI'S FINAL SELF-PORTRAIT: *THE GAZE OF MICHELANGELO*

'Which body? We have several' (Barthes 1977: 60).

Produced by the Instituto LUCE, first screened at the 2004 Cannes Film Festival,[8] *Lo sguardo di Michelangelo* (*The Gaze of Michelangelo*, 2004, 35mm) was made in the wake of the completion of the 'Progetto Mosè' (Project Moses), the four-year meticulous restoration of Michelangelo Buonarroti's monumental complex of the tomb of Julius II, in the Roman Church of San Pietro in Vincoli. The project had an ample audience, and an informational halo: it could be followed live on the internet thanks to a number of well-placed webcams.[9] Subsequent to the completion of the restoration, Antonioni filmed the seventeen minutes of *The Gaze of Michelangelo*, a deceptively simple nonfiction, in which the director goes to San Pietro in Vincoli to admire *Moses* and the other statues.

The short can be read in many ways: as the documentation and exploration of the results of the restoration; as a tribute to Michelangelo; as a study of the *Moses*; as a reflection on the relationship between film and the fine arts; as an exploration of digital technologies and their marriage with traditional filmmaking; as a meditation on the relationship between art and life, permanence and transience; and as a contemplation of death. It can additionally be seen as a retracing and repetition of the many visits Sigmund Freud is known to have paid to the statue which fascinated him so much. After seeing it for the first time in 1901, Freud went to study *Moses* daily, and for many hours at a time, during his summer vacation in Rome in 1912; he then wrote the controversial essay *Der Moses des Michelangelo* in 1914 (see Freud 1953–74).

While being all this, *The Gaze of Michelangelo* is, I argue, primarily a self-portrait of Michelangelo Antonioni; of the self-portrait it has, indeed, all the tenets and functions. Placed at the very end of his career and his life,[10] containing Antonioni's last self-fashioned images, and being undoubtedly his best post-1985 film, it acquires the function and value of a legacy. When Antonioni leaves the church, seemingly on his own legs, at the end of the film, he leaves simultaneously art, the cinema, his audience and life.

As is well-known, since 1985 Antonioni was half paralysed as a consequence of a stroke, which affected his bodily movement and speech for over twenty years, and needed aid to walk. Yet in this film we see him standing and walking without aid (although not talking),[11] thanks to a digital alteration of the image. Antonioni's experimentation with image modification was certainly not new – an example is his testing of colour in the video, then reprinted in 35mm, *Il mistero di Oberwald* (*The Oberwald Mystery*, 1981). As the director has suggested, talking of this film: 'Electronic equipment allows you to add, take away, modify colour, from the whole image or a section of it, while you are shooting. In practice, you "paint" your film there and then, while making it' (in Biarese and Tassone 1985: 60; author's translation).

Digital intervention in the self-portrait is far from being surprising or unheard of or. Self-portraiture was, indeed, used as a promotional tool even by Renaissance artists, who began to think of identity in new ways, so much so that 'in the sixteenth century there appears to be an increased self-consciousness about the fashioning of human identity as a manipulable, artful process' (Greenblatt 1984: 2). While it is possible to identify paintings that appear to be the product of dispassionate self-awareness, and that offer unforgiving analyses of one's image, self-portraits frequently are a means of narcissistically communicating the idea of the self that an artist is most comfortable with and proud of, and wants us to embrace and remember.

It is thus unsurprising that digital technology is today an alluring tool for the refashioning of one's identity: in recent times, for instance, 'Artists eagerly adopted computer-based technology in order to "put themselves in the picture" in the form of digitally manipulated photographs' (Avgitidou 2003: 134). They often did this not in order to 'distort reality but to help redefine the narrow dictates of normality' (Adams 1994: 216). When looking at the possibilities offered by the internet, then, artists 'have engaged in digital culture beyond manipulated photography, in invented (non-existing) personalities, identities shared by a group of people or subjectivities "constructed" by various others' (Avgitidou 2003: 135). The onset of digital technology, in other words, has introduced a whole series of new possibilities in terms of self-fashioning – even though the novelty factor is only relative. As Maureen Turim has convincingly argued,

> the principles of image construction are only in part determined by a technology, since all the techniques associated with that new technology existed before, in a form of prefiguration. [...] With digital video, the artisanal approximation that performed similar processes include the ways art, photography, film, and video prefigure the work of digital imagery through compositional devices, *mise-en-scène*, constructivism, and collage/superimposition techniques. (1999: 52)

For Antonioni, the use of technology (at that time, video) for the purpose of image alteration appeared to realise the director's old wish of 'painting a film as one paints a picture' (in Tinazzi 1996: xxv).[12] It is also important to recall that self-portraits in painting, because of the freedom they afforded the artist, on account of the lack of a commission and the constant availability of the model, often originated as opportunities for technical experimentation: 'Artists could use the self-portrait as a means of drawing attention to the medium and the process of production of the work, to show off their skill, or to experiment with technique or style' (West 2004: 165). And yet, if image construction has always been available to artists (even before the advancements introduced by digital technology),[13] fashioning and self-fashioning, especially when a photographic image is involved, do not necessarily sever the link between such image and its object, or disrupt our ability/tendency to look at it as an indexical trace of reality. As Timothy Dow Adams correctly noted, 'the emergence of computer manipulated photography seems to have done little to shake the belief in a direct, physical link between photographs and their subjects' (1994: 476).

The significance of the digital refashioning of his body by Antonioni in *The Gaze of Michelangelo*, a restoration that echoes the restoration of the *Moses*, will become clearer after an exploration of the features of this ostensibly plain and minimalist, but in truth extraordinarily rich and complex, self-portrait.

Antonioni appeared as himself in footage by other filmmakers, and especially in various documentaries, for instance Gianfranco Minghozzi's *Michelangelo Antonioni storia di un autore* (*Michelangelo Antonioni: The Story of an Auteur*, 1966, TV); Wim Wenders' *Chambre 666* (*Room 666*, 1982, TV); and Enrica

Antonioni's *Fare un film per me è vivere* (*To Make a Film is to be Alive*, 1996, TV), a behind the scenes of *Al di là delle nuvole* (*Beyond the Clouds*, 1995). With regard to self-fashioned images, however, Antonioni's body is almost completely absent from his cinema,[14] as well as from his painting: 'I used to paint even as a child; then, it was faces: my mother's, my father's, Greta Garbo's. Mine, never: because I'm unable to see myself' (Antonioni 1993; author's translation). Despite such almost complete absence of self-produced images, it is possible to argue that Antonioni is immanent in all his films, embedded through his directorial gaze, which is constantly felt by the spectator as a structuring presence; as Sam Rohdie has argued, precisely like his characters, 'Antonioni gazes, equally estranged, on that multiplication and problematisation of looking which extends itself, uncomfortably, to the audience' (1990: 72). It is not coincidental that the title of Antonioni's self-portrait film should be *The Gaze of Michelangelo*.

Such a title immediately evokes a number of themes that are emblematic of self-portraiture: the name, the signature, and the double. While 'Michelangelo's gaze' alludes, in the first instance, to Buonarroti and his 'vision', to his style and his signature, a secondary but obvious reference is to Antonioni himself. The film's title, therefore, attracts our attention to the destiny in a name, which Antonioni shares with another Italian artist, who lived between 1475 and 1564 – a fortuitous, but significant and symbolic coincidence. Antonioni, in fact, fashions his self-presentation in the shape of a mirror image of another Michelangelo. The implications are bold, given Buonarroti's widely recognised status as one of the greatest Western artists – or, more precisely, a multi-talented genius (sculptor, painter, architect and poet) that, as the archetypal Renaissance man, embodies a (the?) peak of Western civilisation.[15]

Is Antonioni drawing parallels with Buonarroti, hence positioning himself as one of the greatest artists of his century – and promoting his own work as a pinnacle of the achievements of the cinema, in its phase of most radical experimentation but also of maturity of his art, before its decline in the second half of the twentieth century? Is he looking at himself as an utterly original artist – precisely as Buonarroti, who, taking as his point of reference the styles of Florentine and Roman classical Renaissance, produced an utterly novel, revolutionary artistic vision?

It is no coincidence that Antonioni's work is widely regarded by critics to be very conversant with, and bordering on, the fine arts. His first artistic production was as a painter;[16] his cinema is noticeably painterly, characterised by a use of framing, lighting and, when relevant, colour that is clearly inspired by an observation of the work of painters. A recurring motif in his work are the 'places which are openly non-narrativised, of a pictorial and visual interest which suddenly takes hold, causes the narrative to err, to wander, momentarily to dissolve' (Rohdie 1990: 51). As evidence of this interest and focus, one can note that 'Antonioni's cinema has always thematised the world of image creation – the cinema, photography, and painting' (Casetti 2002: 5; author's translation). Furthermore, Antonioni was, of course, especially sensitive to architecture – his films always frame the built environment in aesthetically striking ways. His interest in technique and experimentation with style and filmic language is close to those traditionally associated with the fine arts. As Antonioni himself recognised:

I have a great love for painting. For me, it is the one art, along with architecture, that comes immediately after filmmaking. I'm very fond of reading books on art and architecture, of leafing through pages and pages of art volumes, and I like to go to art shows and keep in touch with the latest work being done in art – not just to be *au courant* but because painting is something that moves me passionately. Therefore I believe all these perceptions and this interest have been somewhat assimilated. And, naturally, having followed modern art, my taste and my predilection for a certain style would be reflected in my work. (1996: 44).

If the suggested comparison with Buonarroti may seem immodest, or even tactless, a number of attenuating circumstances should be considered. The principal one is that Antonioni frames himself as visually towered over by the *Moses*. This is also a philological approach – *Moses*, in fact, now at floor level, was initially conceived for a different position in the monumental complex, and was made to be viewed from below; calculations suggest that its head was supposed to be at 6.6m from ground level (see, for instance, de Tolnay 1963: 284; Macmillan and Swales 2003: 69). Antonioni's choice is also suggestive of a viewing position 'from below', almost as if sitting in a wheelchair (he needed one more permanently since 2005).

Furthermore, Antonioni positions himself as an admiring spectator rather than as a fellow artist (no overt reference is made to his role as a filmmaker); and clearly pays homage to Buonarroti as a superior genius, an unmatchable source of inspiration. It is also highly significant that Antonioni's statement about his own status and achievements as an artist is made by means of an utterly small, modest, understated film, which was not destined to be widely seen – in many ways, the opposite of Buonarroti's *Moses*, which is not only imposing, sublime and superhuman, but that in Michelangelo's original plans should have been part of a colossal structure for the tomb of Pope Julius II, previously intended for the impressive setting of St Peter's Basilica. Nonetheless, the comparison with Buonarroti is undeniably introduced by the film; Antonioni here makes his claim to fame for posterity – not for nothing, is the self-portrait, as already suggested, a highly narcissistic genre, deeply linked to self-promotion and the presentation of the way in which the artist positions himself or herself in society.

Part of this positioning is conveyed by the artist's own name, which becomes a true signature – and the self-portrait is always, of course, a form of signature; also because, historically, 'When artists began producing portraits of themselves in the fifteenth century, it was initially as a footnote or signature to another commission' (West 2004: 163). Michelagnolo Buonarroti (as he himself spelled his name) is universally known as 'Michelangelo' – a highly recognisable 'brand name', which stands for a rigorous, commanding, grandiose and austere vision of art and of life, and for a titanic spirit of rebellion against the human condition. The name also becomes Antonioni's signature, which stands for a similarly outstanding and unique, instantly recognisable style, and sober engagement with the subject of the human condition.

It must be noted that the homonymy and the system of correspondences, suggested by the title and implied by the film, also gesture at the uncanny experience of the doubling, which is a persistent theme in self-portraiture. The double is also one of the key figures in Antonioni's cinema – examples are films like *L'avventura* (*The Adventure*, 1960), with Anna (Lea Massari) who is first mirrored and then replaced by Claudia (Monica Vitti); and *Professione: Reporter* (*The Passenger*, 1975), with Jack Nicholson's David Locke taking the place of his döppelganger, the dead David Robinson. For Rohdie, in Antonioni's cinema 'the process of doubling has no starting point: it is not first the reality, then the image of it, first the substance, then the silhouette, but rather the tenuousness of both, their intermingling, the fragility of the line marking them, the constant threat of obliteration and dissolution [...] Subject and object waver, their very existences at stake' (1990: 111–12).[17] In self-portraiture, the subject/object relation is also a threat to identity: the artist looks at herself from the outside as an*other* body, as a reflection, as a split self or, indeed, as a double.

Buonarroti produced several self-portraits; he appears in a number of his paintings and statues, as a young man, as an adult and, finally, as an old man. Many scholars consider his art to be deeply autobiographical – *Moses* included: 'Michelangelo's oeuvre contains autobiographical allusions, though always indirect, generalised, sublimated. Even though idealised, his works are more personalised than those of any other Tuscan master. The faces of Procolus, David, Moses, Brutus reflect his own fierceness and his stern morals' (de Tolnay 1963: 263; author's translation).

One of the most uncanny of Buonarroti's self-portraits is included in the fresco of the Sistine Chapel: here, Michelangelo's face appears, distorted and deformed but still recognisable, in the skin that St Bartholomew carries with him. This rather disturbing self-representation points at another important facet of self-portraiture: the visual representation of oneself, one's double, becomes a mask, more specifically a mortuary mask, implying the ideas of both death and *vanitas*. This aspect is fundamental for an understanding of Antonioni's self-portrait in *The Gaze of Michelangelo*. Antonioni's image is here a mask, a digitally modified double, which hints at questions of demise as well as of instability of the self. Before I come to these all-important issues, one more element of the film's title must be explored: the gaze.

I have suggested above that Antonioni presents himself in his film as a 'consumer', as a spectator rather than as a producer of art, and as a director. This may seem unusual, given the long-standing tradition in visual self-portraiture of representing the author in the act of painting or of photographing, and of including in the representation images of the artist's tools – brushes, easels, canvas and paintings, and cameras. Even when these objects are not present, an emphasis is usually placed on the artist's 'natural' work tools: eyes and hands. Indeed, while Antonioni does not carry a camera, the insistent framing of his eyes and hands is ample evidence of his role as an artist, and specifically as a film director. Even though it may seem logical that the director should privilege his eyes only as instruments of his art, there is plenty of evidence that filmmakers consider their hands to be at least as important as their gaze; probably not only on account of the idea of holding the camera, but of the prominent role of montage in filmmaking, and its persistent association, despite the evolution and computerisation of the technique, with basic manual operations of cutting and gluing. Furthermore, the hands aid the gaze, they assist it in organising and 'framing' the viewed object, as Antonioni's hands clearly do here.[18] It is significant that in filmic self-portraits directors often frame their hands – two examples are the already quoted scene in *The Gleaners and I*, and *JLG-JLG: Self-Portrait in December*, in which a long sequence is dominated by a reflection uttered by Godard over images of his hands.

The gaze in the film's title is, obviously, as polyvalent a term as the name 'Michelangelo'. It refers to Buonarroti's artistic vision; as well as to the stern gaze of the *Moses*, which is studied and almost brought to life by Antonioni's camera. It is known that Michelangelo considered *Moses* to be his most accomplished, life-like creation; upon completion of the statue, he is believed to have struck its right knee and commanded: 'Now speak!'[19] Through a series of close-ups and detail shots, articulated through a montage that constantly varies the angle of vision, Antonioni seems to ask the Moses to 'now look'. Antonioni's framing and montage, however, do more than this; as I have already suggested, they also reconstruct the original viewing position. By moving the camera around the sculpture and by varying and multiplying the point of view, Antonioni annuls its 'alleged disproportionate, monstrous, and satyr-like characteristics' (Macmillan and Swales 2003: 73), which are perceived by a spectator in the current frontal view, and achieves the effect, intended by the artist, of a 'vital, complex, and lively figure' (ibid.).

The gaze is, of course, also the gaze of the cinema, and especially of Antonioni – both the man's gaze (which, now quite opaque but still searching and intense, is often scrutinised by the camera) and the director's 'vision'. By exchanging glances with *Moses*, and to an extent with Michelangelo (if we take the *Moses* to be, at least in some measure, a self-portrait), Antonioni represents himself as the director of a cinema eminently engaged, at an aesthetic, philosophical and linguistic level, with the question of the gaze.

The geography of this visual exchange, reproduced by shot/reverse shot, is a compelling *mise-en-abyme*; the gazes put in circulation by Antonioni's camera are multiple – including, of course, the spectator's. By this process, Antonioni recreates and simultaneously complicates the typical situation of the visual self-portrait, in which the artist stares out of the painting/photograph/sculpture at the spectator; and the spectator, looking into the eyes of the artist's image, is placed in the position of the artist herself, and doubles her gaze. The paradox of an addressee who becomes the addresser is masterfully reproduced. We both look *at* Antonioni (there are at least as many shots of him as of the statues) and *with* Antonioni: several semi-subjective shots, in which the camera is placed just behind Antonioni's head and frames the side of his face (with his glasses in clear evidence), as well as the field of his vision, invite us to look *through* his eyes (indeed, quite literally through his spectacles). In

these shots, the spectatorial identification with the director is also suggested by the photography: while his image is sharp, his field of vision is out of focus. Simultaneously, we exchange glances with *Moses*, and thus look into the mirror of Michelangelo's eyes.[20]

The emphasis on matter, form, body and the activities of fashioning and self-fashioning is overwhelming. One cannot stress enough the importance of the body in the self-portrait, which 'bases itself above all on the experience of the body, of the author's own body as the site and theatre of experience' (Bellour 1989: 10). Framed at some distance, Antonioni, about to turn 92, enters the church with his right hand casually resting in his pocket, and walks slowly but resolutely towards the tomb. The frailty, thinness, quasi-transparency of his body are highlighted and intensified by his apparition: he enters from an open door, through which a blade of light cuts through the darkness of the church. The importance of this door (which literally opens and closes the film, and frames it) is consonant with the prominent role that 'not only archways, but doorways, entrances, exits, thresholds, often windows' (Rohdie 1990: 66) play in Antonioni's cinema, as boundaries between different spaces. The open, lit door of *The Gaze of Michelangelo* recalls not only the eschatological/supernatural dimension (which will acquire importance at the end of the film) but also, of course, the (im)materiality itself of the cinema – the ray of light tearing the darkness of the auditorium. Antonioni's body is, therefore, an ethereal, fashioned filmic body, a play of shadows and light projected on a screen – as well as an iconic image of a real body, preserved and embalmed by the cinema in its function of death-at-work.

Walking through the film's threshold: the opening sequence of *The Gaze of Michelangelo*.

Contrasting masculinities: the titanic Renaissance hero and the Western bourgeois artist.

In the film, Antonioni's is a still-flexible and handsome though aged body; stylishly dressed in Armani, he looks confident, smart and blasé, a refined bourgeois intellectual at total ease with himself – an image that fits in with prevalent forms of self-portrayal by male artists in the late twentieth century, which included 'the tropes of the artist as gentleman, Christ, Bohemian, or technician' (West 2004: 169). The distance of the camera enhances the seamless effect of the digital intervention, which allowed Antonioni to show us his body as he saw it, and as he wanted us to remember it; to express his understanding of his position in society, through choice of clothes, bodily shape and posture; as well as his comprehension/fashioning of his masculinity.

This self-portrait is not, however, that of a false, FX body; neither does it become a sublimated or sanitised version of an old man's body. The camera does get near to inspect Antonioni's face in close-up, to frame it from different viewpoints, to linger on the opaque gaze and the wrinkled skin. Furthermore, Antonioni does not attempt to trick the audience as to the reality of his situation – although in the medium-long or full shots he is seen standing, thanks to the digital refashioning of the image, in the close-ups that include the top of his shoulders he is evidently in a seated position. Hence, his viewing position fully corresponds to his embodied experience (as seen in the view 'from below' of the *Moses*). In Antonioni's cinema, bodies are always historicised (see Rascaroli and Rhodes 2008); and the director's body in this film is no exception. This point becomes unmistakably clear through the comparison he mercilessly sets up between his aged, fragile body, connoting a certain type of modern Western masculinity, and the timeless body of the statue, immortalising the Renaissance vision of a heroic, wilful and imposing masculinity.

Antonioni's film, hence, brings the body to the fore in multiple ways: as the theatre of experience (an experience that, via the emphasis on sight and touch, is marked as fundamentally sensual); as the site of the specific and embodied experience of an artist, and therefore instrument of abstraction, intelligence, craft, sublimation and creation; and as the product of an act of self-fashioning, which attests to the man's vision of himself, within his society and within the history of the arts and of the cinema in particular. And again, as the historicised body of a bourgeois, Western, male intellectual; as a filmic body – a flickering, insubstantial, but intensely iconic and desirable image, which actualises the myth of bodily intimacy between the film's spectator and a more-than-real, magnified and beautified human figure; and, finally, as embodiment of the frailty and imperfection of human matter, compared to the durability of marble, and of artistic creation.

The film evokes death in many ways, and not only because of Antonioni's considerable age at the time of shooting; this is perhaps unsurprising, given that 'there is hardly an Antonioni film in which death is not a central concern' (Rohdie 1990: 106) – and also given that death is the necessary subtext of all self-portraits.[21] The director comes to the church of San Pietro in Vincoli in order to admire Pope Julius II's grave; the church itself inspires thoughts of mortality and transience. The durability of *Moses*, which long outlived its creator, and which will also outlive Antonioni, its admirer, is in contrast to the fragility of this very minor, occasional nonfiction, to which Antonioni entrusted his last (and almost only) self-fashioned images, and which risks being rapidly forgotten, overlooked by the mechanisms of film distribution and, as a result, film criticism.

Aware of being in the process of crafting his final self-portrait, Antonioni does not shun the thought of death; rather, he faces it straight on, and portrays himself in the act of leaving life. When he enters the church through the open door, the chirping of birds invades the silent, dim space of the chapel together with the light – thus giving the impression that the director had arrived from the reality of a bright Roman morning. When he exits through the same door some time later, however, the birds are no longer to be heard; from off-screen comes instead the sound of a distant choir singing the 'Magnificat' by Giovanni Pierluigi da Palestrina.[22] Prompted and almost summoned by the incipit of the sacred, otherworldly singing, Antonioni leaves *Moses* and heads towards the brightness, which now looks like a metaphor for the transfiguration of death. In long shot and without cuts, we observe his slender, beautiful figure turn and give a last look at Michelangelo's statues, then walk slowly towards the door. The camera pans to follow him, then stops and lets him go, continuing to observe him at some distance as, hand in pocket, Antonioni nonchalantly walks away

The ultimate disappearance: Antonioni leaves the church, the cinema and life at the end of *The Gaze of Michelangelo*.

from the lens, and steps into the unknown. The filmmaker of the disconcerting uncertainty of subjectivity, the director of so many uncanny disappearances, performs the final, ultimate disappearance – and walking through the door/limen/frame of the film, transforms himself into the matter of cinema.

Acknowledgement

An earlier version of this essay first appeared as a chapter in L. Rascaroli (2009) *The Personal Camera: Subjective Cinema and the Essay Film*. London: Wallflower Press.

Notes

1   Consider, for instance, the Romantic concepts of 'personality' and 'inner life'.
2   Lejeune's autobiographical pact relates to language (prose), subject (the life of an individual), the author's situation (coincidence between author and narrator), and narrator's positioning (coincidence between narrator and protagonist); see Lejeune (1996).
3   As well as being a road-documentary on gleaning, and a travelogue (see Mazierska and Rascaroli 2006: 124–30).
4   This effect is reached in many of his 1970s videos, for instance *Theme Song* (1973).
5   In this sense, it is significant to note that commissioned self-portraits are traditionally rare. This fact also contributes to explain the scarcity of 35mm self-portraits.
6   As, for instance, does Muriel Tinel (2006).
7   In 1998 Akerman also created a video installation entitled *Selfportrait/Autobiography: A Work in Progress*, which included six monitors showing images from DVDs accompanied by a narrative written and read by the artist, and which was presented almost simultaneously that year in New York, London and Paris. A section of *Cinéma, de notre temps: Chantal Akerman par*

Chantal Akerman is included in the 2007 Carlotta DVD set *Chantal Akerman: Les Années 70*.

8   The film had limited theatrical distribution, and was released as a bonus in the Warner Bros. 2004 DVD edition of the omnibus *Eros*.

9   At the now unavailable website www.progettomose.it Helmut Newton took a series of photographs of the restoration.

10 Only followed by his disappointing instalment in the omnibus *Eros*, *The Gaze of Michelangelo* is, in many ways, Antonioni's true final film. Antonioni died in Rome on 30 July 2007, at 92 years of age.

11 While no word is pronounced, the film is notable for its wonderfully refined soundtrack of noises and sounds.

12 Significantly (and also proving Turim's point in the above quotation), Antonioni had already used artisan-like means to 'paint' some of his previous films. For instance, when shooting *Il deserto rosso* (*Red Desert*, 1964), his first film in colour, he asked his crew to spray paint the vegetation on the set, in order to achieve the desired tonal effect.

13 A fitting cinematic example is Woody Allen's *Zelig* (1983), which achieved ample and seamless image manipulation before the advent of digital technology.

14 Antonioni appears in his ten-minute documentary *Ritorno a Lisca Bianca* (1983, TV, 16mm), a return to the Eolian island of *L'avventura* twenty-four years after the shooting of the film.

15 It may be useful here to bear in mind that this opinion was already championed by biographer and art historian Giorgio Vasari while Michelangelo was still alive.

16 Antonioni was a painter at least since the 1970s; some of his work is currently displayed at the Michelangelo Antonioni Museum in Ferrara, his birthplace.

17 Although I here extended them to Antonioni's entire oeuvre, Rohdie's comments were written about a specific film, the documentary *N.U. Nettezza Urbana* (1948).

18 It is also worth recalling here that 'Antonioni's films are often filled with shots of hands moving, groping, reaching out, in search of something which only becomes clear when it is found and sometimes not even then' (Rohdie 1990: 133).

19 According to the tale, a visible scar on the statue's knee is the mark of Michelangelo's hammer.

20 It must also be noted that *Moses*' gaze (together with his posture, and his manner of holding his beard and the tablets) was a crucial point of interest in dissimilar and even conflicting critical readings of the statue (including Freud's).

21 Once again, I would like to recall the example of Varda's *The Gleaners and I* as a 'portrait of the artist as an old lady'; and especially the moment in which she argues: 'No it is not "Oh rage", no it is not despair, it is not "Old age, my enemy", it might even be "Old age, my friend", but still my hair and my hands keep telling me that the end is near' (translation from the English subtitles of the 2002 Zeitgeist DVD edition of the film).

22 It is significant that, as part of the restoration, the large arch window and the four rectangular openings that Michelangelo had inserted in the monument, and that had subsequently been closed, have been reopened. Through these openings both light and sounds originally came – behind the monument, in fact, the choir of the Canonici Regolari Lateranensi used to rehearse, and Michelangelo meant for the voices to enter the church, as a soundtrack.

References

Adams, T. D. (1994) 'Life Writing and Light Writing; Autobiography and Photography', *Modern Fiction Studies*, 40, 3, 459–92.

Aiken, E. A. (1983) '*Emak Bakia* Reconsidered', *Art Journal*, 43, 3, 240–6.

Antonioni, M. (1993) 'Le montagne incantate', in *Le montagne incantate e altre opere*, catalogue of exhibition held in Ferrara, 30 July–31 October 1993, ed. by Direzione delle Gallerie Civiche di

Arte Moderna di Palazzo dei Diamanti, Ferrara Excerpt on-line. Available HTTP: http://musei.
talete.org/musei/antonioni/docdoc.htm (20 July 2008).

____ (1994) *Fare un film è per me vivere: scritti sul cinema*, ed. C. di Carlo and G. Tinazzi. Venice:
Marsilio.

____ (1996) 'A Talk with Michelangelo Antonioni on his Work' (1961), in *Michelangelo Antonioni:
The Architecture of Vision, Writings and Interviews on the Cinema*. di Carlo. C. and G. Tinazzi,
(eds.) New York: Marsilio: 21-47.

____ (1996) 'Preface to Six Films' (1964), in *Michelangelo Antonioni: The Architecture of Vision,
Writings and Interviews on the Cinema*. di Carlo. C. and G. Tinazzzi, (eds.) New York: Marsilio:
57-68.

Avgitidou, A. (2003) 'Performances of the Self', *Digital Creativity*, 14, 3, 131–8.

Barthes, R. (1975) *Roland Barthes par Roland Barthes*. Paris: Seuil.

____ (1977) *Roland Barthes by Roland Barthes*, trans. Richard Howard. London: Macmillan.

Beaujour, M. (1991) *Poetics of the Literary Self-Portrait*. New York, NY: New York University
Press.

Bellour, R. (1989) 'Eye for I: Video Self-Portraits', trans. Lynne Kirby, in R. Bellour (ed.) *Eye for I:
Video Self-Portraits*. New York, NY: Independent Curators Incorporated: 7–20.

Biarese, C. and A. Tassone (1985) *I film di Michelangelo Antonioni*. Rome: Gremese.

Calatayud, A. (2001) 'An ordinary woman but a filmmaker: *Demain et encore demain* (1997) —
Dominique Cabrera's self-portrait', *Studies in French Cinema*, 1, 1, 22–8.

Casetti, F. (2002) 'Introduction', in Saverio Zumbo, *Al di là delle immagini: Michelangelo Antonioni*.
Alessandria: Falsopiano: 5–6.

de Tolnay, C. (1963) 'Michelangelo Buonarroti', in Massimo Pallottino (ed.) *Enciclopedia Universale
dell'Arte*. Florence: Sansoni: 263–306.

Degli-Esposti, C. (1996) 'Federico Fellini's *Intervista* or the Neo-Baroque Creativity of the Analysand
on Screen', *Italica*, 73, 2, 157–72.

di Carlo, C. and Tinazzzi, G. (eds) (1996) *Michelangelo Antonioni: The Architecture of Vision.
Writings and Interviews on the Cinema*. New York: Marsilio.

Freud, S. (1953–74) 'The Moses of Michelangelo', in *The Standard Edition of the Complete
Psychological Works*, ed. James Strachey, 24 vols. (v. 13). London: Hogarth Press and the
Institute of Psychoanalysis, 211–36.

Gambill, N. (1980) 'The Movies of Man Ray', in *Man Ray: Photographs and Objects*, exhibition
catalogue, Birmingham: Birmingham Museum of Art, 30–42.

Gerstner, D. A. (2006) *Manly Arts: Masculinity and Nation in Early American Cinema*. Durham, NC:
Duke University Press.

Gilbard, F. (1984) 'An Interview With Vito Acconci: Video Works 1970-1978', *Afterimage*, 12, 4,
November: 9-15.

Greenblatt, S. (1984) *Renaissance Self-fashioning: From More to Shakespeare*. Chicago, IL:
University of Chicago Press.

Jones, A. (2002) 'The "Eternal Return": Self-Portrait Photography as a Technology of Embodiment',
Signs: Journal of Women in Culture and Society, 27, 4, 947–78.

Krauss, R. (1976) 'Video: The Aesthetics of Narcissism', *October*, 1, Spring, 50-64.

Lane, J. (2002) *The Autobiographical Documentary in America*. Madison, WN: University of
Wisconsin Press.

Lejeune, P. (1996) *Le pacte autobiographique*. Paris: Seuil.

Lomas, D. (2000) *The Haunted Self: Surrealism, Psychoanalysis, Subjectivity*. New Haven, CT: Yale
University Press.

Macmillan, M. and P. J. Swales (2003) 'Observations from the Refuse-Heap: Freud, Michelangelo's
Moses, and Psychoanalysis', *American Imago*, 60, 1, 41–104.

Mazierska, E. and Rascaroli, L. (2006) *Crossing New Europe: Postmodern Travel and the European
Road Movie*. London: Wallflower Press.

Meyer, A. (2001) 'Interview: "Gleaning' the Passion of Agnès Varda", *IndieWire*, On-line. Available HTTP: http://www.indiewire.com/people/int_Varda_Agnes_010308.html (20 July 2008).

Rascaroli, L. and J. D. Rhodes (2008) 'Antonioni and the Place of Modernity: A Tribute', *Framework*, 49, 1, 42–7.

Rideal, L. (2005) *Self-Portraits*. London: National Portrait Gallery Publications.

Rohdie, S. (1990) *Antonioni*. London: British Film Institute.

Tinazzi, G. (1996) 'The Gaze and the Story', in C. di Carlo and G. Tinazzi (eds) *Michelangelo Antonioni: The Architecture of Vision, Writings and Interviews on the Cinema*. New York, NY: Marsilio, xiii–xxvii.

Tinel, M. (2006) 'Cocteau, Wenders, Akerman, Kramer… Le cinéma et l'autoportrait: de l'expression de soi à l'expérience d'un support', *Hors Champ*, April, On-line. Available HTTP: http://www.horschamp.qc.ca/article.php3?id_article=220 (23 April 2012).

Trilling, L. (1972) *Sincerity and Authenticity*. London: Oxford University Press.

Turim, M. (1999) 'Artisanal Prefigurations of the Digital: Animating Realities, Collage Effects, and Theories of Image Manipulation', *Wide Angle*, 21, 1, 48–62.

West, S. (2004) *Portraiture*. Oxford: Oxford University Press.

Williams, J. S. (2006) *Jean Cocteau*. Manchester: Manchester University Press.

Cycles of Life: *El cielo gira* and Spanish Autobiographical Documentary

Efrén Cuevas

A wide shot of a landscape with a hill and a solitary tree at the top. We hear the filmmaker's voice: 'This is the place that you see from the house where I was born, and therefore, the first thing I saw in the world.' This key moment, close to the beginning of *El cielo gira* (*The Sky Turns*, 2004), seems to suggest a standard autobiographical film about the life of the filmmaker. Instead, we find a portrait of a small Castilian village on the verge of disappearing, composed of long, contemplative shots of the austere landscape and the old villagers who inhabit it. It may come as a surprise, then, to realise that we are confronted with a landmark in Spanish autobiographical filmmaking; a sensitive portrait of a village filtered through the gaze of Mercedes Álvarez, never visible on-screen though present through her calm voiceover commentary. This subtle approach to personal filmmaking somehow speaks of the uneasiness of some Spanish documentary filmmakers about turning their cameras on their own lives. The case of the film *Retrato* (*Portrait*, 2004), with Carlos Ruiz refusing to consider the portrait of his parents autobiographical, seems to underline that idea: 'In fact, autobiography is just a contextual level in which one can discuss many things – time, memory, past and present, being man and woman – and mainly the dichotomy of the son's point of view – myself, in this case – because it is the point of view of the child and the grown-up.'[1]

This chapter intends to delve into that creative milieu, to examine in the first place why Spanish filmmakers have scarcely adopted an autobiographical approach to documentary, while commenting briefly on those that have appeared during the 2000s.[2] Then, I will analyse closely *El cielo gira*, which can be considered the best autobiographical film to date from Spain. Its approach may serve as an example of a certain type of Spanish documentary, where it blends an auterist look with a contemplative style, in order to explore in this case the layers of our country with a microhistorical lens.

MAPPING OUT THE AUTOBIOGRAPHICAL DOCUMENTARY IN SPAIN

Tracing the autobiographical documentary in Spanish cinema, it is surprising to note at first glance the absence of this type of film before 2000, as if the rise of personal documentaries that was happening in America and elsewhere in Europe had no impact on the Spanish documentary. The artistic and industrial context of Spanish cinema, however, was not very different from those other countries, since during these last decades Spain also experienced a growing interest in documentary, in terms of production, exhibition, critical reception and educational resources. Barcelona and Madrid have become the main centres of this activity, but signs of documentary life are cropping up elsewhere as well. Yet even with this growing interest (and indeed production of) documentary, very few if any were made using the first person address.[3]

How can one explain then the absence of autobiographical documentaries during the 1980s and 1990s? It is not easy to find a simple answer, because some contextual explanations that account for the rise of personal documentaries in other countries, like the standardisation of digital technologies, also apply to Spain. One reason that may partially explain that absence could be the limited distribution of the best autobiographical works from other countries up until the 2000s. Names like Alan Berliner, Ross McElwee or Naomi Kawase, widely known nowadays in our documentary community, were quite unknown in Spain a few years ago. Berliner, for instance, became very well known after the retrospective organised in Navarra in 2002, followed by a publication about his work and the release of his films on DVD.[4] Kawase has gradually become better known, but it was not until 2008 that Las Palmas organised a retrospective and published a book about her work.[5] This festival also organised a special programme on film autobiographies in the same year, together with a book on the topic, *Cineastas frente al espejo* [Filmmakers in Front of the Mirror].[6]

Another reason for the absence of this kind of documentary could be the lack of references within Spanish cinema, since the country's most influential documentary filmmakers have not entered the autobiographical fray or they have done so only recently.[7] This is the case of one of the most influential documentary *auteurs*, José Luis Guerín. He has made documentaries with a very personal approach (at times bordering on experimental, as in *Tren de sombras* [*Train of Shadows*], 1997), but not directly related to his own biography. His most successful documentary to date, *En construcción* (*Work in Progress*, 2001), resorts to an observational techniques, though filtered through the distinctively poetic approach that has become a signature of his work. However, his last film, *Guest* (2010), is a travel journal filmed during his trips to present his film *En la ciudad de Sylvia* (*In the City of Sylvia*, 2007) in festivals all around the world. It is worthwhile to note that despite this autobiographical set-up, Guerín rarely appears onscreen and there is no first person voiceover narration, though he is heard from time to time in the interviews he conducts. His film is more reminiscent of an ethnographic travelogue – exploring the ordinary lives of mostly underprivileged characters – than a personal diary. Another key Spanish filmmaker, Víctor Erice, also relies on an observational approach in *El sol del membrillo* (*Quince Tree of the Sun*, 1992). His only 'documentary' work, it adopts a detached point of view, far from the conventions of personal documentary. These examples relate somehow to a strong tradition of realism in Spanish art and literature – from Murillo to Antonio López, from the picaresque novel to Miguel Delibes – which may also help to explain the scarcity of first person documentaries, since their foregrounding of subjectivity might seem to clash with that tradition of realism in narrative and representational arts.

A new direction has begun to develop during the first decade of the twenty-first century, with some filmmakers approaching their work with a style close to the films of Guerín or Erice, but now focused on topics and characters related to their own lives. One might even be able to trace an evolution towards a more autobiographical approach in Spanish cinema following some of the best documentaries of the decade. In 2001, Pablo García made *Fuente Alamo*, a film about a village in Castilla La Mancha. During one summer day, he follows the lives of children, women at work in a small factory, farmers and shepherds, elders at home or at church, and finally the whole village in a summer celebration. There is a sense of familiarity, of observation from the inside, of a shared history, something not easily explained by just examining its textual marks. The meta-textual data reveals the reason for this intimacy: Pablo García is making a film about the village of his parents, where he spent every summer of his childhood. These are his friends and relatives, and the life he is portraying is very much interwined with his own biography.[8] Interestingly, though, this does not find explicit expression within the film. The first person perspective is suppressed, but nonetheless 'felt'. Four years later, *La casa de mi abuela* (*My Grandmother's House*) was released. The film, directed by Adan Aliaga, shows the lives of an old woman and her granddaughter in their daily routines at home, in a house about to be torn down to make way for an apartment building. The film presents the granddaughter's perspective as the one from which to story is told (even resorting briefly to her voiceover in first person) linking therefore the 'my' of the title to her character. But what is never explained is that the person behind that nervous camera silently observing both characters is actually another grandchild, the filmmaker Adan Aliaga. That information is hard to find even on the film's webpage, which is also constructed around the character of Marina, the granddaughter, who introduces Marita as her grandmother, and the filmmaker as a 'man who has followed me and my grandmother.'

A step further in this personalisation of family stories comes from two Spanish/Argentinean co-productions, *Diario Argentino* (*Argentinian Diary*, 2006), and *Los pasos de Antonio* (*Antonio's Steps*, 2007). The latter, directed by Pablo Baur, portrays the daily routine of his grandfather in Cordoba, Argentina, with a focus on his daily walk between his home and the local church. We never see the filmmaker, though on few occasions we hear him off-screen and feel his presence through some awkward camera movements. Furthermore, there is a written text towards the beginning of the film, stating explicitly: 'This film follows my grandfather's footsteps along the streets of Córdoba. He had promised he would walk every day to the local church. For four years, I walked beside him with my camera.' Pablo Baur effaces himself to show the tiny details of the old man walking and his daily routines, with sporadic dialogue or sentences, and very few characters interacting, creating a minimalist impression where habit and repetition overtake the demand for narrative tension. His film therefore proposes a singular detour from the typical observational documentary, following closely the daily life of the protagonist, but inscribing the gaze of the film from an autobiographical perspective, that of the grandson.

Diario Argentino details the trip of the filmmaker, Lupe Pérez, to her native Argentina for vacation. This becomes the catalyst for another 'journey' into the recent history of her country, closely related to her decision to come to Spain with her family, and to her ambivalence about returning to Argentina. It is interesting to note that these films, *Los pasos de Antonio* and *Diario Argentino*, originated in Spain, each beginning as a project of its respective author's MA in Documentary; however, both were made by Argentinean filmmakers, shot in their home country and with a story thoroughly steeped in Argentinean culture and political history. This also confirms the prominent position of Argentinean cinema in the autobiographical arena, with such accomplished examples as *La televisión y yo* (*The Television and Me*, 2002), *Los rubios* (*The Blondes*, 2003) and *Papá Iván* (2000).[9] Despite their stylistic differences, these films nevertheless share a feature not commonly found in Spanish documentary: a reflection on the national history through the personal perspective of the filmmakers and their family stories. This may be due to the more recent nature of the traumatic political events set in motion by the 1973 *coup d'état* and directly or indirectly affecting the childhood of all of these filmmakers, albeit in different ways.[10] By contrast, the current generation of Spanish filmmakers, though more inclined to adopt an autobiographical approach than their predecessors, has not experienced first hand any traumatic historical events like the Spanish Civil War (1936–39) and the difficult postwar years.

The family portrait – the term proposed by Jim Lane (2002: 95–119) for autobiographical films built around family networks – clearly becomes the dominant format among the emergent Spanish autobiographical documentaries. This is the case with medium-length films like *Amor Sanjuan* (*Sanjuan Love*, Luis Misis, 2006), about the grandmother of the filmmaker, and *La memoria interior* (*Inner Memory*, María Ruido, 2002), about the filmmaker's parents and their immigrant experience in Germany. In a feature format, we should also mention *Bucarest, La memoria perdida* (*Bucharest, Lost Memory*, Albert Solé, 2008), focused on the public profile of his father, the politician Jordi Sole Tura; and *Familystrip* (Lluis Miñarro, 2009), based on the daily conversations of his parents during the painting of a family portrait at their home. Another variation on the topic comes with *Yo soy de mi barrio* (*I Am From My Neighbourhood*, 2002), where Juan Vicente Cordoba offers a portrait of his neighborhood, strongly linked to his family history in that place. Two other short films, *Haciendo memoria* (*Making Memory*, Sandra Ruesga, 2005) and *El horizonte artificial* (*Artificial Horizon*, José Irigoyen, 2005), similarly follow family history, but unlike those previously mentioned, these rely heavily on home movies as their visual source.[11]

The family portrait constructed around autobiographical themes continues as the pattern for two documentary features by Spanish filmmakers, in this case ones living outside of Spain: *Le Temps et la Distance* (*Time and Distance*, François Gurgui, 2001) and *Retrato* (Carlos Ruiz, 2004).[12] One might be forgiven for thinking *Le Temps et la Distance* was French, judging from the title of the film and the language of the omnipresent voiceover.[13] However, the filmmaker is from Catalonia (Spain), and the film is strongly rooted there, since it traces the story of his Catalonian grandmother, who had recently died; a feeling reinforced by the use of home movies and family snapshots which increases the connection of the film to his homeland. The second film, *Retrato*, deals with the lives of the filmmaker's parents. He uses his parent's interviews in voiceover, recounting their memories, overlaid with a meandering visual track in the spirit of *Last Year at Marienbad* (1961) comprised of black and white images of his parents in familiar places. Completely detached from the setting and from each other, they appear distant from one another even when they share the same frame. Despite winning an award at Documenta Madrid, *Retrato* never secured distribution in Spain and remains largely unknown even within the documentary community.

The opposite happened to Mercedes Álvarez's film *El cielo gira*. The film had a very successful run at Spanish and international festivals, winning top awards in places like Cinema du Reel in Paris, the Rotterdam Film Festival, and Bafici (Buenos Aires Independent Film Festival), and it quickly became a cult hit within contemporary Spanish documentary. It may come as a surprise to learn that it was her first film as a director, but Álvarez came to this film with many years of experience in film and television behind her, working just before this project as the editor for José Luis Guerín on *En construcción*.

Four years after *El cielo gira*, a new feature autobiographical documentary, *Nadar* (*Swimming*, 2008), was released in selected festivals and theatres in Spain, proving the growing presence of this approach in Spanish cinema. Its director, Carla Subirana, explores her own family identity through the figures of her mother and her grandmother (the latter died during the shooting of the film, which actually spanned several years). Her film is also an exploration of Spanish history, prompted by her curiosity about her grandfather, a mysterious figure executed in 1940, and about whom the grandmother never spoke. Subirana was working on this film while she was one of the cinematographers and assistant directors on another project partially shot at the same time, *Más allá del espejo* (*Beyond the Mirror*), the last film made by Joaquín Jordá, released posthumously in 2006. Jorda's film stands on its own as autobiographical, though it was not promoted as such. The film deals with people suffering agnosia and alexia, brain diseases causing serious perceptual distortion. Jordá, himself a sufferer, becomes the guide of the film as well as one of its protagonists, talking about his problems in the same way as the other

Nadar by Carla Subirana (2008)

Más allá del espejo by Joaquín Jordá (2006)

interviewees, sometimes allowing them to interview him, thus reversing the standard roles of filmmaker and social actor.

EL CIELO GIRA (THE SKY TURNS)

Having examined the panorama of autobiographical documentary in Spain, I will now focus on a closer study of *El cielo gira* – an analysis that will nevertheless maintain some dialogue with the films already mentioned. *El cielo gira* portrays the life of a small Spanish village, Aldealseñor, where only fourteen elderly people still reside. The filmmaker was the last child born in the village, forty years ago. She and her family moved to the city when she was three years old. Now she comes back to film the daily routines of the few remaining villagers over the course of one year. In that period, however, new things happen: a windmill park is built nearby and restoration begins on the old palace to turn it into a luxury hotel.

Within this set up, Álvarez constructs a very compelling film, structured in four chapters, in which she combines an autobiographical perspective with the observational modes of an ethnographer and an austere style which echoes some realist traditions within Spanish art (and especially to Castilla, where Aldealseñor is located). Álvarez is never visible on-screen, but her calm and serene voiceover keeps her present throughout the film. Her presence, however, is not just to be found in the voiceover since she becomes a kind of invisible character within the film. This is more evident at the beginning when she states clearly the autobiographical force of her project. After a prologue, the first chapter of the film opens with a frozen shot of a landscape – a hill

Álvarez's frozen landscape: the hill with holm oak

with a solitary holm oak at the top – with Álvarez saying: 'This is the place that you see from the house where I was born, and therefore, the first thing I saw in the world. Or to be more exact: during the first three years of my life, this spot was the world. The rest takes place beyond that hill. I have frozen the image because, according to those who stayed here, this place has remained unchanged since then. And because it is here that my father lies buried.' The connection of the film with her roots, material and familiar, places her portrait of the village therefore within a clear personal framework.

The challenge facing Álvarez, then, becomes how to retain the requisite distance necessary to offer a faithful portrait of the village of Aldealseñor, while maintaining the personal force behind the project. She manages to find a delicate balance between those poles, offering an engaging variation on the standard ethnographic film, better described in this case as 'autoethnography', following Catherine Russell's terminology (1999: 275–314). The filmmaker's literal kinship with the 'ethnographic subject' provides an intimacy with the people and routines of Aldealseñor that would be otherwise hard to achieve, overcoming the main obstacles traditionally caused by the tensions between ethnographer and subject. She actually applies the same techniques as Pablo García in *Fuente Álamo*, though here taken a step further by the inclusion of the filmmaker's voiceover narration which roots the ethnographic enterprise in her own self-narrative quest.

There is in fact another difference between *El cielo gira* and *Fuente Álamo*: the introduction of an interpretive presence, the nearly-blind painter Pello Azketa, invited into the village and the film by Álvarez so as to paint his impressions of the place. The painter and the village share a related fate with both at intersecting points in their existence: one will soon lose his vision, and the other will soon be lost from vision. Álvarez, while relying on the indexical power of the film medium to capture the people and their routines, seems to need to go further and grasp what is beyond appearances. Azketa stands here as the medium between the filmmaker and Aldealseñor. He helps to achieve that deeper vision that enables the film to penetrate the surface, so as to better portray the soul of the village. As Víctor Erice has written, Azketa 'takes the role of the catalyst of the action – two of his paintings open and close the film – as a kind of blind guide – the ultimate paradox – of the narrator' (2005: 3).[14]

In terms of formal style, she catches the rhythms of the small village in long takes, avoiding any camera movement. She keeps a physical distance from the characters, using a telephoto lens in the few instances that she gets close to the faces of the individual people. Thus, at first glance, she seems to fit well into the observational mode of filmmaking described by Bill Nichols: an exhaustive description of everyday events, sync sound, long takes, rendition of present time, and so on (1991: 38–44). However, in actuality, she moves well beyond the mode of distanced observation, and not only by means of her personal voice-over and the presence of the painter Azketa; she also infuses the visuals with a stylisation perceived in the crafted compositions of each shot, constructed with careful lighting and without room for improvisation. The overall result shows a creative tension between the visual distance of the shots and the proximity of her voiceover that becomes a key element in the creation of the film's mesmerising effect. This approach permeates the entire film, but it is at its most acute in such scenes as the presentation of Pepa or the death of Eliseo. In the first case, we see a foggy view of a street and an old house, with a woman walking in the distance. The filmmaker introduces Pepa in a shot awash in a dream-like morning light, helped by an iterative narration which she links to the moment of her birth: 'The woman I watched coming out every morning was Pepa. She had helped my mother the day I was born. Since then no other baby has been born in the village. I wanted to get a picture of that woman from afar before I entered her house.'

This restraint is further amplified in the scene outside her uncle Eliseo's house. He was very sick and the filmmaker did not want to enter the house with the camera. Instead, she filmed the front with the empty chair where her uncle used to sit every day before he fell ill. Her uncle passes away and we never get to see him or the inside of the house. We do not even have an explicit account of his death; rather, Álvarez shows a similar outdoor shot of the house without the empty chair, plus a sym-  bolic shot of a fox prowling around the place and the sound of a death bell. Clearly the filmmaker is not interested in a straightforward account; instead, she is trying to convey the inner life behind appearances, in sharp contrast to mainstream trends, so enslaved to the superficial spectacularisation of society. In a move as paradoxical as the blind guide, Álvarez's penetrating gaze is achieved precisely through its

Pepa's House

distance; it is through distance that the spectator can find a space for reflection, eschewing the immediacy so vaunted in contemporary television and cinema.

Interestingly, a similar strategy can be found in Carlos Ruiz's *Retrato*, though to quite different effect. Ruiz also intends to create a tension between an intimate voiceover – containing the testimony of his parents – and a detached visual track. Nevertheless, Ruiz aims for something else: while both vectors – oral proximity and visual distance – seem to clash, they are also related in a sense, since his parents speak of their alienation from one another, and the visuals portray them entirely separated, not interacting even when they are in the same frame. Ruiz usually composes the image with his parents in familiar settings, but always posing, still, portrayed in black and white, provoking a strong estrangement effect, clashing openly with the familiarity of the voiceover testimonies. Ruiz wants to retain the indexical force of the images while removing their iconic resemblance, so the spectator is forced to read the images in a de-familiarised context. *El cielo gira*, in contrast, does not resort to such defamiliarising effects. The film instead blends such tensions into a single narrative, with the visual distance working productively alongside the intimacy created by the filmmaker's voiceover.

El cielo gira presents another feature usually linked to observational documentaries: the long shooting period following the same characters and settings. Álvarez shot in Aldealseñor from the fall of 2002 to the early summer of 2003, becoming just one more inhabitant of the village. The long production period allowed her to capture the slow rhythm of the village, so closely tied to the cyclical passing of the seasons. The scenes unfold slowly, letting the villagers express themselves with no hurry, getting the real flavour of life in a small rural village. Her formal approach also allows the filmmaker 'to catch life unawares,' that quality associated with documentary since Dziga Vertov (see Lioult 2005).[15] *El cielo gira* is full of those unexpected situations if we take the whole process of production as the temporal frame. The most unexpected events actually happened in the film's pre-production stage, when Álvarez found out about the construction of the windmill park and the transformation of the old palace. Other unforeseen discoveries include those of the elite Moroccan athlete and the Moroccan shepherd living in the area, with whom she meets serendipitously in the film, offering evidence of the significant demographic changes occurring in the region. Other minor though no less revealing events occurred during the shooting, such as the blaring political campaign songs heard on the soundtrack while the camera filmed some people reciting the rosary in the church, providing a neat palimpsest where crass contemporary politics clash unexpectedly with the more traditional cadences of the village.

Alongside its stylistic approach, *El cielo gira* stands out for its dense articulation of the temporal and spatial axes, around which the filmmaker proposes a fertile reflection on time, memory and history. At first glance, the film deals with a space, the village of Adealseñor. Yet in that space, time is inscribed in different ways, through different layers. As indicated earlier, the most immediate one is the cyclical time imposed by nature, that of the seasons, around which the four chapters of the film are structured. This cyclical time clearly captures the rhythms of the village, still very much dependant on agriculture. However, Álvarez did not make this film simply to capture the life of a small village, but to film the decay of that place, the last days of a village founded one thousand years ago, the place where she was to be the last soul born. Focusing on this final period provokes a reflection, on the historical time accumulated in the different strata throughout the region. In this sense, Aldealseñor is a fascinating place, as it contains remains from the time of the dinosaurs, the Celtiberians, the Romans, the Arabs, and the Middle Ages. Thus the film also reflects on the cyclical nature of human time, with civilisations and generations passing by, one disappearing and another emerging. This perspective helps her understand that she is not in fact witnessing the final stage of that place, but the end of a cycle, just before another begins. This fact becomes even more evident with

the appearance of the elements of a new 'civilisation': aerogenerators, excavators and trucks to build the windmill park and construction workers to transform a derelict palace from a previous era into a modern hotel. Alvarez explains her quest to address those questions:

> Filming time is an ideal, a great ideal, but just an ideal. What is obtained is in any case the trace left by time in those people and objects, its shadow. And I like to think that there are places [...] where it is easier to register those traces. [...] I think that the village and its region was a place like that, with remains of different historical times co-existing in the same space, ruins and buildings indistinguishable from the living trees, a place where the traces of time, like the dinosaur's footprints, have remained. (2007: 175)

El cielo gira goes beyond even the time imposed by nature and the passing of human generations, to introduce the biographical time of the old people living in the village, as well as the autobiographical time of the filmmaker. The villagers' time constitutes a collective memory that goes from some of the major events of the twentieth century in Spain such as the Civil War, to the minor events of the village, like the inauguration of a fountain, or the death of the old elm growing in the middle of the village square. Álvarez collects these memories from the villagers' ordinary conversations, and also by resorting to the only archival material used in the film: old photographs, sometimes commented upon by their protagonists, other times simply juxtaposed. Such juxtaposition is at work in the scene of Silvano playing on the pelota court. Álvarez fades to old pictures of the same court during an official celebration, while slowly blending them into a montage sequence that ends with a photograph of the villagers gathered around a fountain, which dissolves back to the same fountain in the present.[16] The biographical time of the inhabitants of Aldealseñor also includes contemporary time, currently amplified by television. In the film, the Iraq War has not yet begun and we witness an interesting crossover between the everyday remarks of the villagers and the international designs of world powers. The crossover becomes literalised by the military planes seen crossing the skies of Aldealseñor, on their way to the Middle East. Again, it seems as if Aldealseñor retains a magical power as a place where history is condensed, no matter the scale.

Alvarez's interweaving of all these temporalities – the cyclical time of the seasons, the historical time of the generations and civilisations, the biographical time of the current villagers, as well as her own autobiographical time – becomes the main feat of the film, an achievement which gives *El cielo gira* a captivating, transcendental quality. Although the film as a whole can be seen as a meditation on the relationship between time and history, there are some scenes where it finds a more productive expression, as in the construction of the windmill park on a foggy day. In that scene, the film cuts from the image of a life-sized dinosaur – a tourist lure – to images of machines at work, emerging from the fog, as if they were the monsters of our era. Another giant – the wing of an aerogenerator – appears immediately thereafter, completing the invasion of a new time in the region. The filmmaker, ever conscious of this imbrication and condensation of time, refers to the village as 'a complete universe, where time flows from the very childhood of the world':

Places, names, generations, memories of the past, wars, disappearances, alternation of cultures, annual seasons, metamorphoses of nature; all the elements forming the universe and human destiny, under the cosmic sky, were there. To convey this idea became an almost physical need, something that we experienced during the shooting of the film in the village. Then it comes – projected over that profound time – the time of individual lives, of the neighbours of that village. [...] We had to make a fabric with those two temporalities, the linear – biographic, historical – and the cyclical one. Weaving all of them took almost one year of editing. (2007: 175–6)

That temporal interplay also balances historiographical scale, combining the macrohistorical portrayal of the passing of civilisations and centuries with the microhistorical look at the daily life of the people at Aldealseñor. It is obvious that *El cielo gira* does not pretend to be a conventional historical documentary, but it contains a historical tension within it, built on a contrapuntal interplay of scales. The film even materialises that 'play of scales'[17] in the character of Silvano, who makes use of a telescope to look at the stars and of a magnifying glass to spot the people in old photographs. Silvano's actions perfectly echo Paul Ricoeur, who refers to these optical instruments when talking about the historiographical questions related to the macro and micro scales: 'History, too, functions in turn as an eyepiece, a microscope, or a telescope' (2004: 211).

There are some moments in the film where the macro scale becomes more visible, expressed through complex and interpenetrating associations capturing the passing of history. Two scenes stand out in this regard. The first one condenses thousands of years in just two shots, as the filmmaker explains in voiceover: 'There has been a megalithic stone structure since the beginning, and a bit further up a shepherd's hut. If anyone walked from one place to the other on a misty day, they could pass through thousands of years without any problem.' The second takes place almost a full hour later in the film, after we meet the two Moroccans: the shepherd and the athlete. The latter leaves running, in a long shot, while the filmmaker makes another macrohistorical remark in her voiceover: 'The shepherd and the athlete said farewell, and in an instant they were again separated by a thousand years of distance. While that

instant stretched on, I thought that the history of the village, with all its generations, fit in between.' The physical distance is understood in both scenes metaphorically, in the service of the macro scale framework where Álvarez places her portrait of Aldealseñor.

These telescoped historical moments notwithstanding, *El cielo gira* relies more on the micro scale, offering a rich portrait of a small community where history becomes 'fleshed out', as microhistorians like to say. In this sense, the film finds itself closer to approaches like the *Alltagsgeschichte*, a 'history of the everyday life' proposed by Alf Lüdtke (1995), or the Italian *microstoria* of authors such as Giovanni Levi (1991) or Carlo Ginzburg (1992). This film becomes another example of the results achieved when the scale of observation is reduced, giving more relevance to ordinary people as the protagonists of history, with corresponding effects in the historical account (see Revel 1996: 19–20). The contrast introduced, for instance, by the Moroccan characters in the quiet life of the region is one of those events unnoticed by macrohistory. Those characters – and what they talk about in their rather long conversation – bring back historical resonances from the time of the Moorish occupation of Spain, adding new insights in relation to problems like immigration, while showing some of the effects of globalisation, with an elite Moroccan athlete training in this remote area of Castilla.

The scenes showing the impact of the electoral campaign on the village provide more interesting samples of the knowledge acquired through micro scale observation. Two different cars come into the village to leave their political posters in the main square. They work quickly and to the complete indifference of the villagers, as is shown in the almost comical contrast of the energetic political campaigners putting up posters while the whole village takes siesta. This attention to the micro scale does not intend to offer, as Ricoeur says, 'a resurrection of the lived experience of social agents, as if history were to stop being history and link up again with the phenomenology of collective memory'; what we 'must not expect to see is the lived experience of the protagonists. What we see remains social interactions, at a fine scale, but one already microstructured' (2004: 214). This is reflected in *El cielo gira*, which is delicately structured so as to reveal these social interactions. Álvarez organises the filmed material in four chapters following the seasons, as already mentioned, searching for dominant threads to make it expressive, meaningful; a process developed throughout the months of shooting and the year of editing to which the filmmaker refers. Álvarez herself talks about that process: 'When confronted with all the material shot, before editing, I felt like I was in front of a blank page. There it was, the memory of a whole year passed in the village. It was literally like living it again. But now we had to tell it, to plow the memory and take out the narrative hiding in its interior, finding the writing' (2007: 178–9).

Actually, its elaborate interweaving of temporal layers within a singular place seems to call for the kind of chronotopical approach proposed by Mikhail Bakhtin. One can easily perform an analysis of the film focused on the study of chronotopes, those singular combinations of time and space in each work of art where narrative events become specific. As Bakhtin suggests, 'it is precisely the chronotope that provides the ground essential for the showing-forth, the representability of events. And this is so thanks precisely to the special increase in density and concreteness of time markers – the time of human life, of historical time – that occurs within well-delineated spatial areas' (1981: 250).[18] In this regard, we may be tempted to explain *El cielo gira* as a single chronotope, with the region of Aldealseñor as a privileged location showing the condensation of human dynamics through history. Its lands have literally been accumulating different civilisations, which have now become visible to the visitor, as a villager hints in the first scene in relation to the time of dinosaurs – or later on, as a guide explains while showing the ruins of Numancia, a city famous for its resistance to the Romans. However, this approach would not do much justice to the Bakhtinian concept of chronotope, being so general that it takes Bakhtin's ideas merely as inspiration. For the sake of the analysis, therefore, we may single out two places as the main chronotopes of the film: the village square with its missing elm tree, and the hill with its holm oak.

The village square is the most common meeting point of the few villagers remaining in Aldealseñor. It is the place of their quiet conversations, where their reminiscences intermingle with their present routines and concerns. It is also the place to find such points of reference as the church and the fountain. It is the place, finally, where the old elm tree grew, now replaced by a conifer. The elm tree remains the central symbol of that space despite its absence from the square, or perhaps because of it. Álvarez's strong associations with it prompt yet another historical journey, tied to the life and death of that elm. The film thus revisits the history of the village, as we see in the scene when Antonino and Silvano go over old pictures of the village taken in the square, from the time when all the people met around the elm tree. We also witness, through those pictures, the demise of the elm tree and its unearthing. One  photograph reveals several skulls discovered among its massive roots, bringing forth again the density of the temporal markers of the place. The comments of Silvano and Antonino while viewing the pictures serve to underline the thoroughgoing identification of the village with this tree, whose death is seen as a harbinger of the demise of the town:

Silvano: How many years must they [the skulls] have been under it! In five hundred
years that elm tree must have seen a lot of people pass by…
Antonino: It lived for too long, Silvano. In another four hundred years, nobody will
know what had been here.

The clashing of temporalities materialises again when the visible traces of the
old photographs and oral memories of the villagers fade into the lifeless trunk
of the elm tree covered by snow. Later on, the film will come back to that trunk,
with the painter Azketa touching it, as if trying to understand the passing of
time materialised in that trunk now placed next to the palace. The voiceover of
Álvarez assumes in this scene a most poetic tone, referring to the dead tree as
a living being, staring at the future hotel with the different 'faces' visible in the
old trunk, singled out in close-ups by the filmmaker.

The other central chronotope in the film is the hill with a single holm oak
at its top. The filmmaker herself points out the relevance of this space, placing it as a kind of frame of the portrait of the village. After the 'prologue' with
Azketa's painting and the film's title, the first scene of the film is the one already
mentioned, of the frozen view of that hill from the window of Álvarez's early
childhood home. The foundational nature of that shot – coming from its placement at the beginning of the film and from its linkage to the autobiographical
time of the filmmaker – finds its mirror shot towards the end of the film, with
the long scene of Antonino and José walking up that same hill. Álvarez follows
both characters in long shot, while keeping their synchronous dialogue audible.
Their conversation deals mainly with their biographical time, stressing their
being at the sunset of their lives. Their reflections about that sunset, drawing
upon conventional wisdom, reverberate through the whole film, echoing the
leitmotif about the passing of generations and civilisations present throughout
the film, mixing again historical and cyclical time:

Antonino: But now you see what's ahead of you, that you've grown old and you
see what the future holds. You realise that you are moving towards nothing. And
you think, 'Why was it that way for me?' … What a world!
José: The world changes…
Antonino: We don't know who saw the beginning or who will see the end. … Now
you realise that we are only passing through, that life is just a jiff.

Just when they get to the holm oak at the top, the film fades into what could
well be the last painting of Pello Azketa, a landscape of Aldealseñor. The film
closes with that shot, showing Azketa's interpretation of this foundational
chronotope. It is a landscape that shapes Álvarez as much as she has now given

form to it. In its stillness, it evokes the film's reflection on time and history, on their dynamic condition displayed through generations, creating a rich strata of civilisations in which a new one is now on the verge of emerging. It also evokes the need to come back to one's roots in order to build a narrative of the self, as Mercedes Álvarez carries on with *El cielo gira*, a film where first person narration blends with a certain tradition of realism, so ingrained in Spanish art, perhaps providing a prototype of what Spanish autobiographical films may offer us in the future.

Acknowledgement

All images are from Mercedes Álvares, *El cielo gira* (2004), by kind permission of the filmmaker.

Notes

1   Personal interview with the filmmaker, 20 June 2008.
2   In this essay, I will leave aside other approaches to first person filmmaking addressed in this book, restricting the discussion and analysis to the more narrow terrain of autobiographical documentaries.
3   These signs can be read in the number of MA degrees in documentary (at the Universitat Autónoma de Barcelona, and in the Universitat Pompeu Fabra), and the number of documentary conferences and festivals sprouting up in Spain, such as the one held in Cordoba by the Spanish Association of Cinema Historians (AEHC), or the three organised by the Malaga Film Festival. This increasing interest has been instrumental in the growing number of books devoted to non-fiction cinema. New film festivals specialising in documentary seem to crop up every year, with two notable examples being Punto de Vista in Navarra and Documenta Madrid. Exhibitors are also more willing to programme documentaries in theatres, not only the well-known American titles, but also Spanish films, with *En construcción* (José Luis Guerín, 2000) and *La pelota vasca* (*The Basque Ball*, Julio Medem, 2003) having successful box-office returns.
4   I was the co-editor of the (bilingual) book on Berliner, titled *The Man Without the Movie Camera: The Cinema of Alan Berliner*. His films are distributed in Spain by BNC (www.benece.es) and the retrospective was organised by the Festival de Creación Audiovisual de Navarra.
5   The book was edited by José M. López, under the title *Naomi Kawase: El cine en el umbral*.
6   The book *Cineastas frente al espejo* was edited by Gregorio Martín. In the same year, I co-edited another book on filmic autobiography, a bilingual edition focused on the work of Ross McElwee: *Landscapes of the Self: The Cinema of Ross McElwee*.
7   One exception among the main documentary filmmakers might be Joaquín Jordá, who became himself a character in his influential piece *Monos como Becky* (*Monkies Like Becky*, 1999), providing it with an autobiographical aside.
8   This information comes from a personal interview with the filmmaker in November 2005.
9   We may even speak of an Argentinean autobiographical 'spell' if we look, for instance, at the work of Ricardo Iscar, a Spanish filmmaker with a strong tradition of observational documentaries – like *Tierra negra* (*Black Earth*, 2004) or the award-winning *El cerco* (*The Siege*, 2005) – but who recently finished in 2008 his first autobiographical film, *Postal desde Buenos Aires* (*Postcard from Buenos Aires*), a medium-length diary piece about a trip he made to the capital

of Argentina. For a further discussion of the Argentinean case, see Andrés di Tella's essay in this volume.

10 The most directly affected filmmakers explore the phenomena of 'the disappeared', as in the case of *Los rubios* and *Papa Iván*, which deal with the disappearance of the father in the former, and both parents in the latter.

11 *Haciendo memoria* is part of a feature-length film – *Entre el dictador y yo* (*Between the Dictator and Me*)– composed of six pieces made by different filmmakers born after the death of Franco in 1975. *El horizonte artificial* and *Haciendo memoria* are not the first Spanish films comprised of home movies, since there is a well known feature-length film made in 2003, *Un instante en la vida ajena* (*An Instant in Another Life*), compiled from the home movies of Mandronita Andreu dating from the 1920s to the 1960s. However, the filmmaker, José Luis López Linares, had no biographical link to Andreu.

12 François Gurgui lives currently in France, and Carlos Ruiz in Portugal.

13 Furthermore, his original name is not François Gurgui, but (Francesc) Xabier Juncosa i Gurgui. When he moved to Paris years ago, he changed his first name to French and chose the last name of his mother because it sounded more French.

14 All translations in this article are mine, except the English voiceover of *El cielo gira*, taken from the Spanish DVD edition.

15 Lioult is talking mainly about the unexpected happening within the frame, but his remarks can be extended to the whole process of production. As he says, 'filming the real may require setting up formal, sometimes strict constraints that allow the upsurge of the unexpected, the variable, the unsettled within a concrete and symbolic frame which organises and orders spontaneity's meaning' (2005).

16 It is worth noting that Álvarez looks at this historical time from a distant position, despite the fact that she presents herself as part of the fabric of Aldealseñor, an approach rather common in Spanish autobiographical cinema, as already explained. A main exception to that detached position towards history would be *Nadar*. Its director, Carla Subirana, delves into Spanish history, mainly into the time of the Civil War and the postwar period, in search for the truth about her grandfather. She undertakes this quest, placing herself as the visible protagonist, looking at that period with a microhistorical perspective, searching for traces of her family in the official archives, in the original places of the events, or through the oral memories of her relatives. Nevertheless, her search does not unearth much of her family history, and her film ends up as more a reflection about the role of memory in the construction of personal and family identity.

17 That expression, 'play of scales', is how Jacques Revel titles his well-known anthology on microhistory, *Jeux d'echelles. La micro-analyse à la* experience, published in 1996.

18 The chronotopical approach seems to fit the film medium very well, taking into account the spatial and temporal materiality of cinema, as authors such as Michael V. Montgomery (1993) and Vivian Sobchack (1998) have shown. I have also applied this approach to the analysis of Jonas Mekas's *Lost, Lost Lost* (see Cuevas 2006).

References

Alvarez, M. (2007) 'Fragmentos de entrevistas', *Cahiers d'études romanes*, 16, 175–83.

Bakhtin, M. (1981) *The Dialogic Imagination: Four Essays*. Austin: University of Texas Press.

Cuevas, E. (2006) 'The Immigrant Experience in Jonas Mekas's Diary Films: A Chronotopic Analysis of *Lost, Lost, Lost*', *Biography*, 29, 1, 54–72.

Cuevas E. and C. Muguiro, eds. (2002) *El hombre sin la cámera: El cine de Alan Berliner/ The Man Without the Movie Camera: The Cinema of Alan Berliner*. Madrid: Ediciones Internacionales Universitarias.

Cuevas E. and A. N. García (2008) *Landscapes of the Self: The Cinema of Ross McElwee/ Paisajes del Yo: El cine de Ross McElwee*. Madrid: Ediciones Internacionales Universitarias.

Erice, V. (2005) 'Cómo muere un olmo', *La Vanguardia*, 25 May 2005, Cultura, 3.

Ginzburg, C. (1992) *The Cheese and the Worms: The Cosmos of a Sixteenth-Century Miller*. Baltimore, MD: Johns Hopkins University Press.

Lane, J. (2002) *The Autobiographical Documentary in America*. Madison, WN: University of Wisconsin Press.

Levi, G. (1991) 'On microhistory', in P. Burke (ed.) *New Perspectives on Historical Writing*. Cambridge: Polity Press: 97–119.

Lioult, J. L. (2005) 'Framing the Unexpected', *Jump Cut*, 47. On-line. Available HTTP: www.ejump-cut.org/archive/jc47.2005/Lioult/index.html (23 April 2012).

López, J. M. (2008) *Naomi Kawase. El cine en el umbral*. Madrid: T & B editores.

Lüdtke, A. (ed.) (1995) *History of Everyday Life: Reconstructing Historical Experiences and Ways of Life*. Princeton, NJ: Princeton University Press.

Martín Gutiérrez, G. (2008) *Cineastas frente al espejo*. Madrid: T & B editores.

Montgomery, M. V. (1993) *Carnival and Commonplaces: Bakhtin's Chronotope, Cultural Studies, and Film*. New York: Peter Lang.

Nichols, B. (1991) *Representing Reality: Issues and Concepts in Documentary*. Bloomington, IN: Indiana University Press.

Revel, J. (ed.) (1996) *Jeux d'echelles. La micro-analyse à la experience*. Paris: Seuil/Gallimard.

Ricoeur, P. (2004) *Memory, History, Forgetting*. Chicago, IL: University of Chicago Press.

Russell, C. (1999) *Experimental Ethnography: The World of Film in the Age of Video*. Durham, NC: Duke University Press.

Sobchack, V. (1998) 'Lounge Time: Postwar Crises and the Chronotope of Film Noir', in N. Browne (ed.) *Refiguring American Film Genres: History and Theory*. Berkeley, CA: University of California Press: 129–70.

From the Interior: Space, Time and Queer Discursivity in Kamal Aljafari's *The Roof*

Peter Limbrick

Kamal Aljafari's *The Roof* (2006) begins in *medias res*: from a flat, spatially compressed shot of a rain-soaked window, the shallow focus allowing us only the raindrops rather than the view beyond, the film cuts to a close-up of a woman's face silhouetted flat against the glass, then out further to a dark, static two-shot of two figures on opposite sides of a restaurant booth, and silently back again to the woman. As the shot holds on the woman, an off-screen voice, presumably that of her companion, begins to recall the experience of being in a prison room for six and half months with forty others. Without context or explanation, we learn little details: the layout of the cell, that it was a formative experience, that the speaker made many good friendships, and that this all took place during the first *Intifada* (1987–93).

This enigmatic scene operates as a pre-credit prologue to *The Roof* and it crystallises the film's focus on spatiality and temporality. With its first person voice-off from a briefly glimpsed figure – testimony that takes the viewer back almost twenty years yet refuses context or on-screen synchronisation with its speaker — and its equally ambiguous *mise-en-scène* which relies on backlit, indistinguishable bodies, an out-of-focus landscape, and a mundane interior setting, this short scene constructs an interiority that is literal (inside this nondescript hotel or bar), and metaphorical (a man's personal prison narrative brought to conversation). The flattened planes of background, middle-ground, and foreground seen in the opening shot of the window prefigure the many sequences in which Diego Martínez Vignatti's camera tracks along the unfinished walls of a house or the smooth surfaces of the separation wall built by Israel. As a means of setting in place a consistent visual style, then, the scene is formative.

Crucially, however, the sequence also introduces us to the literal voice of the filmmaker. *The Roof*, the viewer later learns, is partly the story of the filmmaker's family and their lives as Palestinians living within the 1948 borders of Israel. The film often places its maker within the *mise-en-scène* and thus builds a first person-ness from the connection between visible body and audible voice. *The Roof*'s first person mode of address, however, is complex and far-reaching in its implications because of the way it exceeds the person of the filmmaker himself and instead speaks from an ambiguous collective position which refuses normative discourses. I will argue here that the film is characterised by a queer discursivity that is irreducible to notions of sexuality or categories of identity and that instead constitutes a particular response to Palestinian and Israeli constructions of temporality and space. In part, I will suggest, the queerness of the film has to do with its focus on 'the interior', that part of Palestine that lies within the 1948 borders of Israel, and all the attendant contradictions of that terrain. But while one can certainly argue that the spatial and temporal anomalies of '1948 Palestine' are both marginal and oppositional to the normativity of the Israeli state, it is the film's particular mix of discursive strategies – among them the long take, the disembodied voice, the muteness of the filmmaker-on-screen, and the focus on the flattened and striated walls of its setting – that cement its particularly queer style. As a poetic first person statement 'from the interior', *The Roof* rejects in a single move the hegemony of the Israeli settler state while also refusing the urgent, at-times melodramatic style of the 'roadblock' or 'checkpoint' documentary and the normativity of the Palestinian-family-as-nation equation that is invoked in some Palestinian films.[1] Aljafari's film instead creates a queer genealogy that is characterised by irony, absurdity, and by the quiet undoing of normative equations between family, nation, diaspora, exile and place.[2]

In this essay I wish to approach the *The Roof*'s first person-ness as a strategy to negotiate a politics of temporal and spatial disjuncture. Rather than create for himself the position of a speaking subject who controls the narration, Aljafari has rendered a first person subject position that is constructed less through his physical presence or literal voice than through other aspects of the film's discourse. Rather than a literal and singular 'I', Aljafari's film creates a fragmented 'we' that exists across the movement of the film's slow tracking shots, or just beyond the frame of its static compositions of streets, rooftops or ruined architecture. *The Roof* maintains a sense throughout that whoever is speaking is doing so through the shards, fragments and sedimented layers of history that make the present a painfully disjunctive moment for Palestinians living within Israel. The film contains relatively few sequences in which people 'explain' history (such explanations are conventionally rendered in other documentaries through the interactive interview, often with the filmmaker's participation or questions effaced) but many in which the effects and manifestations of history are evoked through a sequence of *tableaux vivants*, a lengthy tracking shot, or a staged encounter with everyday banalities. Where *The Roof* offers the director's presence in its *mise-en-scène*, it tends to in fact *dis*engage him from a position of authority through, for example, a distracted look, a deferral to the other's speech, or a static, mute and passive position within the frame. As viewers, we learn just a little about him, not much more about his family, but a great deal about the way that Palestinian history is experienced through spatial and temporal transformation and control. *The Roof*'s first person mode is developed in part as a means to reveal histories and pasts that are threatened or partially destroyed; but, as we shall see, it also questions the processes by which those pasts become spatialised and pathologised in order to offer paths towards newness.

PRESERVING PASTS

After the prologue described above, the film fades to black. A title appears in Arabic (*Al Sateh*) and is subtitled 'The Roof'. The same voice we hear in the prologue begins to speak, in Arabic, in a non-diegetic voiceover that is also subtitled into English:[3] 'It all began in 1948. In May.' When an image appears again, we see a wide shot of the oceanfront at Jaffa with abandoned fishing boats and large blocks of concrete littering the foreshore. The camera is motionless. The voiceover continues:

Over those few days the waves got too big, so they were forced to return.

But when they came back Palestine was already gone.

My grandparents were on a boat on their way to Beirut after their city of Jaffa had been bombed. Over those few days the waves got too big, so they were forced to return… But, when they came back, Palestine was already gone. Their homes were gone as well. The people who remained were forced to live in one neighborhood and they were given the houses of other Palestinians. This was the case of my mother's family in Jaffa. And the same happened to my father's family in Ramle. In 1948 the owners of this house were still building the second floor. Today the house is still the same: my parents live on the first floor and the past lives above them.

Thus begins a first person narration that will anchor us to the events that follow. As the filmmaker's voice entwines personal history with Palestinian history, finishing with the declaration about the past, the camera has begun to track left along the gravelly ground, slowly craning up to reveal the ruins of a cemetery, the stillness within the scene broken only by the movement of a stray cat in the middle distance, by the sounds of birds on the soundtrack, and by the movement of the camera itself. Long after the voice finishes, the shot continues until the camera eventually comes to rest with the tower of *Al-Masjid al-Abyad* (Ramle's 'White Mosque') in the background. A title burns into the right corner of the frame: 'Ramle'.

In this long take, remarkable for its qualities of stillness despite the moving camera, the film quietly evokes the destruction of the built Arab environment that was so radically transformed in the events of 1948. As has been carefully documented by writers like Walid Khalidi (1992) and Meron Benvenisti (2000), Zionist colonisation of Palestine took place through a process of physical destruction that was not a corollary to but a condition of settlement. Such an erasure was not only physical but was enacted through language, as Benvenisti argues, by the reinscription of the landscape in a process of remapping and renaming (2000: 17–20). Ramle, originally Al-Ramla, was one of the few places whose Arabic name remained virtually unchanged through the process of Hebraisation, yet a subsequent sequence of shots in *The Roof* reveals the renaming of individual streets that nevertheless took place – Dr Koch St, Dr Sigmund Freud St, Dr Salk St.[4] The forced resettlement of Palestinian families in the area around Jaffa and Ramle, alluded to in the voiceover, radically changed the relationship of habitation to the built Arab environment and resulted in the kind of asychronicity that Aljafari's family experiences in relation to the unfinished second storey.

After another fade to black, the film introduces two shots around Ramle's streets that, in the manner of later examples, are reminiscent of *tableaux vivants*: the figures in the shot seem frozen in time, embalmed in a relationship to place that suggests no movement or vitality and stresses the confining aspects of their surroundings. We move from there to the roof of a house, and to another shot whose style of flattened, compressed planes is by now familiar. Tracking along the half-built wall that we associate now with the voiceover description of an unfinished second storey, the camera moves slowly enough to allow the viewer to linger on details: an empty bird cage perched on a ledge of corrugated iron; coils of electrical wire that sit unused on the concrete blocks that make up the wall; the colour and texture of the walls themselves, tightly framed without context in the foreground, yet with the other walls of the structure visible in the compressed plans of middle and background. The shot is thus evocative not so much of the now-destroyed, pre-1948 built environment, as in the earlier tracking shot, but the built environment as it was frozen in 1948. The shot is the construction of a moment in time whose pastness speaks to the present more directly than does the director; the unfinished storey is really an unfinished 'story' of Palestinian life within the interior.

From the sequences just described, then, emerges a visual style that must, in the first instance, return us to questions about space and temporality that are so productively raised in the work of André Bazin. For in *The Roof*'s slow tracking shots across the rubble of Ramle's cemetery or along the roof of the Aljafari house, we can observe the camera's production and recovery of indexical traces of an Arab architecture that is either erased or stalled in time; we see 'all that remains' both in Khalidi's (1992) sense of the only things that are left standing, but also in the sense of all that remains to be finished. These remains are recovered from the invisibility that they have acquired within a Zionist cultural narrative and are present in the image as the traces of a Palestinian past.

The images thus carry not only the pastness of the time in which they were cre- ated – the indexicality of the sign – but also the pastness of the actual referents within that sign's iconicity – the buildings and walls that are represented there. Bazin reminds us that as a result of what he termed our 'obsession with realism', we interpret these signifying images as marking the presence of something in the world whose imprint is now made visible to us again. Thus we have affirma- tion that the camera was at some moment actually there in front of the rubble; Bazin invokes the example of a death mask to describe this kind of indexicality (1967: 12). But in his astonishingly productive reading of Bazin, Philip Rosen also elaborates on a related problem of the relationship between the image and the preexistence of the concrete objects in the world that it represents, now 'preserved' in the manner of an embalming by the indexical image itself. The crucial and overlooked role of subjectivity in Bazin's writing, argues Rosen, is that it requires a subject 'obsessed with realism' to not only invest credibility in the image's referentiality to something in the world, but also to believe in the pastness of the moment of recording, that something 'took place' for the camera in the moment of shooting and that it was captured in a moment by the intervention of the lens (2001: 20–3).

What we cannot access in our apprehension of such images, however, is their 'when-ness' or context, so while we understand them to be evidence of some kind of past-ness, Rosen argues that we must infer or 'fill in the gaps' that are raised by the ambiguity of the image (2001: 23). It is this gap between what the image shows (the thing-ness of the ruins or the physical texture of the wall) and the context for its existence as an object that is so productively rendered in this film as a collective first person position. Later sequences on the roof more closely investigate the texture of the concrete in the wall, with its aggregate of shells and stone; another sequence at Jaffa's coast provides a montage of still shots that reveal the fill pushed into the sea to 'reclaim' the coast, fill that is comprised of the remains of Palestinian homes – a beam visible here, a door lintel there. Rather than relying upon an expositional description and defini- tive explanation of these traces, the film instead allows space for the activity of the documentary spectator, 'obsessed with realism', to invest in the image a pastness that carries not just a sense of history but a sense of agency: a 'we' for whom this past exists.

In its photographic rendering of architectural remains and physical struc- tures, *The Roof* might thus be compared to the work of The Arab Image Foundation's project to gather collections of photographs by Arab photogra- phers. In the Foundation's archiving of studio photographers like Hashem El Madani, we see a concern for the recirculation of photographic 'embalmings of time' from across the Arab world, destined to invisibility or deterioration without the intervention of the archivist. Some of El Madani's portraits, which often document exterior settings and backgrounds as much as they do their human subjects, are collected in the volume *Mapping Sitting* (Bassil *et al.*, 2005). Like Aljafari's film, this volume refuses a comprehensive textual explication of what it presents, instead leaving the reader only captions, mere hints of context. Working from memory during the project's curation, El Madani recorded captions for the photographs such as 'A Palestinian coffeemaker, 1950', or, even more simply, 'A Palestinian, 1951'. Presenting the photographs as if on a contact sheet, grouped only into themes like 'riding' (for images of people with bicycles), 'boxing' and so on, the editor-curators reject an explanatory rhetoric, throwing the burden back to the viewing subject to provide a when, a how, or even a 'what' to the images. Thus conceived as a text where the form of the book replicates the accretive and elusive meanings of El Madani's vast archive of photographs, *Mapping Sitting* produces an editorial voice that speaks in the third person – 'here is the archive, here are its subjects' – thus 'mapping' the positions and performances held within it and allowing for its readers the prospect of 'selective – if not fetishistic – appropriations' (Bassil *et al.*, 2005: 0.002). Yet as the book's title suggests, these are also records of 'sitting' for the camera and in the myriad of poses and props chosen by the photographic subjects emerge hints of first person narratives of identity and history.[5]

QUEER SPATIAL PATHOLOGIES

The Roof constructs a first person discursive position that is not organised around a definitive or self-evident identity. Despite its references to the body, voice, family and friends of the filmmaker, the film's speaking position cannot be reduced to that of its director, nor does it inscribe a singular or straightforward politics of Palestinian resistance. Indeed, what I find most compelling about *The Roof* is its anti-normative approach to nation, family and politics, an approach that resists the supposed self-evidence of all those constructions. Put another way, the film's first person speaking position is queer. I am aware that 'queer' may seem like the wrong word to use, since the film at first glance seems not to develop any explicit concern with sexuality or gender. But it is precisely the non-equivalency of its first person position to any explicit directorial statements or representational literalism that helps the film speak queerly. Some of the most startling and productive work in queer studies is that which has refused to organise itself around a notion of queerness as a category of sexual exceptionalism and has instead revealed the ways that queer and non-queer bodies and subjects are implicated within formations of race, gender, class and nation that cannot be wished away by the assertion of a transgressive queer identity. Jasbir Puar, for example, has exposed the nationalist normativities and violences that are produced by some US rhetorics of queerness-as-exception by paying special attention to the cleavages created when queerness becomes an identity of white privilege that relies for its coherence on the figure of the Muslim as other to homo-national secular discourses of freedom. In thus moving queer interventions 'beyond narrowly conceptualised frames that foreground sexual identity and sexual acts' (2008: 10), Puar forcefully argues for the relevance of queer theory to issues of racialisation and state violence and extends the task of queer studies to consider US empire and even Israeli constructions of queer citizenship (2008: 16–18).[6]

In a different context, Amy Villarejo has also addressed the problem of transposing 'queer' to apparently inappropriate contexts by provocatively arguing that queer theory is precisely most useful

> to the degree to which 'queer' is deployed as a catachresis, as a metaphor without an adequate referent. To put it differently, queer theory seems to me most equipped to 'tarry with the normative' when it forsakes its claims to the literal and makes for the more dangerous – but also more commodious – complications of relationality and variegation. Queer is but one name, hurled back with pride, for social abjection, exclusion, marginalisation and degradation; it provides, by this logic, but one opening toward freedom. (2005: 70)

Villarejo's essay, an extended reflection on Rod Ferguson's brilliant *Aberrations in Black* (2003), uses Ferguson's work to ask a series of questions about cinema and, in particular, the potential for queer theory to uncouple the pathologies of symptom from the potential for queer agency (whereas, she argues, Ferguson collapses the two [2005: 74]). While it has become customary to find scholarly readings of queerness that attend to a literal presence of non-normative figurings of gender or sexuality or sex in the text, especially those embodied by a self-identified queer subject, Villarejo suggests that such readings can narrowly delimit or overlook the ways in which queer theory has the potential to unsettle our understandings of normative nationalisms, racialisations, temporalities and their sexualised and gendered logics.

The Roof, I will argue, offers such an 'opening to freedom', as Villarejo calls it, through its refusal to abide by the logics of marginalisation even while asserting a politics of difference. Here I wish to affirm the way in which the film resists the Zionist colonial logic of the Israeli state with respect to Arabs in the interior. Such a logic, as others have pointed out with respect to cinematic and other cultural forms, has racialised Palestinians and other Arabs within Israel in terms that suggest pathology and perversion (see Shohat 2010). But I wish to also recognise the queer agency of the film itself: its active undermining of such pathologising and racialising discourses together with its refusal to counter them with a normative identity-oriented Palestinian nationalism of its own. Rather, the film replies to the processes of radical othering by opening up cracks or ruptures within the Israeli state's logic of exclusion, offering fault lines from which different social relations and political possibilities might emerge. Through discursive strategies mentioned already and those that are delineated further below, Aljafari's film fashions a queer response to the historical situation of 1948 Palestinians.

Because of its attention to racialisation, nationalism and their imbrication with sexuality and gender, 'queer of color' critique (as Ferguson and others' work has become known) is potentially very revealing of the ways in which *The Roof* is organised.[7] Palestinians within the 1948 borders of Israel exist as a population that is paradoxically rendered as 'out of place' (paradoxical since their roots in Palestine are long established) and culturally illegible to the normative space of nation: Palestinians register fundamentally in terms of their deviancy from the Zionist national norm and in their potential to 'unsettle' the colonial settler state, most dramatically in their perceived affinity for terrorism, a representational trope attaching to Arabs that also continues to resonate within a post-9/11 United States (see Puar 2008). Like the Mizrahim or Arab Jew, Palestinians are culturally marked within Zionist discourses by associations to that which Ferguson (2003), speaking of African Americans in US racialised discourse, has described as the 'aberrations' of deviancy, perversion, pathology or (more generally) non-heteronormativity. Palestinians, in other words, may constitute a recognised minority within the Israeli state but, as non-Jews, are simultaneously expunged from the ideal of nation which the state constructs and, indeed, from many of its actual mechanisms, as Saree Makdisi points out (2008: 144–5).[8] Nationality in Israel, therefore, is not only organised around normative expressions of race, gender and sexuality, but is definitionally Jewish.

The discourses of the Israeli state thus organise Palestine's marginalised and 'perverse' subjects in ways that cut across nationality and that place them within racialised logics of gender and sexuality. Arab-ness in general, rather than Palestinian-ness alone, is made deviant. As Ella Shohat (1988) incisively argued some years ago now, the historical role of 'victim' to Zionism's racialising and nationalising frame is one that has been shared – albeit not in identical ways – by Palestinians and Mizrahim, those Sephardic or Arab Jews whose presence was solicited for the structural and demographic efficacy of the fledgling Jewish state. More recently, Raz Yosef's *Beyond Flesh* (2004) has detailed the way that Mizrahi masculinities are feminised and racialised within Israeli cinema and culture in a manner that resembles an Ashkenazic colonial fantasy. In referencing theories of colonial discourse in the work of writers such as Frantz Fanon (1966) and Edward Said (1978), Shohat and Yosef reveal Zionism's operation as a colonial discourse which racialises Palestinians and other Arabs while reserving the mantle of nationality only for Jews, thus admitting the Arab who is a Jew but not the Arab who is a Palestinian.

As *The Roof* demonstrates, Palestinian life within the interior is organised through connected practices of spatialised marginality that construe Palestinian zones or neighborhoods as aberrant, when they are not already invisible. Such spatial disjunctures within the state are acknowledged in multiple ways by the film. Early on, for example, two Arab men on the streets of Ramle approach the camera and one begins to speak of the differing status of Palestinians before and after 1948. Noting the economic centrality of Ramle to Palestinian society prior to 1948, he bemoans the fact that now Jewish immigrants of any other nationality have become Israeli nationals, controlling the everyday economy while the Palestinians, as he puts it, 'became useless': 'This is our country and we became its tail.' He gestures to the spatial transformation that has occurred as Russian and other immigrant Jews supplanted Arabs and took over the businesses and the interview is followed by the sequence of three shots mentioned above in which we see the Ashkenazi Jewish street names that have supplanted the Arabic names.

Shortly afterwards is a sequence in which the filmmaker takes a driving lesson, one that might be better thought of as a lesson in spatial segregation. With the camera situated outside the vehicle at ground level, we follow a brand-new-looking Volkswagen as the filmmaker stutters and starts along suburban, tree-lined Ramle streets. As the car takes a left turn towards a derelict-looking open lot with houses in the distance, we hear on the soundtrack the instructor caution that 'We're on a rough street with lots of holes … this street leads to the Arab neighborhood of Ramle. We've seen how easy it is to drive on a normal street. Here it is more difficult because the car could be damaged.' In extreme long shots, we see the car negotiate buildings that are surrounded by demolition debris, navigate unpaved potholed streets, and traverse a railway crossing that is neither signed nor signalled. Here, then, the film reveals the way that Palestinian space is segregated from the logic of 'the normal street'; the literal ghettoisation of Palestinian life in Ramle is brought into the filmic discourse as a moment of spatial and cognitive disjuncture.

The starkest example from the film, however, of the state's spatialising logic of deviancy and non-normativity is found in the ongoing references to Palestinian imprisonment. Indeed, the film makes of this a consistent theme, evoked through the first person testimony of the filmmaker in the opening scene of the film, then visualised through the shots of barred windows and flat walls that follow later. In fact, the audience's most direct contact with the first person subject of the film is found in a sequence in which Aljafari stages a phone call with Nabieh Awada, a prison-mate of whom he has spoken in the film's first scene. The spatial fragmentation of Palestinian lives is articulated here through the contradictory logics of states (Nabieh, as a Palestinian-in-exile now living in Beirut has more movement around the Levant than has Aljfari as a citizen of Israel) and the ever-present suspicion of being a terrorist is made apparent through Nabieh's story of border detention at Jordan while attempting to travel to a rock concert. Significantly, the audience in fact never learns what it was that led to Aljafari's earlier imprisonment. That ambiguity, in keeping with the way in which a collective and queer first person address is deployed in the film, directs our attention to the generalised confinement and criminalisation of a population rather to any trauma confined to the personal circumstance of the filmmaker.[9]

The film graphically realises this theme of criminalisation and walled imprisonment in the later sequences in which the filmmaker and his sister drive around the separation wall in East Jerusalem. Stopped by an Arab soldier in Israeli Defence Force uniform, they are eventually allowed to pass and in long, almost silent takes, the film takes us along the twisted route of the separation wall as it carves out an unauthorised border between Israel and the Occupied West Bank.[10] The sequence rhymes with others in which we study the surface and texture of various walls, and in this sense builds on the film's emphasis on Israel as a space of ideologically organised destruction and re-construction of built environments.[11] Yet it also seems to signify the other sense in which these walls, all of them, register: as the enclosing surfaces of a prison that incarcerates those Palestinians within Israel, exiled not without but within their own country, made into the other of a Jewish majority and then rendered as a queer population associated with backwardness and the threat of terrorism (as the filmmaker's sister affirms when she relates that, if she speaks Arabic in Jerusalem, 'people react is if they don't know Palestinians live in this country; as if they were afraid.')

QUEER TEMPORAL PATHOLOGIES

The temporal associations of Palestinians with 'backwardness' are something that the film exposes throughout. This is its second function with respect to pastness: not only does it attempt to reconstruct or recover Palestinian histories that are made invisible to the state, as we have seen with respect to its visual style, but it also addresses the pathologising temporal shifts that confine

Palestinians to a time of backwardness or premodernity. *The Roof* suggests that the spatialising colonial logic that organises Palestinians within Israel is also temporal in its practice, and that it queers Palestinians in relation to the normative time of the state. Elizabeth Freeman has argued for the necessity of understanding the 'chronopolitics of development' as a normative and violent discourse within state formations, one that queer theory and politics must recognise and challenge. Chronopolitics, she suggests,

> extends beyond local conflicts to the management of entire populations: both the state and the market produce biopolitical status relations not only through borders, the establishment of private and public zones, and other strategies of spatial containment, but also and crucially through temporal mechanisms. Some groups have their needs and freedoms deferred or snatched away, and some don't. Some cultural practices are given the means to continue; others are squelched or allowed to die on the vine. (2005: 57)

Freeman crucially identifies such vulnerable populations as those who are 'forced to wait or startled by violence, whose activities do not show up on the official time line, whose own time lines do not synchronise with it' and recognises the ways in which a chronopolitics of development, 'at once racialised, gendered and sexualised', has set Western modernity in relation to a 'slower premodernity figured as brown-skinned, feminine and erotically perverse' (2005: 58).

Freeman's insights beautifully elucidate the ways in which *The Roof*, through the quiet accumulation of shots and through the uncanniness of its first person address, makes evident the shape of the chronopolitics that binds Palestinians in the interior. The image above recalls one moment in the film where that occurs. Marking 1948 as a definitive moment, the voiceover articulates the way in which henceforth his people will be 'too late', backward, or stuck within a 'dead time', rendered fully out of step with the national project of Zionism and its claims to modernity, futurity and progress. The shots that follow, of the ruins of the mosque and cemetery, stand in eerie contrast to the modern-looking Tel Aviv that appears in a later scene and that will be discussed below. The driving lesson, described above in terms of its spatialising aspects, evokes temporally opposed qualities as well: driving the most modern and European of vehicles, the filmmaker subject makes halting, broken progress through the gears and, as the lesson turns towards the Palestinian quarter of Ramle, there is the sense of travelling not just into a spatially segregated and marginal area, but one that is temporally backward too, with its unpaved streets and inadequate technologies. Things seem stalled, frozen, embalmed, like the unfinished roof which cannot be restored or continued within the present – the filmmaker suggests at the end of the film that it should not be finished since the house really belongs to someone else; his mother replies somewhat elliptically that 'they've all left'.

The 'chronopolitics of development', as Freeman refers to it, becomes the particular focus of those scenes in the film that are set in and around Jaffa. These scenes are remarkable for their invocation of first person intimacies of embodied subjecthood as the filmmaker appears, again mutely, on screen, while they simultaneously historicise and queerly politicise the destruction and 'development' of the Jaffa/Tel Aviv area. In a key sequence, Aljafari and his uncle sit on a sea-wall at Jaffa in a two-shot while the uncle, Salim, describes in detail how the family was stalled in Jaffa while attempting to flee. He then continues to describe the way in which Arab homes in Jaffa were later demolished and used as fill for the foreshore. The destruction of Arab architecture and dwelling places in Jaffa and the Tel Aviv area is well documented[12] and the practices of displacement and redevelopment there continue into the present and are the focus of Aljfari's next film, *Port of Memory* (2009) and other work.[13] *The Roof* visualises for viewers the way in which the temporalising logic of the nation-state functions to ignore or, more drastically, erase the present and past realities of Palestinian lives within the bounded space of the interior.

Such visualisation is done within the terms that the film establishes early on: through long takes in which the focus is architectural remains, rubble, or the dissonance of a demolished dwelling condemned to exist only in a suspended past. Following Salim, we discover a stately Arab home that has had its front

wall removed 'by mistake' by an allegedly errant Israeli bulldozer, and there is a shot in which the untouched interior of the house is revealed within a frame of demolished walls, constructing a visual image that resembles a doll-house. The house's owner, her furniture, her keepsakes and photographs, and the very details of her domestic design and furnishing are framed as if now transformed into a miniaturised past, something of curiosity rather than vitality. The sequence, with its explicit questioning of terms like 'redevelopment' by those Palestinians who arrive to marvel at the site, signals the way that the developmental chronopolitics of Israeli gentrification construct a timeline in which Arab homes and families are 'premodern' or backwards in relation to the dictates of the market. A subsequent sequence of traveling shots taken inside a car cements the point: Salim drives, silent, as the sound of Souad Massi's music creates a smooth and evocative frame through which to observe the movement across the changing landscape of Jaffa, littered with construction trucks, piles of earth on empty lots, and signs of new building.[14]

It is within the next scene, however, that the extent of the film's first person critique of normative Israeli temporality is perhaps clearest. This section of the film, in fact comprised of three scenes, begins with a close-up shot of a preface of a book, revealed in the next shot to be a page from *How to Make a Jewish Movie* (Shavelson 1971). The book is held by a pair of hands that do not 'belong' to anyone in the frame but that suggest themselves as the filmmaker subject's. There is a cut to a new location, and here the filmmaker stands in the empty observation floor of a tall Tel Aviv tower, framed in long shot and silhouetted as the camera takes in the view beyond him. A voiceover begins, which we quickly realise is an audio tour in American-accented English, introducing 'the city which some refer to as the cultural centre of Israel – Tel Aviv'. Over the strains of a classical string concerto, this voice points out the 'ancient city of Jaffa' and proceeds to narrate a history that situates it as a Hebrew city that 'fell into the hands' of a long list of people, a list that incidentally includes 'the Philistines' and Arabs, and wraps up by recounting the arrival of 'the British conquest and, finally, the Israelis. What a history!' Such a packaged history corresponds to LeVine's description of a twinned mythology that is central to Zionist constructions of Palestinian and Israeli history, namely 'that Jaffa, like the rest of Palestine, was mired in a period of stagnation and backwardness until the "arrival" of Europeans at the end of the nineteenth century. The second, related myth is that its daughter city, Tel Aviv, was born literally out of the sands, a parturition that denied Jaffa any role in the construction or rapid development of "the first modern Hebrew city in the world"' (2005: 124–5). Thus obsessed with Tel Aviv and its municipal spaces, turning to Jaffa only as an 'ancient' example that neatly omits any specific reference to Palestinian Arabs, the audio tour is recontextualised by a shot of a silent, expressionless Aljfari who listens on headphones while surveying the primitive/modern dichotomy of Jaffa-Tel Aviv.

From that static vantage point, the ironies of the 'found' soundtrack resonating against the long take of filmmaker and city, the film cuts to an unusual close-up shot of a white cup and saucer, full of milky coffee, on a nondescript faux-wood laminate table. An arm breaches the frame and at its end, a hand holds a sugar sachet imprinted with a picture of former Israeli president Golda Meir. Throwing it on the table, the arm reaches for another sachet, then another, each imprinted with the face of an historically significant Israeli or Zionist leader, such as former presidents Chaim Weizmann and Yitzhak Ben-Zvi. As the El Avram Group's 'I Believe' plays over, the Zionist sugar packets cover the table and there is a cut to a long shot of the filmmaker slumped in a hotel lobby chair as the singer intones 'I exist, I exist, I'm the son of Israel!' Building on the scene before it, this one seems to ironically juxtapose the body of the filmmaker within a commodified *mise-en-scène* of Jewish nationality that here exceeds its own limits and tips into self-parody. But the function of each sequence is not simply to undermine through ironic humour; in fact each emerges as a profound articulation of a first person subjectivity in the film, a subjectivity that sound and image here construct as muted and dis-articulated from an Israeli spatial environment. The passivity and relative silence of the subject's disposition throughout might suggest that the film succumbs to a kind of quietism in which loss of agency is treated only as a symptom of dispossession. However the film's queer discursivity lies in the paradoxical way that it

turns the pathologies and chronopolitics of dispossession and marginality into a position of political energy and agency.

QUEER DISCURSIVITY

That *The Roof*'s discourse is not like that of some other Palestinian documentaries was a fact not lost on the film's German television producers, who rejected the director's first cut of the film because it lacked conflict; they wanted an explanatory voiceover throughout, thought that Aljafari's family looked 'too Italian' and spoke too softly, and that the film would be better if it presented conflict. In short, says Aljafari, they believed that 'you can't make a film about Palestine/Israel without having the Israelis shooting [...] and Palestinians falling down and crying and being the victims' (Aljafari 2008). In rejecting such histrionics, Aljfari also rejects an equally essentialising national narrative of Palestinian identity that could be counterposed to the spatial and temporal pathologies of Israeli state and market formations. For example, drawing on Marcia Landy's work on the melodrama of the national narrative and its typical functioning through discourses of the family and normative gender constructions (1995: 175–6), and referring to films by Rashid Masharawi and Michel Khleifi, Livia Alexander notes that some Palestinian films resist a Zionist national narrative of Palestine by invoking the unity of family as a collective force standing for the Palestinian nation in the face of the violence inflicted on it by the Israeli state and its disruption or betrayal by exilic Palestinians (2005: 158–9). *The Roof*, however, resists the potential normativity of such strategies.

Despite the presence of the filmmaker and his family in many scenes, the film does not make of them a heroically national collectivity that might offer a narrative of resistance to the state – productive though that tendency has been for the films that Alexander describes.[15] Instead, the family is presented in this film as if stalled or imprisoned within the logic of pastness and backwardness that the state has ascribed to it: a father and son in a tyre shop, not speaking over the constant drone of the TV; a mother seated passively at home in the house with no roof; an uncle and great aunt caught between the remembered realities of the pre-Zionist past and the present of under- and unemployment. The fractures are further exploited by one daughter's apparent class mobility and, of course, by the extradiegetic fact of the filmmaker's own diasporic situation. *The Roof* makes of its family the grounds for an agency that lies elsewhere: not wholly within the diegesis, nor outside of the text, but within the discourse itself. That is, its first person discursivity as described throughout this essay is the vehicle for creating rupture within what could appear solely as an elaboration of a symptom: Palestinians as anachronistic to the modern state of Israel. In detailing the many ways in which that pathology is elaborated temporally and spatially within Israel, *The Roof* offers a way of seeing and knowing that generates its own, contradictory, ambiguous and anti-normative form of resistance. Seizing the possibility for rupture within the fabric of 'the interior', the film creates new possibilities for what Villarejo terms 'relationality and variegation', for meaningful relations of difference that are not yoked to a national counter-narrative or to the familiar slogans or icons of Palestinian nationality, but rather to gestures and hints of other lines of connection that might serve to produce newness for Palestinians within Israel. As points of rupture in the film, these might include such things as the experience of prison and its formative role on political consciousness and social intimacy for the narrator, or the dislocatingly productive possibilities of migration and return in which the film, through its director's own transnational training and production strategy, had its beginnings.[16]

The final shot of this film is its longest tracking shot as the camera moves along the still-fascinating surfaces of the unfinished second floor, revealing every scrap of debris and detail along the way, while end credits burn into the image. In its perverse and excessive attention to these flat, overinscribed surfaces the film finally offers the viewer a queer discourse that is not about explicitly articulated sexual or gendered identity – not of the filmmaker, of its subjects, or of a nation. Rather, the film's queer discursivity emerges from its radical, first person response 'from the interior' to the complex political and social density of Palestinian life within Israel.

Notes

1 As Janet Walker has generously reminded me, this should not be the place to signal a rejection of melodrama as a politically subversive mode, nor do I mean to suggest that the roadblock or checkpoint film must by definition lack in subtlety or political nuance. What I do wish to argue, however, is that *The Roof* articulates its politics in a manner that fully exploits – rather than attempting to contain – the ambivalent position of Palestinians within the borders of a settler colonial state. By necessity, then, this film will adopt different discursive strategies for articulating that position, especially as it concerns nation, than might a film located in the West Bank.

2 On the potential for queer theory to unsettle normative constructions of nation and diaspora, see Gopinath (2005).

3 Since, at the time of writing, my spoken Arabic is not yet strong enough, my 'reading' of the film here is accomplished partly through a literal reading of subtitles. While such a reliance always renders the text differently, in ways that can be problematic, here subtitles add another layer to a film that is constructed within a polyglossia of Arabic, Hebrew and English (see Shohat 2010: 263) and that is composed throughout of images of layers and over-inscriptions. For this reason the first two frame enlargements I present here become especially interesting for the way they embed the title as another layer of meaning upon the image.

4 On 'Hebraisation' and the political intent of renaming, see Benvenisti (2000: 18); on the survival of some Arabic village names, see Benvenisti (2000: 36).

5 A later publication from this longer project (Le Feuvre and Zaatari (eds) 2004) tacitly acknowledges the reader's desire for contextualization and presents considerably more material about El Madani and the photographs themselves, including an essay by Lawrence Wright (Wright 2004) framing that particular collection of portraits in terms of their frequently transgressive gender codes.

6 See also 'Queer Politics and the Question of Palestine/Israel,' a special issue of *GLQ*, 16, 4 (2010); many of its essays interrogate neoliberal constructions of gay identity and nationalism and ask how queer politics might challenge our understandings of cultural production and activism in Palestine/Israel.

7 For an introduction to some of this work, see some of the essays included in the special issue

of *Social Text*, 'What's Queer About Queer Studies Now?', edited by Eng *et al.* (2005), along with as the books, already cited, by Puar (2008) and Ferguson (2003).

8   Makdisi argues that by withholding *nationality* to Jews alone, while allowing citizenship for Palestinians within the 1948 borders, Israel is able to say that all its citizens are treated equally while in practice discriminating heavily against anyone who is not a national (2008: 144–5). For other work on Palestinians within Israel with respect to social conditions and colonial control, see, for example, El-Asmar (1975), Zureik (1979), Lustick (1980), Davis (2003), among many others.

9   This could be a place to reveal how trivial was the pretext that put him in prison during the *Intifada*. In a Q&A with my students in 2008, the filmmaker explained the situation that led to his imprisonment and contextualised it within the logic of Israeli state control and criminalisation of Palestinians; yet to repeat that story here seems to me to work against the power of the film's own rhetoric of openness and ambiguity. I am aware that to even suggest that there is an explanation, and that it confirms my point about the criminalising of a population, may perhaps function to reassure the anxious viewer/reader that Aljafari 'is really not a terrorist'.

10 On the wall and Israel's architecture of control, see Weizman (2007).

11 See LeVine (2005: 350) who adopts Holston's (1989) term 'erasure and reinscription' to describe this process.

12 For a compelling history of Jaffa in relation to modernities, colonialism and nationalism, see LeVine (2005). A more intimate and immediate impression of the politics of everyday life in one of Jaffa's old neighborhoods is found in the blog 'Occupied' (see 'Yudit').

13 *Port of Memory* takes up the story of Salim and his sister and their imminent eviction from their home in Jaffa. His video installation *Al-Bum*, for the Home Works IV programme in Beirut in April 2008, consisted of static shots of unfinished balconies on Palestinian homes in Jaffa.

14 Aljafari returns to this home in *Port of Memory*. For an extended analysis of that film and his other work, see Limbrick (2012).

15 For an excellent discussion of the shifting discourses of nationalism in Israeli and Palestinian cinema, see Shohat's 'Postscript' in the new edition of her book *Israeli Cinema* (2010: 249–325).

16 Aljafari produced this film from a German production base. For more on his German-based work, and a fuller account of the production controversies of *The Roof* described above, see Limbrick (2012).

References

Alexander, L. (2005) 'Is there a Palestinian Cinema?', in R. L. Stein and T. Swedenburg (eds) *Palestine, Israel, and the Politics of Popular Culture*. Durham, NC: Duke University Press, 150–72.

Aljafari, K. (2008) Public lecture and discussion, University of California, Santa Cruz, 9 April.

Bassil, K., Z. Maasri and A. Zaatari (eds) (2005) *Mapping Sitting: On Portraiture and Photography*. Second edition. Beirut: Mind the Gap/The Arab Image Foundation.

Bazin, A. (1967) *What is Cinema, Vol. 1*. Berkeley, CA: University of California Press.

Benvenisti, M. (2000) *Sacred Landscape: The Buried History of the Holy Land Since 1948*. Berkeley, CA: University of California Press.

Davis, U. (2003) *Apartheid Israel: Possibilities for the Struggle Within*. London: Zed Books.

El-Asmar, F. (1975) *To be an Arab in Israel*. London: Pinter.

Eng, D. L., J. Halberstam and J. E. Muñoz (eds) (2005) 'What's Queer About Queer Studies Now?', special issue, *Social Text*, 23, 3–4.

Fanon, F. (1966) *The Wretched of the Earth*. Trans. C. Farrington. New York, NY: Grove Press.

Ferguson, R. A. (2003) *Aberrations in Black: Toward a Queer of Color Critique*. Minneapolis, MN: University of Minnesota Press.

Freeman, E. (2005) 'Time Binds, or, Erotohistoriography', *Social Text*, 23: 3–4, 57–68.

Gopinath, G. (2005) *Impossible Desires: Queer Diasporas and South Asian Public Cultures*. Durham, NC: Duke University Press.

Holston, J. (1989) *The Modernist City: An Anthropological Critique of Brasilia*. Chicago, University of Chicago Press.

Khalidi, W. (1992) *All That Remains: The Palestinian Villages Occupied and Depopulated by Israel in 1948*. Washington, DC: Institute for Palestine Studies.

Landy, M. (1995) 'History, Folklore, and Common Sense: Sembène's Films and Discourses of Postcoloniality', in G. Rajan and R. Mohanram (eds) *Postcolonial Discourse and Changing Cultural Contexts: Theory and Criticism*. Westport, CT: Greenwood Press.

Le Feuvre, L. and A. Zaatari (eds) (2004) *Hashem El Madani: Studio Practices*, Beirut: Arab Image Foundation.

LeVine, M. (2005) *Overthrowing Geography: Jaffa, Tel Aviv, and the Struggle for Palestine, 1880–1948*. Berkeley, CA: University of California Press.

Limbrick, P. (2012) 'Contested Spaces: Kamal Aljafari's Transnational Palestinian Films', in A. Mensch and T. Ginsberg (eds) *A Companion to German Cinema*. Oxford: Blackwell, 218–48.

Lustick, I. (1980) *Arabs in the Jewish State: Israel's Control of a National Minority*. Austin, TX: University of Texas Press.

Makdisi, S. (2008) *Palestine Inside Out: An Everyday Occupation*. New York, NY: W. W. Norton.

Puar, J. (2008) *Terrorist Assemblages*. Durham, NC: Duke University Press.

Rosen, P. (2001) *Change Mummified: Cinema, Historicity, Theory*. Minneapolis: University of Minnesota Press.

Said, E. (1978) *Orientalism: Western Conceptions of the Orient*. London: Penguin.

Shavelson, M. (1971) *How to Make a Jewish Movie*. London: Allen.

Shohat, E. (1988) 'Sephardim in Israel: Zionism from the Standpoint of its Jewish Victims', *Social Text*, 19/20, 1–35.

____ (2010) *Israeli Cinema: East/West and the Politics of Representation*. Revised editon. Berkeley, CA: University of California Press.

Villarejo, A. (2005) 'Tarrying with the Normative: Queer Theory and Black History', *Social Text*, 23, 3–4: 69–84.

Weizman, E. (2007) *Hollow Land: Israel's Architecture of Occupation*. London: Verso.

Wright, L. (2004) 'Falling Into His Eyes', in Le Feuvre and Zaatari (eds) *Hashem El Madani: Studio Practices*. Beirut: Arab Image Foundation, 5–10.

Yosef, R. (2004) *Beyond Flesh: Queer Masculinities and Nationalism in Israeli Cinema*. New Brunswick, NJ: Rutgers University Press.

'Yudit'. 'Occupied'. On-line. Available http://yuditilany.blogspot.com/ (23 April 2012).

Zureik, E. (1979) *The Palestinians in Israel: A Study in Internal Colonialism*. London: Routledge.

FIRST PERSON PLURAL

Jennifer Fox's Transcultural Talking Cure: *Flying: Confessions of a Free Woman*

Angelica Fenner

A co-production for Danish public television, the six hour-long episodes comprising Jennifer Fox's longitudinal documentary *Flying: Confessions of a Free Woman* (2007) share a similar impetus to that underpinning feminist confessional literature and ethnographic filmmaking. During five years of travel to seventeen countries, she became habituated to living with the handheld digital camera as the means of examining the assumptions implicated in her own gender socialisation as well as that of women around the world. She also passed the camera among her participants to enact a dialogical mode of communication that could weave a 'red thread' across cultural differences. This essay investigates how confessional discourse articulates Fox's belated feminist awakening, but also betrays specifically Western assumptions about the production of truth and unified subjectivity. Moments of footage that escape narrative determinism reveal that, as technologies and signifying practices cross borders, they do not necessarily and inevitably induce greater self-understanding or emancipation.

THE CONFESSIONAL TURN IN VISUAL MEDIA

In an oft-cited passage in the *History of Sexuality* Michel Foucault pronounces the rhetorical mode of the confession 'one of the West's most highly valued techniques for producing truth' (1990: 59), centrally implicated in such institutional procedures as criminal investigations, juridical proceedings, medical diagnoses, pedagogical strategies, and psychoanalytical and therapeutic sessions. Much earlier, Theodor Reik recognised its emergence as a veritable 'inner compulsion' (1945: 300), one whose sequelae across a wide array of contemporary media corroborate Foucault's conclusion that we have become 'a singularly confessing society' (1990: 59). As television scholar Mimi White (1992) has observed, a wide cross-section of contemporary American programming, such as gameshows, religious broadcasts, advice shows, and shop-at-home advertising, now utilise therapeutic discourses predicated upon confession-ality. While confessional transactions on television all too evidently become commodified in the service of network ratings, internet chat rooms, blogs and vlogs offer a venue relatively detached from commercial motivations. Michael Renov also finds redemptive, even utopian possibilities in the experimental work of American video artists such as Sadie Benning, Wendy Clarke, Lynn Herschman and George Kuchar. He suggests that 'first-person video confession is uniquely suited to its moment. Born of late-stage capitalism, it endows therapeutic practice with exchange value', yet it may also 'facilitate understanding across the gaps of human difference, rather than simply capitalize on those differences in a rush to spectacle' (1995: 97).

Renov's pronouncements can also be applied to American documentarist Jennifer Fox's six-hour autobiographical series *Flying: Confessions of a Free Woman*. Co-produced with the Danish Film Institute, the series first aired on Danish Public Television (DR-2) and was then broadcast on the BBC, Sundance Channel and several Scandinavian networks. It has been circulated widely at high-profile festivals such as IDFA and HotDocs, and continues to screen at local art-house cinemas and college campuses. Situating herself as both pro-tagonist and director of the unfolding drama of her own life shot across a span of five years, Fox's most personal project to date foregrounds confessional authorship in its title and utilises a *mélange* of film languages deriving from the documentary mode and serial television melodrama to capture the attention of female audiences. Regarding its remarkable success, the filmmaker concedes: 'Nobody would have thought that people would want to see six hours about how women speak [...] there really isn't another film like it out there' (in Fenner 2009: 33). *Flying* fuses ethnographer Jean Rouch's cross-cultural deployment of the camera as 'psychoanalytic stimulant' (Levin 1971: 137) with the autho-rial interiority of Sarah Jessica Parker's voiceover musings about sexuality in the HBO series *Sex and the City* (1998–2004), while also evoking the mel-ancholic whimsy of the eponymous heroine of Jean-Pierre Jeunet's *Amélie of Montmartre* (2001) – an association reinforced by using several Yann Tiersen compositions in the soundtrack.

Fox was also influenced by a highly personal approach to documentary filmmaking she encountered while teaching production at the National Film School of Denmark in the late 1990s. This style gained widespread interna-tional visibility when a Danish cohort applied its principles (including handheld cameras, natural lighting, no props or extra-diegetic music, and location shooting only) to fiction filmmaking. The infamous 'Vow of Chastity' was drafted in 1995 under the premise that the imposition of specific constraints can actually liberate creativity in unforeseen ways (see Elster 2000). Productions approved by the Dogme 95 group displayed a spontaneity reminiscent of *cinéma vérité*, with the director often viscerally involved as a cast member.[1] Fox describes her own parameters as follows:

> I had no idea what kind of plot would evolve. I didn't know what would happen to me in the course of that time period. All I knew was that I would film myself, my girlfriends, the women in my family, and women I would arrange to meet here and around the world, to add the element of strangers and the unknown. And that I would pass the camera with these four groups over time and investigate the way women talk and try to represent that. (In Fenner 2009: 29)

Her transnational journey explores the complex contradictions attending women's status in rapidly changing societies around the world to discern possible commonalities in discourse and communication. In the film's opening voiceover she asks: 'What is this strange modern female life we are living?' 'Is there a red thread that connects women across the globe?' 'Do women have a special language?' These questions constitute the epistemological core of much feminist theory, fraught though it always has been with the possibility of forging solidarities at the price of espousing universalism or essentialism.

The stylistic hybridity of *Flying* parallels the scope of its geographical and cultural coverage; however, its politics are not immune to the pitfalls media theorist Ella Shohat elsewhere associates with global feminism, which has too often 'privileged a specific narrative that revolves exclusively around European and Euro-American feminist trajectories and that is cast exclusively around terms of sexual difference' (2001: 1270). The film's focalisation may incline towards what Shohat has coined the 'sponge/additive approach' to multiculturalism; in other words, 'paradigms that are generated from a US perspective are extended onto "others" whose lives and practices become absorbed into a homogenising, overarching feminist master narrative' (ibid.). My ensuing analysis nevertheless suggests that Fox's innovative use of the camera for dialogical production of knowledge and understanding also enacts the relational form of multicultural feminism Shohat promulgates. Such an alternative practice should extend 'beyond a mere description of discrete regions and cultures' to involve 'the translation of ideas from one context to another,' achieved by addressing 'the operative terms and axes of stratifications typical of specific contexts along with the ways these terms and stratifications are translated and reanimated as they travel from one context to another' (2001: 1271). The camera becomes a 'technology of confession' circulating among a cast of women entering into a dialectic of vulnerability and control in the face of cultural differences. If *Flying* inaugurates a veritable transcultural talking cure, confessionality itself also undergoes disclosure as an essentially Western mode of production of subjectivity and local truth, one that may become 'lost in translation' when applied in certain non-Western settings. My analysis draws on feminist theories of autobiography, poststructuralist and psychoanalytical approaches to confessionality, and film theoretical mediations on the interrelation of camera technique and ideology, both to pinpoint the fundamental impasse at the core of Fox's therapeutic endeavour, as well as to acknowlege the productivity of confronting global spectators with the very limit points of discourse itself.

Flying represents an aesthetic and ideological deviation from Fox's earlier productions, one triggered by what she acknowledges as a belated feminist awakening. Throughout her 25-year career, she has consistently produced pioneering work, earning her a place within the contemporary league of highly successful documentary *auteurs* able to choose their projects. Her contributions to the field have been predicated upon border crossings of a formal, thematic, political, geographical and technological nature, beginning with *Beirut: The Last Home Movie* (1988), for which she dropped out of NYU film school. A brilliant metacommentary on the seductions of war, *Beirut* documents daily life in an aristocratic family stolidly esconced downtown in their nineteenth-century mansion while the Lebanese Civil War rages around them. The film was broadcast in twenty countries and won seven international awards, including Best Documentary at Sundance. With each successive film, Fox has employed a different narrative structure, predicated less upon inherited documentary forms and more upon adapting genre conventions and paths of spectatorial identification traditionally associated with fiction filmmaking. Thus, *Beirut* could be said to be modelled after Anton Checkhov's *Three Sisters* (1901), while her ensuing ten-hour foray into the longitudinal form, *An American Love Story* (1999), recalls the family sitcoms of the 1970s, such as *The Brady Bunch* (ABC, 1969–74) or *All in the Family* (ABC, 1971–79). That work received a Gracie Award for Best Television Series and was named 'One of the Top Ten Television Series of 1999' by the *New York Times* and four other major American newspapers. In the series, Fox documents daily life in multicultural America by virtually moving in for a year and a half with the biracial Wilson-Sims family in Queens, New York. Both of her previous films involved rethinking the politics of objectivity and observation, consistently imbricating the personal with the political by actually living with her subjects and, thus, serving not only as a witness to history but also as its participant.

Fox's most recent project upped the ante, when a crisis in her own romantic life became the impetus for turning the camera upon herself. In her late thirties, her lifestyle as a successful documentary *auteur* was defined through autonomy and mobility – what she describes as 'a very autonomous male life' (in Fenner 2009: 27). To her mind, this meant successfully negotiating a profession inhabited almost exclusively by male practitioners, while privately involved in a steady succession of (heterosexual) relationships. Yet she recognised 'it wasn't the men that were holding my life together, it was these amazing conversations I had with my women friends' (ibid.). She found herself wondering why her life had ended up so different from theirs, as she weighed her professional achievements against the rapidly foreclosing biological possibility of motherhood in the context of marriage or a stable relationship.

CONFESSIONALITY AND FEMINIST CULTURAL PRODUCTION

Fox's decision to turn the camera on herself and make a film about a classic 'mid-life crisis' is congruent with the terms of feminist confessional literature associated with the women's movement of the 1970s and 1980s in the United States and in Western Europe. As Rita Felski has observed, 'the questioning of self is frequently inspired by a personal crisis which acts as a catalyst' (1989: 88): questioning socialism in Christa Wolf's *The Quest for Christa T.* (GDR, 1968); debilitating mental illness in Marie Cardinal's *The Words to Say It* (France, 1975); changing gender roles in Verena Stefan's *Shedding* (FRG, 1975); cancer in the case of Audre Lorde's *The Cancer Journals* (US, 1980) and sexual identity in Anja Meulenbelt's *The Shame is Over* (Netherlands, 1980). The link to this feminist genealogy is also signaled in the film's title, which recalls Erica Jong's semi-autobiographical novel *Fear of Flying* (US, 1973), in which the explicit adventures of protagonist Isadora Wing serve as a thin foil for the author's own marital malaise and Kate Millet's *Flying* (US, 1974) about a crisis triggered by the loss of a lover. Fox may further be building upon the allusions to emancipated sexuality metaphorised in the term 'flying', but her title also references the fact that her father, a professional airline pilot, exemplified the freedom and mobility she craved as a girl growing up under the restrictions imposed by her full-time mother, two aunts and grandmother. Needless to say, flying also references the mode of travel that shaped her lifestyle during four years of visiting seventeen countries to gather footage for her transnational documentary.

As a subgenre of autobiography, the confessional narrative is distinguished by the painful intimacy of the details recounted – details only disclosed under the compelling terms of personal crisis. Critical studies of its history in Western culture frequently identify it as a rhetorical mode grappling with the dualism characteristic of the early modern era, when the body became the arena of conflict and the site of a perceived unruliness. Confessional literature spanning the fourth to eighteenth centuries in Europe testifies to the mind's endeavour to overcome the body through religious dictates and cultural practices.[2] In Fox's own endeavour, the body's territorialisation through gender and sexuality becomes a similar source of preoccupation. Her voiceover in the opening installment of the series poignantly identifies the veritable cross-gender identifications which shaped not only her childhood but also her personal and professional choices in adulthood. Amidst a montage of Super-8 footage from the Fox family archive, she recalls:

> I never wanted to be a girl the way girls were supposed to be. I grew up practising take-offs and landings with my father on Sunday mornings in a two-seater plane. My Dad was everything to me. He could do anything. He left the house early in the morning and got to explore the world. He built buildings and had important meetings with interesting men and travelled everywhere. I adored my father. I wanted to be a boy. They could do anything they wanted.

Conversations later in the series reveal a life ruled by a heightened degree of sexual autonomy, whose motivations are rationalised in the same opening voiceover when she goes on to describe her mother as 'stuck with us kids and she kept having more, one baby after another until she had five. I decided I would never have children, and I said to my mother that I would never get married like her, nobody would ever tell me what to do. I wanted to be like my father – I wanted to be free.' The segue into the present drama concludes:

> So there I was. A free woman, 42 years old, living the life I thought I wanted in New York City. I travelled around the world alone, I made a career as a filmmaker and teacher. I slept with whom I chose and fell in love with those I wanted. I knew I didn't fall into common roles, but I didn't care. It was more important to be free, and I thought that life would go on forever like that.

A close-up of a pregnancy test wand displaying the double band of a positive reading constitutes the narrative hook, which draws the viewer into the film's more immediate diegesis, as Fox's voiceover trails off: 'I was pregnant, and I didn't know what to do.' In ensuing episodes, challenges are posed to achieving the settled structure of partnership and family. When she belatedly explores the path of biological motherhood, she painfully confronts the literal limits of her body, i.e. the manner in which fertility subsides across the seasons of a woman's life. She succumbs to repeated miscarriages while trying to get pregnant with then, and current, partner Patrick.

Her body's betrayal by aging triggers a crisis of purpose and identity. When the core of one's identity is jeopardised, the act of confession enacts a narrative journey towards reconstruction of the self, mastering the trauma by rendering identity legible again within the symbolic field. Specifically within feminist confessionality, Felski identifies a bifurcation in rhetorical structure and political function – one that 'exemplifies the intersection between the autobiographical imperative to communicate the truth of unique individuality, and the feminist concern with the representative and intersubjective elements of women's experience' (1989: 93). Fox enacts a similar double maneouvre by going simultaneously inward and outward, turning her personal crisis into a globe-trotting journey that involves speaking with women from vastly disparate cultures in order to understand how their sense of personal fulfillment could be shaped by, as well as resist, culturally specific norms of gender socialisation:

I couldn't find a reflection of myself in the world. There were no images out there for the life I was leading. I'm a so-called 'single woman', yet I've always been in a relationship. I'm leading this very autonomous male life – I don't have children, I'm not married – and yet I'm a woman. So I felt that there wasn't a representation or a mirror for me in the world, which is why [...] for the very first time I decided to self-film. (In Fenner 2009: 27)

If Fox's camera hereby becomes as a specular device for confronting gender dysphoria, such recourse exemplifies a Bazinian faith in the ontology of the photographic image, whose indexical trace of the real may help us 'to admire in reproduction something that our eyes alone could not have taught us to love' (1967a: 16). What Bazin describes as 'the essentially objective character of photography', (1967a: 13) offers a therapeutic or redemptive potential that Fox embraces:

We all walk around with layers of baggage obscuring the way we perceive our family, our society, and the events that have taken place in our lives [...] I think inherent in the camera, much like in psychotherapy, is the neutral observer. People concede to be on film because they perceive the camera to be an objective witness. (In Fenner 2009: 27)

DIALOGICAL ETHNOGRAPHY: MAKING WOMEN'S DISCOURSE VISIBLE

Contrary to one member of the New York Film Critics Circle, who panned the series as 'a mind-numbing exercise in narcissism' (Musetto 2007), I would suggest that Fox's camera is not deployed exclusively as a speculum but also to facilitate an encounter of a more dialogical nature, shifting the gaze outward to connect with other women. Fox sought to capture on film and make visible the palpable healing she felt regularly took place in conversations with women, about which she remarks:

> ... they went on for hours; they were circular; they were non-goal-oriented, meaning we weren't necessarily trying to solve a problem, although problems sometimes were solved. And they often raised subjects that resurfaced again and again over the course of several years of shooting: relationships, work, or children. (In Fenner 2009: 28)

To transpose this mode of communication into cinematic terms, Fox devised the practice she coined 'passing the camera'. Although reminiscent of the 'talking stick' used in some First Nation cultures to regulate speech within a ceremonial setting, 'passing the camera' actually inverts this function, because the person holding the camera is not so much authorised to speak as to elicit speech from her filmed interlocutor. The camera operator poses questions and listens attentively until moved to respond at length, or until the person being filmed asks a leading question that prompts the camera's exchange. Fox's own mother lost her reticence about speaking before the camera once she realised that she could, in turn, ply her daughter with questions on topics otherwise taboo in their ambivalent relationship.

Fox's utopian claim is that 'passing' erodes the distinction between camera operator and filmic subject, enabling qualities of spontaneity and authenticity so coveted in documentary to emerge:

> I am looking for reality on film. [...] And what is reality? Most of the time you bring a camera out and people disappear. It's like, you can see them back up into themselves and a wall comes up and they become a construction: 'Let me tell you about my life.' And they weed out all the good things, usually. You know, they do a presentation. As a filmmaker, I'm not interested in that. I'm interested in something else and I would call it presence. [...] In this particular film, I knew that if we put someone there observing women talking, they would leave emotionally and mentally, and all the intimacy would go away. A film is made up of bits of images, but those images can be real or false, depending upon if people really show up or not. (In Fenner 2009: 27–8)

Fox is working towards a more nuanced relationship between the camera and the human subjects positioned on either side of its lens. If the filmed subject in her true persona is to 'show up' and hereby generate 'presence', the role of the indifferent witness – a position the documentary filmmaker or camera operator has historically occupied – needs to be eliminated. Only then can the consequences of a dialogical approach to communication be rendered visible and audible to the audience.

Eschewing the 'fly on the wall' approach distributes the terms of enunciation across a continuum of participants in ways reminiscent of how film ethnography has been reframed by theorists such as Trinh T. Minh-ha, who stresses 'writing in the feminine' and 'speaking nearby or together' rather than 'speaking for and about' (1989: 101). Also pertinent is Jean Rouch's 'shared anthropology' developed upon discovering that the recording technology used in visual anthropology could, in contrast to other forms of documentation, be shared with those appearing in the footage, inviting comment and reflection on the document and also on the ethnographer's role. Fox's heightened sensitivity to the camera's influence matches Rouch's awareness of how his anthropological subjects are changed by the audiovisual encounter and may modify their comportment as a result of his presence. Janet Harbord describes his approach as one in which 'the apparatus of the production appears as a discursive two-way mirror through which the filmmakers themselves become visible subjects' (2007: 111).

Fox enacts within the digital era a rethinking of the relationship between technology, its human agents and representation – effectively, a search for a new film language – which previously inspired the febrile experimentation of the *cinéma vérité* movement between 1958 and 1960. In homage to Dziga Vertov's *kinopravda*, Edgar Morin sought to underscore the immediacy and closer contact between film subject and camera operator enabled by portable synchronous sound technologies and elimination of large crews (see Morin 1960, cited in Feld 2003: 14). To avoid any abstract claims for truthfulness, Morin and Rouch later adopted the term *cinéma direct*, stressing only the necessity of direct contact and the ongoing potential for the camera to serve as a catalyst, triggering speech and action that might otherwise remain unspoken or unaddressed. Thus, Rouch abnegated the use of film crews, tripod shooting, and the zoom lens for reinforcing an almost theatrical distance between the recording technology and its object of study (see Rouch 1973). From Rouch's intersubjective deployment of the camera to elicit a truth otherwise inaccessible, one can trace a genealogy leading to Fox's strategy of 'passing the camera' to elicit 'presence'. The type of realism at work among both documentary practitioners enacts 'the ritual connotation of representations that have actual effects on reality and in particular the reality of profilmic bodies' (Margulies 2001: 1). As Fox describes it:

In this room, we're all affecting each other. If one person leaves, the room will change. If someone else enters, the room will change. So we are creating this unified field. If I'm a filmmaker and I'm behind the camera, I can affect the scene by my awareness. Now, I can also affect it in another way, by passing the camera, which is a way to get people to be present with the camera and not disappear. (In Fenner 2009: 27)

Fox also shares Rouch's keen sense of dramaturgy. It was not his ambition to extract empirical or scientific facts from his footage; instead, he regarded the ethnographic film as itself a form of cultural production drawing in imaginative ways from fiction formats and surrealist techniques of representing dreams. Similarly, *Flying* adheres to the popular format of serial melodrama, in which television viewers become caught up in and identify with family and relational dynamics focalised through a central character or intimate cast. Each hour opens with a remixed montage of archival family footage of Fox's childhood and youth, accompanied by her voiceover outlining the backstory that sets the stage for ensuing developments. Each closing sequence similarly hooks audience interest in the next episode by alluding to imminent narrative complications.

SEX AND THE GLOBAL CITY

If *Flying* sometimes feels like a transnational documentary version of *Sex and the City* for the forty-something crowd, the similarities are more than coincidental. When Fox and her editor, Niels Pagh Andersen, were cutting the footage and searching for a viable dramaturgical template, the HBO series was at the height of its international popularity. While building upon the proven popular appeal of female friendship and frank discussions of sexuality, relationships and lifestyle choices among an ensemble of independent-minded professional women, *Flying* also represents a sobered and globally conscious post-9/11 upgrade from *Sex and the City*'s admixture of cultivated cattiness and shrill sarcasm. In *Sex and the City*, journalist Carrie Bradshaw (Sarah Jessica Parker) takes a pseudo-anthropological approach to studying sexual behaviour among the urban populace of 'the cruel planet that is Manhattan' (McMahon 1998: 21). Each episode opens on Carrie's voiceover as she poses questions and later, in closing, draws conclusions, while the camera dollies forward or back to reveal her poking away at her laptop or staring pensively into space within her studio apartment. Fox similarly utilises voiceover to elicit interiority and focalise the ensuing peripatetic journey, but replaces Carrie's Macintosh Powerbook with the Sony PDX digital camcorder as the medium of authorship. While the first installment is launched from the kitchen table of her Tribeca loft, the scope of her ethnographic investigation also expands beyond the 'Big Apple' to encompass other sites of globalising modernity.

Fox's jaunts into the developing world were undoubtedly risky and physically taxing, as she had to cross multiple time zones, combat jet lag, come to terms with unfamiliar food, unpredictable lodging, and navigate daily life in diverse foreign languages – circumstances that would stretch the patience, confidence and inner psychical reserves of most any traveller. Where Carrie's musings remain esconced in a normativised white middle class, with ethnicity and proletarian identities serving as a textural backdrop that reinforces existing class hierarchies and racist clichés, Fox probes further, meeting women of disparate cultural and class backgrounds in geographically distinct settings. What unifies those women is an emancipatory ethos whose proximity to human survival surpasses that of Samantha Jones's search for the perfect dildo or Miranda Hobbes' peevish post-partum body-size consciousness: Amina is a Somali in London educating women about their options to resist female genital mutilation, Chanthol runs a shelter for trafficked women in the Cambodian sex industry, Paromita is a grassroots community organiser and civil rights lawyer in India. Yet passing the camera, to the extent that it could even be passed in cultural contexts where a camera is perceived as a violation of privacy, can only go so far to overcome what remains, at the level of editing and focalisation, a tourist's gaze, however empathetic and self-reflexive. *Sex and the City* and *Flying* share a similar authorial positioning: that of the Western woman with a popular feminist (or, in *Sex and the City*, postfeminist) consciousness. The profound privilege as well as utopian longing bound up in the fantasy of complete autonomy and freedom are themselves the product of an extended Western philosophical tradition – that of the (implicitly male) transcendental subject, whose impossible omniscience women now also claim the right to explore in screen fictions and realities alike.

Both series legitimise women's voices using marketing strategies that build upon notions of female spectatorship and fandom.[3] Whereas the website for *Sex and the City* is more explicitly driven by consumption (for example, free screen savers, a tourist guide to NY locations covered in the series, merchandise for purchase), *Flying* publicises itself as a mode of popular consciousness-raising, including interactive tools such as 'Pass the camera', where women from various countries have uploaded typed entries or video diaries broaching personal concerns such as single motherhood, relationship to aging mothers and self-image.[4] An educational DVD of excerpts from the series has been organised into topics such as abortion, divorce, sexual abuse, illness and female genital mutilation; it can be ordered from the website together with a downloadable discussion guide for classroom or workshop settings. The link 'Take Action', moreover, includes web addresses for women's advocacy organisations in the US such as Our Bodies Our Selves and the National Organization for Women.

'WHAT ARE YOU HIDING?'

Flying resists the status of terminal text, not least because the real lives of its multiple protagonists continue to evolve. The conversation continues, as it were, by figuratively and literally passing the camera to audiences worldwide. Nowhere is confessionality as explicitly valourised as emancipatory strategy as in the web link soliciting videos for a seventh episode of the series and offering a $500 grand prize. In a promotional clip linked to YouTube, Fox recalls the initial difficulty of filming her own life:

> Once I did it, it was truly liberating. Now I've made it my personal mission to get other women to open up about their lives. Women around the world are granted more autonomy and freedom than ever before in history. And still, we hide so much about our everyday lives from the people around us. And for what? So women, let's stop living our personal lives in the closet. [...] Give yourself a voice! What are you hiding?[5]

Jumpcuts in which diverse women playfully repeat Fox's demand 'What are you hiding?' precede the closing exhortation 'Submit your videos!' projected in white text on a black screen. Although couched in the spirit of outreach and solidarity, this direct address towards a duplicitous spectator in denial of her 'true' self also solicits a mode of feminine authorship Trinh has elsewhere described in critical terms: 'Eager to create a meaningful world and/or to unveil her ignored/censored, deeper self, she adopts a series of strategies liable to ensure a transparency of form through which content, intelligently constructed, can travel unhindered' (1989: 30). Recalling Freud's talking cure and the autonomous self of American ego psychology, the ambition is that of bringing the repressed to consciousness – 'where Id was, there Ego shall be' (1964: 80) – and thereby overcoming neuroses resulting from unconsciously internalised social dictates.

Although Walter Benjamin similarly suggests that 'the camera introduces us to unconscious optics as does psychoanalysis to unconscious impulses' (1968: 237), I believe he had in mind a more nuanced perception of how the repressed comes to betray its content almost despite itself, rather than overtly flaunting it. For Jacques Lacan, as well, the pychoanalytical symptom differs from the conventional medical understanding of the symptom as a 'natural index':

> ... it is in the disintegration of the imaginary unity constituted by the ego that the subject finds the signifying material of his symptoms. And it is from the sort of inter-est aroused in him by the ego that the significations that turn his discourse away from those symptoms proceed. (1977: 137)

Lacan's understanding of the unconscious as structured like a language (1977: 147) may offer a more apt paradigm for the sense-making process of autobiographical filmmaking. The operations of the signifier – for example, condensation and displacement – find their visual corollary in the mirror that cannot but offer a series of misapprehensions of the self. Where Fox valourises the therapeutic value of the video camera's imputed indexicality, Lacan would argue that the analyst should function instead as an empty mirror or a blank screen, i.e. a site for projection.

In many ways, the larger a 'project' *Flying* has become through its marketing and reception evinces the dialectic dwelling within the contemporary auto-biographical or confessional endeavour, which has been explicated by cultural theorists and philosophers alike as a tension between freedom and constraint, display and concealment, avowal and repression. Ever since the linguistic turn spearheaded by Louis Althusser, Roland Barthes and Michel Foucault, the autobiographer has come to be understood as interpellated or subjected, made to define herself through discourses that pre-exist her and that enable this ulti-mately only illusory naming of the self as bounded entity accountable for her actions. The very title of Fox's documentary performatively displays this same tension between the social circumscription of subjectivity which the confes-sional stance entails, and Fox's perception of herself as a 'free woman', in other words, as an autonomous subject.

At the level of the film apparatus, a similar contradiction inheres between the manner in which cinematography necessarily functions as ideology, that is, hailing a specific subject into being, and Fox's observation that passing the camera unfetters a pre-existing subjectivity, thereby eliciting that elusive quality summated in the term 'presence'. What happens in the intersubjective encounters between women in the absence of a third party camera operator may be a more Foucauldian endeavour altogether, namely, a mutual internal-isation of the camera as surveillant authority and confessor *par excellence*. If we situate the technique along the historical timeline of other disciplinary regimes, the spatial geography seems to have evolved significantly: from the confined private space of the Catholic confessional box, where it assumed almost exclusively aural form, to Jeremy Bentham's Panopticon, in which the scopic regime encompasses the prisoner's internalisation of the Other's gaze. 'Passing the camera' fuses the dialogical talking cure with visual signs proffered for audience scrutiny in the form of facial expressions, movements of the body, and posture – all of which betray nuanced layers of subtext.

The apparent pervasiveness of the portable camera in Fox's personal life, moreover, embodies the capillary form of power as Foucault prophesied its proliferation, involving voluntary surrender to – indeed, embrace of – (self)-surveillance. In her role as nodal point among a cast of characters in an epic drama derived from real life, Fox maintains she became habitualised to living the camera to the point where her natural inhibitions and inevitable inclination to perform for the camera were eroded:

> I worked with the camera for a really long time to make it not important to me. I made rules: I can't dress up or put on make-up for the camera, I'm not going to prepare at all. I would force myself to take it everwhere – to the bathroom, to the bedroom – you see all that. I would only get dressed up if I was getting dressed up anyway. I would film all the time, every day, even if I'm having the most stupid day in the world. Film when there's nothing going on, so that I'm so used to filming I even manage to take the camera out when something important goes on. (In Fenner 2009: 30)

The assumptions underpinning this approach fly in the face of Jean-Louis Comolli's reasoning in the pages of *Cahiers du Cinéma* in 1971. He took issue with fellow theorist Jean-Patrick Lebel's conviction that the camera is merely 'a passive recording instrument, which reproduces the object or objects filmed in the form of an image-reflection constructed according to the laws of the rectilinear propagation of light waves' (1971: 71; here, citing the English translation in Comolli 1990: 216). Comolli's materialist reading recognises camera technique as part of a larger signifying system that is historically contingent and ideologically motivated. While Fox would hardly disagree, she also claims her technique more fully accesses the ontological. Ironically, whereas André Bazin's 'supra-realism' outlined in 'The Evolution of the Language of the Cinema' (1967b) valourises deep focus and long takes with minimal editing, the documentary realism Fox espouses at the level of shooting is also wedded to a foundational editing technique of classical Hollywood, generating the suture associated with shot/reverse-shot by eliding the inevitable wobble resulting from a running camera transferring hands. Thus, the aura of 'presence' Fox claims to have captured may more accurately be attributable to our spectatorial conditioning by what Daniel Dayan (2000) coins 'the tutor-code' of classical cinema, a system of enunciation reminiscent of the Lacanian unconscious, in that 'it speaks' while similarly eliding its point of enunciation. In Dayan's words, 'the film-discourse presents itself as a product without a producer, a discourse without an origin. It speaks. Who speaks? Things speak for themselves and of course, they tell the truth. Classical cinema establishes itself as the ventriloquist of ideology' (2000: 224).

THE CULTURAL SPECIFICITY OF CONFESSION

Ventriloquism is also salient to Fox's deployment of the camera as a technology of confession. In her project, it becomes a means for producing the truth of the subject within a quasi-juridical framework requiring adherence to specific rules *á la* Dogme:

> The camera had to be passed and it needed to involve a definitive amount of time, meaning, you know, 1–3 hours. We basically created the conditions to enable women's conversations, and food and drink was usually present. [...] I had other rules: everyone had to agree to be on camera – there could be no witnesses. Nobody could say, 'Oh, I'm just going to watch while you guys talk.' (In Fenner 2009: 28)

If this technique facilitates mutual sharing, it would be false to claim that power is obliterated altogether, for as Foucault points out, 'truth isn't outside power' (1984: 72). The implementation of rules proves that, whatever the emancipatory ideology underpinning the camera work, in Foucault's words, it is ultimately 'not a matter of emancipating truth from every system of power [...] but of detaching the power of truth from the forms of hegemony within which it operates' (1984: 74). Although Fox seeks to undercut the power differentials associated with ethnographic filmmaking, it is nevertheless she who sets the parameters, which, in turn, hail into being a culturally contingent and historically specific form of gendered subjectivity perhaps most discernible at the site of a distinct cultural differential. Among women acculturated in Western industrial contexts – in her home territory of New York, in the American Midwest, in London, Berlin and South Africa – the camera seems to merely trigger an already engrained literacy in the confessing mode. In certain regions of India, Pakistan, Indonesia and Vietnam, however, Fox encounters women less accustomed to interacting with a camera. They do not immediately grasp it as a tool for either self-display or confessionality. In Episode Five, when Fox explains to a group of Pakistani women, 'one of the ideas of this movie is that everyone uses the camera', we witness in their perplexed gazes and continued silence how culturally peculiar or Western the filmmaker's assumptions are. What ensues is a series of shots where little passing seems evident, despite an editing style that sutures the spectator by cutting rapidly between the faces of different Pakistani women while maintaining sound continuity; instead, they appear to be patiently and haltingly directing their comments to Fox, explaining to a cultural outsider – the ethnographer – the terms of their lives. These scenes remain stylistically distinct from the types of intimate revelations her Western interlocutors share with striking ease, and reinforce the thesis that the confessing mode is a Western construct, a ritual in which the social subject is performatively called into being through exteriorisation of a perceivedly interior and private self.

Although engaged in what Trinh calls 'writing in the feminine', Fox is not immune from the dangers of 'the Priest-God scheme', wherein 'Woman (with a capital W) may therefore kill women if she loses the contact and speaks of herself only according to what she wants to hear about herself' (1989: 28). The terms and implications of appearing on camera remain vastly different in certain cultures, where being associated with and displayed on that recording device could endanger a woman's social reputation and even her life. Indeed, in Pakistan, we hear and see her local guides repeatedly exhort her to turn off her camera as they enter public areas where men are present. That she resists doing so far longer than is comfortable for her escorts foregrounds how intrusive even the imputedly benevolent camera can be. 'Passing the camera' in itself cannot elide existing economic and social disparaties or degrees of either social or geographical mobility, leading one film critic to conclude: 'Over the six hours spent with Fox as she jets around the globe, a picture emerges, not only of a modern woman contemplating herself, but of Western society boasting of its freedom to a world struggling for mere survival' (Miller 2008).

Fox's transnational aesthetic may appear to homogenise her female subjects into so many variations of womanhood emancipating itself, but fissures most certainly remain that ultimately enrich and lend complexity to the project. Those fissures reveal that, as technologies and signifying practices travel across borders, they do not necessarily and inevitably submit to a self-evident teleological progression towards ever greater transparency and enlightenment. Indeed, these ruptures are possibly the site of the project's greatest realism, if we think of realism, as Bazin did, as best captured in the incidental, contingent and marginal, i.e. in that which escapes narrative determinism. For example, questions of (exclusively hetero-)sexual desire and fulfilment assume nearly banal contours when Fox discusses them with her Western friends, but become the performative site of Derrida's notion of *différance* (1982: 7) in her encounters with Somali women in London and with Paromita in India. The communicative impasse that results reveals the cultural specificity of sexuality, legible only in the context of a series of other local rites and practices that constitute the symbolic order. When Fox asks Paromita whether she ever masturbates, the openly baffled woman seems not to understand the phenomenon nor can she locate a word in her language to identify it. When Fox mischievously waves her index finger to signal the means of achieving pleasure, Paromita can only wiggle all her fingers back at her in bemused incomprehension. Similarly, when Fox asks a 'circumcised' Somali woman whether she feels any pleasure during intercourse, a similar deferral of either a yes or no response occurs. Female desire here becomes the very apotheosis of the *différend*, only incompletely accessible to meaning through its precarious and highly contingent location along a chain of other cultural signifiers. While it remains unclear what rela- tionship these two women ultimately do harbour to pleasure or orgasm, the topic may not simply be taboo in the Western sense but actually constitute both an organic and symbolic lacuna. Of course, the film's Western sexual paradigm evinces its own lacuna, that of lesbian desire, which is never directly broached nor even obliquely acknowledged. What does become evident is that Fox's implicit correlation between orgasm and emancipation – an equation pervasive in *Sex and the City* – eludes easy translation across languages and cultures.

PASSING THROUGH THE MARGIN AND THE CENTRE

Fox's Western focalisation may render her fallible, but precisely that vulner- ability holds up to the West a painfully honest mirror of its own confused encounter with the aporias of cultural difference and historical non-simulta- neity or *Ungleichzeitigkeit* (see Bloch 1962: 96).[6] Few of us would risk having such moments memorialised on film for our own moral examination, let alone that of global audiences. Armchair critics of her project could benefit from illumination about the impossibility for any autobiographical venture in the *verité* style to be free of moments of inadvertent solipsism or disavowal. In response to the label 'self-indulgent' so often attached to personal documen- tary, Michael Renov has pointed out that 'it could hardly be otherwise' (1995: 86). What Fox's literal and figurative border passages evince is a woman com- ing to terms with the fact that she herself occupies at once the centre and the margins. The discursive 'im-passe' identified early in my investigation results not least from the multiple connotations of 'passing', which can be understood as a coping mechanism for Fox throughout her biography, as well as referring to the discursive framework for her cinematography, and indeed, serving as paradigmatic for the project itself as a therapeutic traversal mythologised in Lacanian psychoanalysis as 'the pass'. In the latter controversial rite of pas- sage, the analysand achieves closure on her analysis (which, after all, is not intended to be interminable!) by giving an account to a third-party committee of the analyst's interventions, the handling of the transference, and how she now understands this to have operated at the level of her unconscious. The motivation to undergo the pass is, as Anne Dunand expresses it, a 'calling [...] particularly when it finds its roots in the wish to convey to others how psychoanalysis worked for one individual' (1995: 252).

In analogous fashion, the impetus for *Flying* originated in Fox's desire to performatively enact the therapeutic effect of women's conversations. The shooting process itself redoubles the analytic process by bringing to consciousness via the digital camera the terms of an ongoing misrecognition of identity, one which, in this instance, inculcates in ambitious women a haunting sense of their imposter status (see Clance 1985) – or what Fox has expressed as the lack of a coherent mirror in her social and professional surroundings for the life she was leading. At first glance, she appears to occupy a position of privilege: raised in a bourgeois family, whose archival footage reveals a childhood that included equestrian training and archery lessons; now occupant of a Tribeca loft; at middle age, one of America's most successful documentarists. Yet, on the inside, she is riddled with insecurities: the desire for external approval and for love – from family, friends, colleagues or lovers – now belatedly compounded by concern to fulfill the mainstream definition of femininity and of societal worth by settling with a secure spouse and bearing children. As a child, Fox subconsciously sought to 'pass' in boys' activities; as successful director, she 'passes' in a male-dominated industry; in her filmic interactions she attempts to 'pass' as cultural insider among women of differing backgrounds precisely by 'passing the camera' as means to dialogical communication. What her footage captures is not an ontological truth, but the truth of her ongoing subjection by discourse, as well as her lifelong resistance to the mostly gendered constraints so rigorously enforced since childhood. There is, of course, a corporeal component to that subjection. The five-year therapeutic journey of sharing stories leads to the gradual extraction of the 'truth' of the lived body, namely, its territorialisation through encounters with others – men and women alike. When discussing female genital mutilation with Amina in the fifth episode, for example, she sees a corollary between the matriarchs of Somali society, who conduct the cutting of young girls, and the strict surveillance of her own bodily person by her mother, aunts and grandmother. She concludes that, in both instances, female elders were perpetuating inherited practices intended to secure a woman's marriage prospects and hence, a stable position in society.

Her insights exemplify the therapeutic effects of the Freudian talking cure, in which conscious understanding of how the body has been worked upon enacts a form of mastery. Yet before overcoming past trauma, a state of injury must first be ascertained. From a Foucauldian point of view, the confessional rhetoric invoked in the film's subtitle and technologically induced through mutual 'passing' not only offers a socially sanctioned format for expurgating otherwise taboo topics, its operations are, in fact, performative: to utter within this rhetorical framework is to incriminate oneself as a transgressive and abjected subject. Thus, in the opening voiceover to Episode One Fox may proclaim of her past history, 'I slept with whom I wanted', yet in the course of her journey, she comes to regard herself as a victim of misencounters with men. One turning point involves the recollection of her first sexual encounter at the age of twelve with a gym teacher. The film's construction offers the impression that the experience had long been repressed; only after learning of other women's victimisation does it resurface as an understanding of herself as abused. There is no denying that the gym teacher's past behaviour constituted an egregious abuse of authority and power; nor is there any reason for Fox to feel guilty for what happened at an age when she could not have ascertained the inappropriateness of the teacher's behaviour or the lasting negative psychical consequences for herself. Yet what interests me is how past events in Fox's memory only become inscribed with specific moral meaning following the exchange stories with other women: confessionality implies guilt (and in this case, perhaps retroactive shame), and guilt, especially when unjustified – as it is here – triggers denial, best enacted by professing one's status as, in fact, a victim.

These circumstances bear some affinity with the operation of Nietzschean *ressentiment*, in which the disempowered transform their perception of themselves as weak into one of moral superiority. Within that dialectic, Fox's journey of emancipation also performs her discursive entrapment and is perhaps even predicated upon that rhetorical maneuovre. In his historical survey of confessionality, Jeremy Tambling elaborates:

> The 'human-all-too-human' state of *ressentiment* and the reactive spirit with its will to truth produces marginalised and confessing figures. The hysterical, the mad, the sexually perverted and women are produced as the other of the (now) bourgeois subject, assumed to be male, normal, heterosexual and white. [...] The history of confession is that of power at the centre inducing people at the margins to internalise what is said about them – to accept that discourse and to live it, and thereby to live their oppression. (1990: 6)

This geography of centre and margin holds territorial, social, economic and discursive import for the present instance. While Fox launches her autobiographical foray from within the cultural and economic epicentre of New York City, her indefatigable traversal of numerous national borders and cultural divides gradually redoubles into an identification with the position of the margin occupied by her numerous interlocutors. In the course of their con-versations, she comes to perceive herself as plagued by negative self-image and gender dysphoria, as moreover implicated in the misuse of sexuality, and as wrestling with sexism in what indisputably remains a man's world.

These cross-identifications take place not only within the footage but also at the level of storytelling, as exemplified in the cross-gender ventriloquisms of (male) editor Niels Pagh Andersen. In Lacanian terms, the shooting of *Flying* constitutes Fox's self-analysis in the rough, with Andersen serving as what is known as the *passeur*, whose role is 'to carry the message s/he has been entrusted with' to a wider audience (Dunand 1995: 253). Of course, like a film editor, the pass-bearer 'cannot but filter what has been told them according to their own interests and structures' (ibid.). By the filmmaker's own admission, the imperatives of sustaining narrative continuity and a coherent protagonist result in 'an incredibly constructed object' (in Fenner 2009: 27). The montage and accompanying voiceover that opens and closes each installment becomes the location for assembling the spine of the story:

> By frontloading the archive, Niels created the subtext that will run through the entire series, namely that everything that I'm doing in my life is shaped by the fact that I never wanted to be a girl. It was really amazing for me to see this. Film is a collab-orative medium and Niels brought a lot to this process. It's not just my interpretation of reality, it's also his. [...] But the latter three hours of the film, where the more painful issues of being a woman are addressed – it was something he really didn't understand and it was a hard thing for me to explain and for us to work through. (In Fenner 2009: 32–3)

Through self-discipline and self-analysis during shooting and post-production, Fox's confessional stance has enacted a stabilisation of her identity. As such it constitutes a very public version of 'the pass', inaugurating the analysand's transition into the role of analyst serving others. An emergent understanding of her own gender socialisation equips Fox to more fully grasp the norms that shape the lives of women across cultures. If this maneouvre verges on totalis-ing 'the female condition' in ways reminiscent of second-wave feminism, it is also the ideological linchpin of a *fait accompli* that has inspired identifications among audience members worldwide and provoked discussion of the uneven and gendered distribution of power, agency and self-esteem under globalisa-tion. In unpacking the film's underlying rhetorical strategies, I by no means seek to discredit *Flying* as an important social intervention; rather, I wish to acknowledge that its discourse cannot, nor should it, be disencumbered from its various political and ideological use-values.

Acknowledgements

This research arose out of Jennifer Fox's visit to the University of Toronto in Fall 2007, which was funded by the Cinema Studies Institute, the Centre for Transnational and Diaspora Studies and the Institute for Gender and Women's Studies. A shorter version of this essay appeared in a Special Issue on Transcultural Mediations and Transnational Politics of Difference published by the *Journal of Feminist Media Studies*, 9, 4 (2009). It is reprinted here with permission from Taylor and Francis Ltd.

Notes

1 Early exemplars by the movement's Danish founders include Thomas Vinterberg (*The Celebration*,1998), Lars von Trier (*The Idiots*, 1998) and Soren Kragh Jacobsen (*Mifune*, 1999). In total, 239 international films have been initiated into the Dogme annals. In June 2002, the Dogme Secretariat officially discontinued certification on the grounds that the Vow was never intended as a genre formula, and that its founders have moved on to explore other experimental forms; see Hjort and MacKenzie (2003).

2 See Saint Augustine (1961); the medieval writings of Margery Kempe in Staley (1996); Jean-Jacques Rousseau (2000); and the nineteenth-century confessions of Saint Thérèse Martin (2006).

3 *Sex and the City* also held niche appeal for its 'barely occluded gay sensibility' (Greven 2004: 44) evinced in, for example, the heightened focus on designer labels and fashion and the ongoing retinue of naked male bodies proffered 'as objects rather than wielders of the gaze' (2004: 40). Simultaneously, this queer approach to gender frequently also bordered on 'misognystic and homophobic' (ibid.), expressed through several 'male freaks', for example Charlotte's exaggeratedly horny and hairy boyfriend, and later husband, Harry, and Amanda's encounter with an overweight man with gluttonous eating habits.

4 See www.hbo.com/city and www.flyingconfessions.com.

5 The clip is now archived under the title 'What Are You Hiding?' and can be searched via this title and Jennifer Fox's name on www.youtube.com

6 I am thinking of Ernst Bloch's utopian rearticulation of that Marxian concept, such that different historical temporalities are understood to cohabit under the terms of contemporary globalisation: 'Not all people exist in the same Now. They do so only externally, through the fact that they can be seen today. But they are thereby not yet living at the same time with the others. Instead they carry earlier elements with them; this interferes. Depending on where someone stands physically, and above all in terms of class, he has his times. Older times than the modern one continue to have an effect in older strata' (1962: 96).

References

Augustine, St. Bishop of Hippo (1961 [398]) *Confessions*. New York: Penguin.

Bazin, A. (1967a) 'The Ontology of the Photographic Image', in A. Bazin, *What is Cinema? Vol. 1*, trans. H. Gray. Berkeley, CA: University of California Press, 9–16.

_____ (1967b) 'The Evolution of the Language of Cinema', in A. Bazin *What is Cinema? Vol. 1*, trans. H. Gray. Berkeley, CA: University of California Press, 23–40.

Benjamin, W. (1968 [1935]) 'The Work of Art in the Age of Mechanical Reproduction', in H. Arendt (ed.) *Illuminations: Essays and Reflections*. New York, NY: Shocken Books, 217–52.

Bloch, E. (1962) *Heritage of Our Times*, trans. N. and S. Plaice. Cambridge: Polity Press.

Cardinal, M. [1975] (1983) *The Words to Say It*. Cambridge, MA: VanVactor & Goodheart.

Clance, P. (1985) *The Imposter Phenomenon: Overcoming the Fear that Haunts Your Success*. Atlanta, GA: Peachtree Press.

Comolli, J. (1990 [1971]) 'Technique and Ideology: Camera, Perspective, Depth of Field', in N. Browne (ed.) *Cahiers du Cinéma: 1969–1972: The Politics of Representation*, trans. D. Matias. Cambridge, MA: Harvard University Press, 213–47.

Dayan, D. (2000) 'The Tutor-Code of Classical Cinema', in J. Hollows, P. Hutchings and M. Jancovich (eds) *The Film Studies Reader*. Oxford: Oxford University Press, 217–25.

Derrida, J. (1982) 'Différance' in J. Derrida *Margins of Philosophy*. Trans. A. Bass. Chicago: Chicago University Press, 1-28.

Dunand, A. (1995) 'The End of Analysis (II)', in R. Feldstein, B. Fink and M. Jaanus (eds.) *Reading Seminar XI: Lacan's Four Fundamental Concepts of Psychoanalysis*. Buffalo, NY: State University of New York, 251–7.

Elster, J. (2000) *Ulysses Unbound: Studies in Rationality, Precommitment, and Constraints*. Cambridge: Cambridge University Press.

Feld, S. (ed. and trans.) (2003) *Ciné-Ethnography: Jean Rouch*. Minneapolis, MN: University of Minnesota.

Fenner, A. (2009) 'The Dialogical Documentary: Jennifer Fox on Finding a New Film Language in *Flying: Confessions of a Free Woman*.' *CineAction*, 77, 25–33.

Felski, R. (1989) *Beyond Feminist Aesthetics: Feminist Literature and Social Change*. Cambridge, MA: Harvard University Press.

Freud, S. (1964 [1933]) 'Dissection of the Psychical Personality', *New Introductory Lectures on Psychoanalysis*, ed. and trans. J. Strachey. New York, NY: W. W. Norton, 71–100.

Foucault, M. (1984) 'Truth and Power', in P. Rabinow (ed.) *The Foucault Reader*. New York: Pantheon, 51-75.

_____ (1990 [1976]) *History of Sexuality. Volume I: An Introduction*. Trans. R. Hurley. New York, NY: Vintage.

Greven, D. (2004) 'The Museum of Unnatural History: Male Freaks and *Sex and the City*', in K. Akass and J. McCabe (eds) *Reading 'Sex and the City'*. London: I.B. Taurus, 33–47.

Harbord, J. (2007) *The Evolution of Film: Rethinking Film Studies*. Cambridge: Polity Press.

Hjort, M. and S. Mackenzie (2003) *Purity and Provocation: Dogma 95*. London: British Film Institute.

Jong, E. (1973) *Fear of Flying*. New York: Rinehart & Winston.

Staley, Lynn, ed. (1996) *The Book of Margery Kempe*. Kalamazoo, MI: Medieval Institute Publications.

Lacan, J. (1977 [1966]) *Ecrits: A Selection*, trans. A. Sheridan. New York, NY: W.W. Norton.

Lebel, J. (1971) 'Cinéma et Idéologie', *Nouvelle Critique*, 34.

Levin, G. R. (1971) *Documentary Explorations. 15 Interviews with Filmmakers*. New York, NY: Doubleday.

Lorde, A. (1980) *The Cancer Journals*. New York: Spinsters.

Margulies, I. (ed.) (2002) *Rites of Realism: Essays on Corporeal Cinema*. Durham, NC: Duke University Press.

Martin, T. (2006) *The Story of a Soul: The Autobiography of St. Therese of Lisieux*, trans. and ed. R. Edmundson. New York, NY: Paraclete Press.

McMahon, E. (1998) *Evening Standard*. 13 July.

Meulenbelt, A. (1980) *The Shame is Over*. Trans. A. Oosthuizen. London: Women's Press.

Miller, P. (2008) *Newsblaze.com*, 15 May.

Millet, K. (1974) *Flying*. New York: Knopf.

Morin, E. (1960) 'Pour un nouveau cinéma vérité', *France-Observateur*.

Musetto, V. (2007) 'Overlong and Flying on Empty', *New York Post*, 6 July.

Reik, T. (1945) *The Compulsion to Confess: On the Psychoanalysis of Crime and Punishment*. New York, NY: Farrar, Straus, and Cudahy.

Renov, M. (1995) 'Video Confessions', in M. Renov and E. Suderberg (eds.) *Resolutions: Contemporary Video Practices*. Minneapolis, MN: University of Minnesota Press, 78–101.

Rouch, J. (2003 [1973]) 'The Camera and the Man', in S. Feld (ed. and trans.) *Ciné-Ethnography: Jean Rouch*. Minneapolis, MN: University of Minnesota Press, 29–46.

Rousseau, J. (2000 [1782]) *Confessions*. Oxford: Oxford University Press.

Shohat, E. (2001) 'Area Studies, Transnationalism, and the Feminist Production of Knowledge', *Signs: Journal of Women in Culture and Society*, 26, 5: 1269–72.

Staley, L. (ed.) (1996) *The Book of Margery Kempe*. Kalamazoo, MI: Medieval Institute Publications.

Stefan, V. (1978 [1975]) *Shedding*. Trans. J. Moore and B. Weckmueller. Los Angeles, CA: Scott and Daughters Publishing.

Tambling, J. (1990) *Confession: Sexuality, Sin, the Subject*. Manchester: Manchester University Press.

Trinh T. M. (1989) *Woman Native Other*. Bloomington, IN: Indiana University Press.

White, M. (1992) *Tele-Advising: Therapeutic Discourse in American Television*. Chapel Hill: University of North Carolina Press.

Wolf, C. (1979 [1968]) *The Quest for Christa T.* Trans. C. Middleton. New York, NY: Farrar, Straus & Giroux.

Secrets and Inner Voices:
The Self and Subjectivity in
Contemporary Indian Documentary

Sabeena Gadihoke

The first decade of this century has witnessed a vibrant independent documentary movement in India that emerged out of a series of developments in the 1990s. One of these was the dismantling of a traditional model of state control over cultural production. Economic liberalisation ushered in radical changes in the Indian media through satellite broadcasting, the internet and a digital revolution. Responding to this change as well as the concommitant rise of identity politics, documentary filmmakers started to address fractured urban middle-class subjectivities. A range of first person films explored the private but contested arenas of gender and sexuality, the family or questions of religious and ethnic identities. This essay will map this journey of the self, exploring how these filmmakers also challenge stubborn historical links between documentary and the 'visible'. More comfortable expressing external realities, non-fiction film in India has often marginalised interiority. Using the example of three documentaries made in the last decade, this essay will focus on the filmic representation of the private, looking at the ways in which they dare to articulate a range of cultural silences and taboos.

Quite apart from more overt expressions of subjectivity in national and regional forms of Indian literature, cinema, poetry, songs and theatre, the history of non-fiction film in India followed a different trajectory.[1] The state-controlled Films Division was the sole producer of documentary films after independence. With few exceptions these early films privileged a collective identity linked to nationhood and nation building where the filmmaker remained distant or invisible.[2] The utility value of the documentary was emphasised over its poetic possibilities. India did not have an experimental film tradition like that of the *avant garde* in North America. By the 1970s the disillusionment with the undelivered promises of the nation state gave birth to a number of political documentaries that focused on protest movements or struggles against the State.[3] Part of a global moment, particularly in conflicted parts of the Third World, the makers of these films (many allied with the Left) focused on marginalised subjects. Largely embedded in a realist style, they eschewed the personal and tended to foreground the public persona of their subjects. Moreover, given their ambitions to give 'voice to the voiceless', it was a widely shared assumption that the filmmakers themselves would not be the protagonists in these films. As Jyotsna Kapur (2003) notes, perhaps it was felt that any reference to the subjectivity of the middle-class filmmaker might deflect attention away from the lives and experiences of the underprivileged. During the next decade, private funding for non-fiction films was dominated by international aid agencies and the NGO sector. Driven by the developmentalist agenda of funders, these commissioned films too had little scope for first person filming. There were some early grassroots initiatives with participatory filmmaking. One such initiative was the Video *SEWA* project in Ahmedabad that encouraged marginalised women to make films about their own lives.[4] In many of these videos the self emerged through a distant and disembodied voice-over.[5] Constrained by their form, moreover, these alternative video practices relied on a language of realism that shied away from interiority.

In 1998 Amar Kanwar's *A Season Outside* marked a significant move towards first person filmmaking through its use of a poetic voiceover and evocative imagery. With some autobiographical strands, the film was an insightful exploration of the nature of violence in South Asia. Kanwar's film had been preceded by other films that had made some attempt to foreground subjectivity. For instance, the powerful *Eyes of Stone* (Nilita Vacchani, 1990) focused on the phenomenon of possession and the subjectivity of one woman in a rural family in Rajasthan. Made in the classic traditions of direct cinema, the film was marked by the absence of the filmmaker. Others such as *Khel* (Saba Dewan and Rahul Roy, 1994) attempted to foreground the filmic encounter, while *The Hidden Story* (Ranjani Mazumdar and Shikha Jhingan, 1995) revealed aspects of the power relations between the filmmaker and subjects. The awarding of the first prize to *A Season Outside* at the Mumbai International Film Festival for shorts and documentaries (MIFF) in 1998 was an acknowledgement of the arrival of more personal modes of expression that foregrounded the experience of the filmmaker. A 'submerged' self would appear in several subsequent documentaries that deployed autobiographical vignettes about the filmmaker within films that focused on other issues.[6]

As in the West, the turn to more open forms of first person filming emerged out of identity politics and the feminist and queer movements in particular.

Some of the first films to approach the autobiographical with confidence were a cluster of cross-border films that emerged from journeys made from and to a rapidly globalising India. In 2000 a powerful film commissioned by the National Film Board of Canada went almost unnoticed. This was *Desperately Seeking Helen* (Eisha Marjara, 1998) about a Canadian Indian woman's return to her origins. Screened for the first time in India at MIFF, the film was dismissed as self-absorbed very likely because it spoke openly of the self and used narrative strategies unfamiliar to documentary discourse in India at the time. With its reflexive use of humour, whimsy and a fictive structure in which the filmmaker staged her own body, Marjara's film did not easily fit popular conceptions of documentary.[7] Deeply personal, *Desperately Seeking Helen* was a complex and layered film, ostensibly about the construction of femininity but also hinting at more internal trauma and tragedy.

The cross-cultural family was the theme of *My Mother India* (Safina Oberoi, Australia, 2000). The film's title is significant because of its reference to her Australian mother who settled in India after marrying the filmmaker's Sikh father in the 1960s. *My Mother India* moves from being a humourous commentary on a white mother to the dark days of the anti-Sikh pogrom in 1984 and its impact on this family.[8] The refrain of being able to go away and reflect on identity recurred in another important autobiographical film, *Summer in My Veins* (Nishit Saran, USA/India, 1999). Made by a gay filmmaker, the film documents his mother and aunts as they travel to Harvard for his graduation ceremony. Using the trope of the home movie, *Summer in My Veins* had an exceptional climax when Saran comes out to his mother while shooting her with the camera. One of the major shifts made by the three films described above was their engagement with the personal experience of the filmmaker.

Other films emerge today out of a more vibrant tradition of independent documentary practice. Less expensive digital equipment, a greater circulation of diverse kinds of images, and informal networks of distribution make it possible for the independent filmmaker to survive outside of institutional support. There are a number of film schools in major cities that encourage the study and production of documentary. Most filmmakers have access to a range of regional and international films through global travel or networks of piracy. These changes are accompanied by a refiguring of the realms of public and private experience in urban India. Blogs, YouTube and social networking sites have encouraged a new kind of public visibility of what was formerly considered to be the domain of the private. A variety of approaches mark the ways in which the self appears in the Indian documentary today.[9] These include openly autobiographical films, those that approach the autobiographical through biographies of others and films that use autobiographical elements to interrogate the nature of the filmic encounter. This essay takes as its focus three such films. Both explicit and hidden, they are representative of the different ways in which the self appears in the new Indian documentary. The three films under discussion are *Sita's Family* (Saba Dewan, 2002), *Bare* (Santana Issar, 2006) and *Tales of the Night Fairies* (Shohini Ghosh, 2002)

Commissioned for television by the Public Service Broadcasting Trust (PSBT), Saba Dewan's *Sita's Family* is a film about three generations of women in her family. Saba and her partner/camera operator Rahul Roy film Saba's mother Manorama, and her aunts as they make a journey to an ancestral home to reminisce about their now absent parents. Manorama's parents were 'freedom fighters', who took part in the struggle for Indian independence. The film focuses particularly on Saba's grandmother, Sita Devi who was a feminist icon for the family. This exterior journey is intercut with a more interior journey being made by the filmmaker one winter to understand the roots of a crisis. We are never told this explicitly, but the film hints at it through self-conscious and subjective imagery and words. *Sita's Family* opens with the extended family on the train as Saba's mother, Manorama, and her two sisters travel to visit their brother and family home in Jullunder, Punjab after nearly twelve years. The purpose of this journey is referred to by Manorama in one of the opening sequences. She has visited home before but this time it feels different: 'It doesn't feel like a trip to make a film. I feel I am going to meet my parents.' As the siblings remember the past, the narrative of the second generation of the family is a more public one through memories, laughter and tears. Proud of parents who were public figures, they are also torn by the pain of revisiting an insecure childhood as a result of the incarceration of their parents as political prisoners. The role of the film in evoking several emotional moments is indirectly acknowledged as one of the sisters explains that they never had time to mourn: 'It is important for families to get together and have a catharsis. We however put up a brave face and went back to our lives.'

In contrast to the more public expression of emotion, the filmmaker's reverie is reflected through an elliptical narration and performative visual sequences as she struggles to make sense of her current isolation where 'moving out in the present seemed possible only by going back in the past.' Her subjective experience is expressed through evocative words, music and images: 'One winter, I lived in a glass jar while life flowed all around me. Other people lived and laughed and fought and went to work and hoped. Desperately seeking the sun, frozen to the bones, I would momentarily be awestruck at so much living, but soon the wonder would freeze to a hard crystal.' In the first of these impressionistic sequences, the camera lingers on the familiarity of everyday objects and the possibility of reaching out to more tactile living experience. It moves in close to the blooming flowers in Saba's terrace garden as her lazy cats stretch themselves in the winter sun. In contrast to one kind of subjectivity suggested by the tranquility of these images of domesticity, her personal subjectivity is expressed by a bleak world that is out of control. The alienated presence of the filmmaker is heightened by a composition that cuts out her face and part of her body, both turned away from the camera. There is a cut from an extreme close up of her eye to a blur and blaring sounds of traffic outside: 'Vast spaces of emptiness welled up inside. Brittle, blinding, brightness. Outside.' In another sequence Saba sits in a room full of memories stacked with unused furniture, books and trunks from which she pulls out brocade saris, searching for something that she doesn't seem to find. Her words hint at some of the possible roots of her current predicament: 'In a vast rambling house, a woman retained one room for herself. Her daughter too always had a room of her own and in turn gave her little girl similar space. The only advice she gave the little girl was to walk alone and to walk proud. Over the unfolding years the daughter almost forgot the words but never quite. At the most unexpected moments they would tip toe in and turn her world inside out.'

Parallel to the theme of a strong first-, second- and third-generation feminist identity is the thread of insecurities and expectations among some in *Sita's Family*. Handling home and career, Manorama follows Sita's footsteps. Her time described tellingly by the filmmaker – 'precious, productive, practical' – is to be guarded sternly. A life of multi-tasking is suggested through the ticking of different clocks in the house and the constant ringing of the phone. Manorama has similar expectations from her daughters: 'What she hopes I will be.' The daughters' expectations from their mother seem less resolved though. Saba lives in her mother's home but, 'Seeking her is an endless task. Sometimes I am able to find her but most times I keep searching.' This conflict plays out through the use of recurrent words over a high-angle shot of the filmmaker sitting alone in the centre of a courtyard: 'You have to be a brave girl. There is so much you have to do in life. You have to be a brave girl. You have to learn to cope on your own. You have to be a brave girl and stop following me around.' Her mother's phone rings incessantly in the background. Another sequence in the film has the filmmaker and her sister Sameera laughing at themselves as children in family snapshots. Also revealed in these light-hearted moments are the dilemmas of the children. As a child Sameera felt nervous when her mother would put on her lipstick to leave the house. Moving between candid moments of family narratives that can be spoken of easily and more self-reflexive sequences that hint at the silences hidden behind, the film illustrates Annette Kuhn's ruminations about 'family secrets': 'the other side of the family's public face, of the stories families tell themselves, and the world about themselves' (1995: 2).

The photographs also gesture to some of the intersections between personal and public memory. The relationship between Manorama and her husband, both journalists, is traced in the family album through a history of Nehruvian India.[10] There are photographs of journeys made together to cover the Indo-Pakistan summit in Simla, to Syria and Iran or with public figures close to India such as President Nasser of Egypt and the Palestinian leader Yasser Arafat. The feminist dilemmas of the film, set against a background of early nationalist history are not without irony. In one of the sequences of the film, Manorama and her siblings sit around the television. A flag-hoisting ceremony being tele-cast on the occasion of a national commemoration day becomes a trigger for personal remembrance.[11] The older siblings recount the story of their mother's subversive actions in the 1940s. This was when other inmates and Sita stitched a national flag and replaced the Union Jack with it in prison. While the trans-formation of the struggle against colonialism into the current ritual of official nationalism on television is asserted ironically, there is also the question of what participation in the nationalist movement did for women. Sita Devi may have fought many battles for independence and been a good mother, home-maker and feminist but she remained subordinate to her partner. This was true for Manorama as well. Despite a more public presence as a journalist, she had to similarly limit her career options and life. As she says to the camera/film-maker: 'It is not only a man's privilege to be disorderly, to have leisure, to have an afternoon siesta. I think a woman needs it more.' Her incantation to her other daughter, 'That's why I want Sameera to be something ... besides being a good wife and mother. [...] She has to be something on her own', echoes again as Saba watches her mother – this time as the filmmaker, looking at the footage on a monitor. Central to this sequence are the beginnings of a shift in subjec-tivity from that of filmmaker as traumatised child to that of filmmaker as adult woman and ally of her mother.

In her work on the first person representation of the Jewish family, Alisa Lebow draws attention to films where the filmmaker/child uses the medium to 'repair' childhood trauma (see Lebow 2008: 47). Her work also points to the possibility that childhood memory can be conservative in its recall. One of the characters in Saba's film is an absent presence, an adored father who appears through photographs and flowers: 'Had Papa been here we would have gone for long walks in the sun. On the way he would have recited poetry ... and the cold crystals might have melted into an easy flow of words, laughter and sunshine. But Papa is no more and with mummy it is different.' This memorialisation of their father by the daughters is interrogated in the climax when Sameera confronts her mother for having grown up with insecurities. Questioning their lack of expectations from their father, Manorama suggests the need to refigure this romanticised childhood image. The filmmaker gives space to her mother now: 'Ever since this film started, you have asked me lots of questions. I now have a fundamental question for you … was it just Mummy's responsibility to do everything? Why not Papa too? … Sometimes I do feel hurt that despite being women, you have never tried to understand the struggles your mother waged.' Located at the complicated intersection of motherhood and feminist positioning, the film allows for an understanding of different kinds of subjectivities; the insecurity of a child, the role of a parent and the aspirations of a woman.

If *Sita's Family* can be seen as an attempt at familial reconciliation on the part of the filmmaker/child, Santana Issar's *Bare* gestures towards empathy even when reconciliation is not possible. Also funded by the PSBT, *Bare* is a deeply personal film about a daughter's attempt to reach out to an estranged alcoholic father. This film is made by re-editing home videos shot by the parents during her childhood. Most of the footage was recorded on a ship as Issar's father was in the Merchant Navy. The family's present is constructed through an additional soundtrack composed of phone conversations. Recorded over the two months of making the film, these conversations take place between the filmmaker and her father, her mother and her sister Simran. The film is framed through the memories of different protagonists. It opens with a shot of the two little girls dressed in party frocks performing for the father's camera, as they sing 'Happy Birthday' for him. The first rupture in this celebratory narrative of a family video is made through a phone conversation. The filmmaker asks her sister Simran if she has been in touch with their father in the past two years: 'Because I have been calling up and speaking to him. And I have made the same mistake of falling into the same trap … And then I want to meet him again and see him all over again', Simran tells her sister, 'I speak to him very rarely. I avoid his phone calls … I have no respect for him. He has no place in my life, none at all.' Spoken over a sequence where the footage of the two little girls is slowed down, the sister's closure of this relationship appears over the younger Simran leaving the frame. An amateur pilot, Simran's mother is introduced through the image of a plane in the sky. This is the only time in the film that we hear exhilarating music. In contrast to Simran, the mother makes a distinction between the filmmaker's childhood memories of a caring father and the experience of the present, suggesting that both are valid. Over footage of the past where the mother films playful moments with her husband, her voice pushes Santana to make her own choices: 'When it was beautiful, accept that it was beautiful. Today's assessment may be totally different. It turned bad? Yes. Did it turn unbearable? Maybe. What is important is not to remember anything with distortion … There was a time when it was my job to push and to decide for you. Today is not that time.'

None of the protagonists in *Bare* are ever seen in the present. However, it is the absence of the father that stands out most. In choosing not to show him in the present, the filmmaker addresses the ethics of shooting possible dys-functionality without informed consent. Meanwhile this omission serves to protect her childhood image of a youthful, caring and fun-loving father. Filmic ruptures in these visions of a happy childhood are created by the slowing down of action during the telephone conversations. The more amicable relation-ships indicated by the spatial formations of the protagonists and conversations between them in the footage are also contrasted ironically with the voices of the same protagonists in the present. For instance the voice of the filmmaker's father talking to his daughters is disrupted by a mention of his alcoholism in a phone conversation between the sisters as the footage is slowed down. The use of looks, gestures or juxtapositions between sound and image are other such ruptures. Over footage of the young father playing with the children, we hear a telephonic confrontation between the father and filmmaker. A half-finished bottle of beer next to him in the archival images takes on another layer of meaning as he hangs up on her. In a subsequent conversation, his verbal alien-ation ('I just drink to be happy' – 'But are you happy?' – 'Frankly speaking, no.') is matched by bleak images of the ship at sea hinting at another kind of isola-tion. As he asks, 'How can I make you happy if I am not happy myself?' there is a juxtaposition of an image of the little Santana stepping backwards in alarm as she looks up towards the camera. This is followed by a very distant shot of the father eating his meal in solitude. These filmic interventions become ways in which the filmmaker both invokes an idyllic childhood and simultaneously brings the present to bear upon these memories. The constant switch between the home video footage and its more self-reflexive versions is also illustrative of the conflicted nature of the adult Issar's feelings toward her father unlike her mother and sister who have resolved this issue for themselves. Towards the end of the film the filmmaker is cautioned by her sister about the dangers of being vulnerable to their father: 'Alcoholics are dangerous people. They bring everything around them down.' The two daughters, one who has moved on and the other who cannot break away, argue over their status in relation to their father: 'You *were* his daughter – I *am* his daughter.' Simran's final question to her, 'You are his daughter, (but) where was he?' appears over the ships' deck where the child Santana is being filmed by her mother. As the mother prompts her, 'Where is Papa?', the child looks for her father repeatedly asking 'Where are you Papa?' She hears his voice calling to her from the bridge of the ship ('Can you hear me?') but can't see him. The film fades out as she searches end-lessly for her father on the empty deck.

Unlike the placement of interiority against a larger public canvas in *Sita's Family*, there seems to be no obvious link in *Bare* with the world outside. Like family albums that make sense only to insiders, the home videos are strangely de-contextualised, filmed as they are on undisclosed holiday locations or in the insulated world of a ship in the high seas. Despite its intensely personal content, however, *Bare* is able to forge a wider identification. Describing such films as 'domestic ethnography' Michael Renov asserts that 'its sleight of hand is the rendering public of private-sphere material, but not ... as spectacle' (2004: 226). Giving the home footage a critical edge in *Bare* is the deployment of a form of 'memory work', by the insider/filmmaker where she reworks childhood memory by layering these personal images with other surrounding knowledge (see Kuhn 1995: 4). In so doing, she draws attention to the gaps within the familiar and generic nature of family portraiture. Hidden behind the banality of home movies and family albums are untold and at times dark stories that reside on their margins. Some of these stories can only be recovered by the filmmaker/insider through a critical re-working of the performed/imagined family in representation. The autobiographical film about *one family's secret* becomes autoethnography in its possibility of interrogating the nature of *family secrets*. A different sort of 'memory work' that connects secrets about the self with a world beyond the biological family is seen in the third and last film under discussion, Shohini Ghosh's *Tales of the Night Fairies*. Unlike *Sita's Family* and *Bare*, that emerge out of moments of crisis and are more openly autobiographical, there is no crisis in this film. About a collective of sex workers in the city of Calcutta,[12] the autobiographical in this film is fragmented and peripheral. Based on the first person accounts of five sex-worker protagonists, the film is linked together by autobiographical vignettes of the filmmaker's childhood in Calcutta. Hinted at but not spoken of openly is Shohini's own queer identity. By implicating the filmmaker as a 'sexual outlaw' the film forges bonds across difference and different kinds of sexual transgressions. As she notes, 'The film would not just be about the "other" but about how that "otherness" actually constituted the "self"' (Ghosh 2006: 341).

A film about consensual sex work, *Tales of the Night Fairies* traces the lives of four female and one male sex worker. The easy slip from respectability to non-respectability and the transfer of this stigma to all women who transgress is a recurring motif in this film. Parallel to the stories of the central protagonists is the peripheral presence and voice of the filmmaker. The camera follows her as she traverses the labyrinthian inner lanes of the city of Calcutta. A body that cannot be marked easily in terms of conventional notions of femininity, she is often the subject of curiosity and a reversed gaze during the filming of sex workers: 'One of the women loudly wondered whether I was a boy', Shohini muses in voiceover. Queerness and difference is also signposted through other characters in the film. One of the sex worker protagonists is a cross-dressing man. His femininity is invoked through songs and the staging of his body during performance, and a carnival held by the collective foregrounds queerness through the presence of other cross-dressing and transgendered men.

The revisiting of the filmmaker's childhood in *Tales of the Night Fairies* is not nostalgic. Instead these memories are used to question conventional constructs of gender, sexuality and space that she grew up with. While loitering on the streets has traditionally been seen as a prerogative of men and the sex worker, the filmmaker 'grew up playing cricket on the streets with the boys'. The same streets would also teach her about love and desire, conjuring up all kinds of fantasies including ones in which the world of the prostitute was a pleasured terrain. Simplistic notions about the sexual innocence of children are challenged as the filmmaker stages a childhood act of gazing at sexually explicit film posters. The filmmaker's mother's story in the opening narration reflects anxieties around the moral demarcation of space in the city: 'I grew up in the decent respectable neighborhoods of Calcutta. This was my Calcutta, the only Calcutta I knew. Unlike my mother whose work took her to different parts of the city, including the inner cities of hushed whispers. One day she came back from Shonagachi (the red light area) with a story. She said that some of the houses in the area had put up signs that said, "these houses belong to decent people". It crossed my mind to ask but who lives in the other houses? My mother's story ended where all questions began.' Followed by a song that warns of the dangers of straying,[13] the film cuts to a sequence where Shikha Das, a sex-worker protagonist, attempts to demarcate the red-light areas from the so-called respectable neighborhood. As she points to the streets below, the camera pans over similar homes, suggesting the impossibility of making distinctions between them.

One of the significant ways in which the autobiographical is negotiated in *Tales of the Night Fairies* is through its intangible association with the world of representation. The songs used in the film offer all kinds of additional clues to cultural 'insiders' especially when they privilege queer readings. One instance of this is a sequence where the filmmaker visits the cinema with one of the sex-worker protagonists. Huge posters of *Devdas* (2002), a filmic adaptation of a famous literary text, dominate the frame. While the choice of this film is significant because of the prominent figure of the courtesan in the story, a reflexive soundtrack uses the opening refrain of a song from the film that featured two women dancing with each other. Another such moment occurs during the filming of a boat ride against the backdrop of the Howrah Bridge on the river Hoogly. Iconic symbols of the city, images of the bridge and the river have circulated widely in tourism photography and popular cinematic representations. A boat ride with the filmmaker and her sex-worker companion, Mala, against this *mise-en-scène* throws up an unexpected *vérité* encounter. Drifting along the water, they start to hum a song from a popular film of the early 1970s. As an abandoned barge suddenly appears in the frame, I (as the camera operator of the film) refer to this intrusion and along with the filmmaker we start to berate the boatman. 'You have ruined the scene – You have ruined our *Amar Prem*.' The laughter that follows emerges out of a shared cultural understanding about this reference. *Amar Prem* (*Everlasting Love*, Shakti Samanta, 1971) was a popular Hindi film about the love between a sex worker and one of her married customers. Played by famous stars Sharmila Tagore and Rajesh Khanna, the song (*'Chingari'*) was performed in the same setting. As the sex worker identifies with the 'fem' heroine in this parody, she gestures toward Shohini as her hero, calling her 'my Rajesh Khanna'. Significant in this simultaneously candid and performative sequence is not just a queer moment but also the sharing of a collective memory between several actors across class and other differences. The film and its famous song are recognised by all the protagonists present on screen such as the sex worker, the filmmaker and the boatman. It is also potentially recognised by the off-screen participants; the sound-recordist and camera operator as well as the insider-spectator. In contrast to popular screen representations of the sex worker where she had to be symbolically 'punished' (being killed at the end was usual), *Amar Prem* had a 'happy ending' where the sex-worker protagonist acquired a non-biological family. Drawing links with popular memory, the film allows for several additional vectors of meaning for cultural insiders.

While pointing out the possibility of alliances being forged across difference, *Tales of the Night Fairies* attempts to resist romanticising these bonds. Upholding the rights of women in the profession, it locates its arguments within the domain of consensual sex work. The class differences between filmmaker and the sex-worker protagonists are not ignored either. In one sequence Shikha Das and Shohini sit in an open commons watching a game of golf being played by upper-class women. Completely unexposed to this game, the working-class sex worker wants to know if they are playing hockey. Despite these differences, there are some erasures that cut across class. The filmmaker's own queerness is one such silence that is acknowledged in a more oblique way towards the end: 'Closures are never easy. Resolutions are not inevitable. My story began with where my mother's story ended. My film ends where other stories begin. "What would you like to do ten years from now", I had asked Shikha. "I would like to go to Delhi with a camera and ask you for your story", she had said. Storytelling is a journey without end [...] My film was a search for a Calcutta that had eluded me in my childhood. A search for women who were different. Ones who belonged and yet did not. Ones who had the courage to tell their story, because I did not. Some of us can only tell our own stories through that of others.' While this 'coming out' is not explicitly stated, the groundwork for this assertion of difference has already been laid out through a variety of clues about gender ambivalence in the film. These sentences are a last clue offering a revelation about the self. While many 'coming out' films situate the filmmaker-subject in the familial order, a de-centered reading of this advocacy film suggests that some kinds of 'coming out' may take unexpected detours through childhood memories while engaging surrogates of the self to perform the telling. It also suggests that these revelations may not be mediated by biology but by alliances of 'difference' forged with other kinds of families.

The three films discussed in this essay articulate different ways in which the murmurs of inner voices have emerged in recent Indian documentary. Sometimes direct and at other times lurking and surreptitious, they foreground subjectivity using a variety of strategies. Far removed from the distanced national voice of the Films Division, these voices are located at the intersections of plural identities. They emerge out of experiences of the home and the world outside, of childhood and adult life and of personal and cultural memory. If the politics of *Sita's Family* and *Bare* are located within the family, *Tales of the Night Fairies* gestures towards the possibilities of dialogic encounters beyond the family. Using a creative filmic representation of interiority, *Sita's Family* allows for conversations within feminist understandings of motherhood and nurturing. Wrestling the gaze of a childhood home video turns *Bare* into a critical form of memory work while *Tales of the Night Fairies* demonstrates the power of collective resistance and alliances built at the intersections of personal and cultural memory. All three films use a form of 'time travel' into the past but the interrogative nature of these journeys make them neither romantic nor nostalgic. Sometimes painful and contested and at times gaining strength from unexpected allegiances, they also offer the possibility of healing. In their attempts to express the unspoken and the silenced, all of them become 'coming out' films of a kind that push the boundaries of a subjectivity long denied to non-fiction in India.

Notes

1 See the work of Arnold and Blackburn (2004) that lays out a diversity of life-writing genres in India ranging from traditional horoscopes to women's writing and diaries of political figures. The self also emerges in domestic ethnographies through the mediums of family photography and the home video/film.

2   Srirupa Roy (2003) notes how the documentary film had to be re-invented as the handmaid of a national rather than a colonial state after independence. Part of a larger enterprise of re-imagining the new postcolonial India, there was a need to express 'Indian-ness' through a collective national identity.

3   From the late 1970s filmmakers like Anand Patwardhan, Tapan Bose, Suhasini Mulay, Manjira Dutta and Meera Dewan were to make films on social and political issues.

4   Video SEWA was established in 1984 as a communication and advocacy wing of the Self Employed Women's Association, a collective of non-literate women working in the informal sector.

5   The problems of romanticising participatory filmmaking have also been alluded to in writing on other similar video experiments suggesting that conventional formalistic devices do not automatically get wished away by 'handing over the camera' (see Frota 1996: 271–2; Moore 1994: 128). Also see Angelica Fenner's contribution to this volume.

6   Amar Kanwar's subsequent body of work including King of Dreams (2000), A Night of Prophecy (2001), The Many Faces of Madness (2002) and Lightening Testimonies (2007) used a similar first person voiceover. More peripheral autobiographical vignettes can be seen in Kumar Talkies (Pankaj Rishi Kumar, 1999) and Paradise on the River of Hell (Abir Basheer and Meenu Gaur, 2002).

7   The performative staging of the body has become more common today, for instance in the films of Paromita Vohra and artist N. Pushpamala.

8   Thousands of Sikhs were killed in riots following the assassination of the then Prime Minister Indira Gandhi in 1984 by her Sikh bodyguard. Safina and her siblings migrated to Australia soon after. My Mother India is an example of the 'first person plural'. In an interview the filmmaker describes it as 'about my family, not only in the deepest and most personal sense, but also in the broadest and most political sense'. Online version at www.upperstall.com/films/2001/my-mother-india. Another significant cross-border film made more recently is I for India (Sandhya Suri, UK/India, 2005), discussed in Alisa Lebow's essay in this volume. The film uses Super 8 family footage and audio tapes to tell a personal story of immigration to the UK.

9   This essay attempts to give a broad overview to the terrain of the first person documentary and the films discussed are by no means exhaustive. Some films that explore family biographies and histories include For Maya (Vasudha Joshi, 1998) Snapshots from a Family Album (Avijit Mukul Kishore, 2003), Shadows of Freedom (Sabina Kidwai, 2004) and The House on Gulmohar Avenue (Samina Mishra, 2005). Themes of returns to former homelands recur in Tell Them, 'The Tree They Had Planted Has Now Grown' (Ajay Raina, 2002) and Way Back Home (Supriyo Sen, 2003). In the past five years there have been many more first films ranging from ones that directly speak of the filmmaker/subject such as I am (Sonali Gulati, 2011) to those that use the self to negotiate broader questions of identity and belonging. See for instance The Ghetto Girl (Ambarien Alqadar, 2010). Also see My Camera and Tsunami (R. V. Ramani, 2011) and In Camera (Ranjan Palit, 2010), for their exploration of the subjectivity of the camera person/body.

10 Jawaharlal Nehru was India's first Prime Minister from 1947 to 1964 and the Nehruvian era is representative of the optimism of early post-independence India.

11 The footage on television depicts the official flag-hoisting on Republic Day which is a national holiday in India to celebrate the formal adopting of its constitution on 26 January 1950.

12 The Durbar Mahila Samanwaya Committee or DMSC is a collective of sex workers set up in Calcutta in 1995.

13 The words of the song Who Chali ('There She Goes') can be loosely translated as 'Don't go there my dear, Don't go there alone/lest the looters of love find you there alone'.

References

Arnold, D. and S. Blackburn (eds) (2004) *Telling Lives in India: Biography, Autobiography and Life History*. Bloomington, IN: Indiana University Press/Permanent Black.

Frota, M. (1996) 'Taking Aim: The Video Technology of Cultural Resistance' in M. Renov and E. Suderburg (eds) *Resolutions: Contemporary Video Practices*. Minneapolis, MN: University of Minnesota Press, 258–82.

Ghosh, S. (2006) '*Tales of the Night Fairies*: A Filmmaker's Journey', in *Inter Asia Cultural Studies*, 7, 2, 341–3.

Kapur, J. (2003) 'Why The Personal is Still Political: Some Lessons from Contemporary Indian Documentary', In *Jump Cut: A Review of Contemporary Media*, 46. On line version at www. www.ejumpcut.org/archive/jc46.2003/indiandocs.kapur/ (23 April 2012).

Kuhn, A. (1995) *Family Secrets: Acts of Memory and Imagination*. London: Verso.

Lebow, A. S. (2008) *First Person Jewish*. Minneapolis, MN: University of Minnesota Press.

Moore, R. (1994) 'Marketing Alterity', in L. Taylor (ed.) *Visualizing Theory: Selected Essays from V.A.R. 1990–1994*. New York, NY: Routledge, 126–39.

Renov, M. (2004) *The Subject of Documentary*. Minneapolis, MN: University of Minnesota Press.

Roy, S. (2003) 'The Postcolonial State and Visual Representations of India', in R. Sumathi (ed.) *Beyond Appearances? Visual Practices and Ideologies in Modern India*. New Delhi/London: Sage, 233–63.

In the Eye of the Storm:
The Political Stake of Israeli i-Movies

Linda Dittmar

'Running under the euphoria ... there is something not quite right.'

Jacqueline Rose (2005: 63)

'For those who bewail its absence, honesty is a moral problem. For those who try to achieve it, it is a technical one.'

Dai Vaughan (1999: 9)

The following discussion occupies an unstable space, somewhere between personal, political and academic writing. As if mirroring my subject matter, it grows out of my own life but opens up to embrace much more than itself. Most recently, it taps my collaboration with photographer Deborah Bright, researching and photographing traces of Israel's forcible expulsion of Palestinians from their homelands in 1947–49 – the *Nakba*, as it is called in Arabic. This project began quite accidentally when we detoured from the direct road to the archaeological site of Beit Sh'an to a secondary road marked 'scenic' on our map, near the border north of Jenin. As our car wound its way through a wispy pine forest planted by the Jewish National Fund (JNF), there came a moment, out of nowhere it seemed, when we registered that scattered among the trees and JNF markers commemorating the donors of saplings to this reforestation project, were hand-hewn stones characteristic of Palestinian construction. In this bucolic setting and not that long ago, we realised with a jolt, stood a village whose destruction is just one of many such chapters in the larger story of the *Nakba*. Struck by the enormity of what such stones signify throughout the country, we have been locating and recording traces of the *Nakba* for several years. But why take on this punishing quest?

Unlike Deborah, who is not Jewish and approaches this work mostly with a critical photographer's image-making eye, but like the Israeli filmmakers who are the focus of this chapter, I carry into our work dismay, anger and guilt. For us Israelis, to dwell on the *Nakba* as a foundational event in our national history is to risk Freud's 'return of the repressed' – a compulsive, recursive probing of a barely-named wound that refuses to heal. In this instance the wound concerns a sin of origin traceable back to Israel's national emergence and its determined stake in land ownership. The repressed are not the facts and consequences of its occupation of the West Bank and Gaza in 1967, but the violent depopulation that occurred during the war of 1947–49 and beyond it – events that shaped a painful history that is still in the making. At issue are the markers of the *Nakba* inside Israel, within its 'green line' armistice's borders (operative until June 1967) and its continuing destructive effects on both its Palestinian victims and its Israeli beneficiaries.

While the damage caused by this prolonged war is immediately and visibly born by the Palestinians, its corroding effects could not help but leach into Israel's Jewish society as well as its Palestinian counterparts. Felt though barely named within Jewish Israeli culture, an awareness of culpability and anxiety about the consequences of this history hovers across a terrain where bulldozed urban wastelands and disintegrating farm and orchard terracing stand as the 'voice' of the unspeakable. And indeed the unspeakable is evident everywhere in this contested land, where such markers as untended fig and pomegranate trees, mosques and holy shrines, cemeteries, crumbling buildings, untended prickly pear hedges, or reservoirs disguised by newly planted forests, all bear witness to the violent dispossession on which Israel's modernity uneasily rests.

Considering that the landscape is littered with such visible markers, it takes determined repression to remain blind to the reality that keeps reasserting itself at every turn. It is no accident that Noga Kadman's excellent study of the *Nakba*'s destruction is titled *Erased From Space and Consciousness: Depopulated Palestinian Villages in the Israeli-Zionist Discourse* (2008). The book's evocative Hebrew title is even more to the point: 'At the Roadside and at the Margins of Awareness' (my translation). Registering but not naming what exists just beyond the road's edge and at the periphery of awareness, this title suggests that awareness is a matter of choice. To claim, as I do above, that Deborah's and my awareness came 'with a jolt', is to name the feeling of the moment but not its truth. The jolt occurred when the mechanism of denial momentarily lost its hold, when we allowed ourselves to name what until then lingered at the periphery of our vision.[1]

This dialectic of repression and recognition is hard to escape in Israel. It is a struggle I share with the first person documentary filmmakers whose work is at the core of this discussion. In this land, where history is a palimpsest of disparate national, ideological and ethical narratives, the pressing need is for full accounting as a step towards peace. But is full accounting possible? Inevitably, Jewish-Israeli first person documentaries that engage with Israel's national formation grapple with contradictory forces: a belief in a Jewish birthright to that country (by heritage, birth and daily practice), and a recoil from the brutal consequences of that belief. Thus, while to date the *Nakba* is barely addressed in Israeli cinema, unease about the country's foundational history does seep into both its fiction and its documentary films. The realities of conquest and ethnic cleansing that underlie the heroic narratives of a land 'redeemed' by Jewish sacrifice and endeavour refuse to disappear. These realities continue to lurk in the fissures of the national narrative where the *Nakba* is a ghostly, rarely-named presence that nonetheless won't go away.[2]

What makes such naming difficult is Israel's foundational narrative – a mythic account that does not match up with Israeli history since the beginning of Zionist immigration in the 1880s. This narrative of national redemption (a mix of Leo Tolstoy's social utopianism, Jean-Jacques Rousseau's 'natural man' and social contract, German Romanticism and the pragmatism of Labor Zionism) rests on trust in honest labour, communal solidarity and an ethical people's army that honours *taharat ha-neshek* ('the purity of the weapon', i.e. ethical warfare). This narrative extols the struggle of the few against the many; victims against attackers; the rational and scientific New Man against the irrational man; the cultured and enterprising against the listless and backward. In this narrative the few, the attacked, the enlightened, the righteous and the enterprising are the Jews. The 'Arabs' are the intractable primitive – a fixed, static part of nature, not culture. It is a narrative propelled by Zionism's founding call for settlement in 'a land without people for a people without land', as the deceptively neat slogan puts it, voicing a prevailing colonial refusal to see, to literally see, the colonised.[3]

This ideological morass draws Israeli filmmakers into conflicting allegiances, further exacerbated by the documentary genre's complicated relationship to indexical 'truth', as theorised extensively by Bill Nichols (1991), Michael Renov (2004), Frances Guerin and Roger Hallas (2007) and others. Here the imperative of factual honesty comes up against a powerful master narrative that lays claims to loyalties that, in one's better moments, one might want to repudiate. After all, how can one stave off the insistent demand for national consensus when the master narrative cites biblical destiny and is inscribed in the blood of the heroic fallen? How can one resist conformity when monuments, museums, memorial albums, poems, songs and national ceremonies re-inscribe the nation's righteousness at every turn? Considering that most filmic references to the vaguely named 'conflict' come from the Israeli political Left, the difficulty of flying in the face of this powerful consensus to sustain questionable 'truths' can be overpowering. Israel's very existence as a Jewish homeland is broadly felt to be at stake when it comes to any departure from the iron-clad national narrative. The internal hesitations, encryptions, ruptures and elisions that so often mark these films, point to a shared anxiety about violating a social imperative of this magnitude.[4]

Yet this very difficulty is also an opportunity for Israeli documentarists, an invitation to chart a course through a labyrinth of conflicting claims and self-punishing doubts. The first person documentary genre is particularly well-suited to this task precisely because it legitimises subjectivity as it negotiates the relation between the private and the public. Freeing filmmakers to interrogate their personal position within the public sphere, first person narration moves its audience quite explicitly from the realm of evidentiary 'truth' to the unstable realm of introspective discourse. It creates a space where Israeli filmmakers can examine their relation to their 'Israeliness' as a national, cultural and, indeed, familial template for their individual and collective identity. The very weight that the genre attaches to the narrating persona as a soul-searching and interrogating individual serves as a hook for the audience's projective identification, engaging us with the author/narrator's sensitivities, attempted honesty and dissimulation. At the same time, we cannot help but notice the performative aspects of this discourse as each work channels its substance through its author/narrator's very presence on the audiovisual tracks as well as formally through the conception, style and organisation of each documentary's crafted materials.

Inevitably, then, the personal documentary is steeped in doubts, foregrounding as it does the author/narrator's essential subjectivity and irreducible difference. Truth-seeking but suspect, knowing yet obtuse, performative in its substitutions, superimpositions and correspondences rather than transparent (see Rascaroli 2009: 171), this sub-genre is ideally suited to articulating the contradictory impulses within the Israeli Left. Bundling together love of homeland and its disavowal, hand-wringing anxieties and frustrations, testimony and doubt, such films can draw viewers into scrutinising the text's troubled ideology in relation to their own unresolved or perhaps not fully articulated investments. Fittingly, given the unsettled politics currently afflicting the region, such scrutiny does not yet point to anything even approximating closure regarding the issues with which it grapples.

Not surprisingly, the obsessive turn towards the unhealed wound which this lack of closure necessarily calls for has also inspired a remarkable body of first person documentaries. While these vary both thematically and in their discursive practices, they share an ethical and political struggle to position themselves critically in relation to Israel's foundational myths and their consequences. An insightful point of entry into these films' shared effort is proposed by Israeli film scholar Shmulik Duvdevani (2010) in his study of i-movies – a term I will be adopting for the rest of this discussion. Significantly, his study, and mine too, carves out of this vibrant body of documentary production what might be thought of as a sub-genre of politically engaged works, notably ones that are characterised by a generational struggle of second-, third- and even fourth-generation Israeli-born ('sabra') filmmakers against the legacy of their 'fathers'. This body of work burgeoning after the first *Intifada* (Palestinian uprising, 1987–93), questions the political trajectory Israel has taken since its founding in 1948, including the ideological legacy of national reclamation handed down to these younger filmmakers by the founding generation.[5]

Duvdevani's analysis of the role of 'fathers' (and therefore, implicitly, the filmmakers as 'sons') relies persuasively on a rich vein of psychoanalytic scholarship regarding collective traumas of violence and guilt, loss and dispossession, confession, memory, bearing witness and generational struggle, as seen through a Freudian/Lacanian lens. He sidesteps this risk of de-contextualising the films under discussion by situating them within a supposedly universal psychoanalytic discourse while reading them within a clearly specified Israeli political arena.[6] Rather, the real risk here is of a masculinist bias – a proclivity endemic in Israeli society as well as dominant in psychoanalytic theory. To date not much has been written about the position of Israeli women as willing/unwilling partners in Zionism's production of the 'New Man' and the generations of 'sons' that follow. That old Freudian question, 'What does a woman want?', acquires new permutations given the complexities of cross-gender identification that war and patriarchy force on Israeli women.

In Duvdevani's account, guilt for Zionism's 'original sin' (of colonising a populated land and thus causing the dispossession of its inhabitants) saturates the collective Israeli unconscious, ready to erupt. While applications of psychoanalysis to social theory and politics have been used to analyse to a range of trauma-based cultural practices globally, its privileged place within trauma and Holocaust studies (see Felman and Laub 1992; Caruth 1995 and 1996; Walker 2005) injects bitter irony into the present discussion. On the one hand, existential trauma works to justify the notion of survival at all costs, but at the same time it also becomes self-perpetuating, as Jacqueline Rose (2005) argues, where a people traumatised by their own victimisation and decimation may perpetuate the damage by re-directing it at others. This is a central theme in

Asher Tlalim's documentary, *Al Tigu Li B'Shoah* (*Don't Touch My Holocaust*, 1994), where he uses the play *Arbeit Macht Frei* to reflect on the intersecting trajectories of the holocaust and the *Nakba*.[7]

Israel's version of the cult of masculinity is lodged in the ideals of the muscular, labouring, pioneering New Man – a Jewish version of the heroic Soviet template – on the one hand, and the demands of a battle-ready national culture of militarism on the other (see Peled 2002). Both are sustained by a heritage that repudiates the abject diasporic Jew of the diaspora and converge in the 'sons', presenting them with the untenable choice of either rejecting the 'fathers'' life's project or justifying the 'fathers'' guilt for bequeathing their 'sons' a settler-state and the virulent conflict it creates. The challenge for the 'sons', then, is to find a way of responding to the knowledge that the victim can also be a victimiser, that Jews threatened with extinction can nonetheless do likewise to others, that the ideals of 'the purity of the weapon' are negated by the practice of brute conquest, and that the land was never without people. Finally, at issue is one's daring to refuse to bear the burden of the 'fathers'' dreams – dreams deeply implicated in the contested ethics that tainted the project of state-building as practiced by the 1948 generation and are being re-enacted by its heirs.

Seen through this framework, the decidedly patriarchal cast of all this discourse of fathers and sons is more than just a Freudian derivative. Within the context of Israel's history and ideology, this masculinist bent has compelling investments in a desperate need to regain power, dignity and a sense of agency. Resting on a centuries-old Western (and Middle Eastern) view of 'Man' as a stand-in for all of *man*kind, Israel's settler-state's need to valourise brawny pioneering and militarism as survivalist necessities carries layers of symbolic investments. Though this survivalist impulse is supremely pragmatic, it is underpinned by modern Judaism's repudiation of a heritage of Jews accepting their decimation like 'sheep led to slaughter', and by a language (Hebrew) that is intrinsically imbued with gendered valuations. In this sense the masculinist diction of national formation reflects but also perpetuates the exigencies that define the Zionist project.

I-movies cannot escape this heritage. Inevitably gender leaves fingerprints on the origins, themes, reception and authority of these films. Still, while the following discussion does register this fact, it is not my central concern. Rather, my focus is on a generational restiveness in which women as well as men participate. Though the films discussed below are amenable to gendered analysis, my emphasis is on the restiveness which marks their directors' wrestling with the injunction to silence regarding the history into which they were born. That history is not simply a personal matter. Their speaking 'I' casts their personal and often anguished enquiries as a stand-in for a repressed national discourse.

Unlike David Perlov's epic benchmark i-movie *Yoman* (*Diary*, 1973–83), the politically inflected i-movies of younger filmmakers situate the personal within the political and the political within the personal quite deliberately, as seen in films by Udi Aloni, Michal Aviad, Yulie Cohen, Danae Elon, Ari Folman, Amit Goren, Dan Katzir, Avi Mograbi and Dorit Na'aman, among others. While the tone, focus, narrative strategies, politics and output of their documentary films vary, and though gender is a directorial concern for some, taken together their work posits that the personal voice is mainly a conduit and template for the national collective it interrogates, challenges and loves, however perversely. In this sense, and in contradistinction from the Western tradition that is the focus of such studies as Laura Rascaroli's *The Personal Camera* (2009), in these Israeli i-movies the ethics of truth-seeking and the performance of subjectivity intervene quite deliberately in the politics of representation (see Renov 2004: 171–81; Vaughan 1999: 54–83; Bruzzi 2000: 40–50).

Perlov positions the apparatus to record linear sequences of events as these present themselves to a camera 'eye', mostly filmed from high up and at a distance, through a constricting high-rise apartment's window frame. Only occasionally does he turn the camera inward into his apartment, and it is even less at street level. In his hands the apparatus is mostly static; the banal and contingent insists on being attended to; emotion would seem numb were it not for the suppressed tension that strains the text as significant fragments of history force their way into this constrained rendition. But while the duration of the gaze is a key mediating signifier in Perlov's *Diary*, urging viewers to dwell on the minute tremors that occur within the text's tightly controlled regularity, recent i-movies are turbulent in their structure and address. Consisting of heterogeneous materials, mobile cinematography, dynamic editing and ample authorial commentary, their discontinuities of location, genre and discourse are key signifiers where textual turmoil mediates inner strife and unresolved argument.

Seen in its historical context, this turbulence captures Israel's move from near-silence regarding the events of 1948 to a much more troubled sense of its history. The years since 1967 saw the Israeli Left's decline over Rabin's assassination and the breakdown of the Oslo negotiations; the opening of archives that allowed for historical revision; two major *Intifadas*; a rise in critical NGO activism and international censure; an increase in ideological draft and military service resistance; and a sharp rise in expansionist religious extremes. Dan Katzir's i-movie *Yatsati L'chapes Ahavah – Techef Ashuv* (*Out for Love… Be Back Shortly*, 1997) captures poignantly the relative innocence of the days immediately preceding some of these developments. Not surprisingly, for politically engaged filmmakers today – Israeli, Palestinian and international

– the post-1967 occupation cannot but provide crucial and often reiterated themes: the curfews and closures, the separation wall, settler assaults, suicide bombings, uprooted olive trees, targeted assassinations, house demolitions, deaths and births at checkpoints, relentless missile attacks, grieving at funerals on both sides, demonstrations by all parties, and more. In a media-conscious world this history demands (and to some extent gets) urgent representation.

In the current climate of increased self-examination via revisionist history and geography, documentary i-movies have become a compelling medium in Israel precisely because their combined confessional and performative address lets them explore both the ethical resonance of personal choice and its collective political consequences. Tapping into historical accounts that challenge the dominant view of Israel's destiny, the personal enquiries they unfold anchor the individual within the national. Selected examples include Yulie Cohen tracking her relationship with a terrorist who almost killed her (*Hamechabel Sheli* [*My Terrorist*], 2002); Danae Elon filming her reunion with the Palestinian man who was her childhood caretaker (*Another Road Home*, 2004); Michal Aviad struggling with her decision to have her children grow up in Israel (*Layeladim Sheli* [*For My Children*], 2002); Udi Aloni striving to join Arab and Jew in spiritual paths to peace (*Mala'ach Mekomi: Fragmentim Te'ologim-Politiyim* [*Local Angel*], 2002); and Avi Mograbi assaulting Israeli self-righteous complacency regarding the conundrum of land ownership and Palestinian dispossession (*Yom Huledet Sameach Mar Mograbi* [*Happy Birthday, Mr. Mograbi*], 1999). Relying on carefully edited and sequenced compilations, these and other i-directors foreground the interpolated 'I' as framing the possibility of communal as well as individual change. The very act of speaking – the performative address of the 'I' to a collective 'we' – affirms that possibility. By exposing their crafting as a dynamic invitation to an engaged reception, these films posit processes of dialogic construction, not fixity, as modes of understanding. Their destabilised organisation and especially their use of a troubled, enquiring authorial/narrating *personae* mediate the ethical and personal struggle that propels these films – the struggle to shake off, or at least question, the 'fathers'' legacy.

As is to be expected, within the shared struggles sketched above, differences do exist. In some instances the tone can be angry and confrontational, as happens in Avi Mograbi's i-movies. In contrast, Dan Katzir (in *Out for Love... Be Back Shortly*) charms with its youthful voice of discovery, while Udi Aloni conveys a tortured choking of will. Danae Elon's truncated reporting sets up a constrained discourse; Michal Aviad's reflectively affectionate tone elicits empathy and trust in her judgement precisely because it shuns facile answers; while Yulie Cohen, more centrally than Aviad, mourns the vanishing of a wishful fantasy of a purer and better Israel – that secular Zionist utopia for which her parents fought, that myth that could have never come into being. Given Israel's particular inflection of gender within its prevailing ideology of militarism and virility, including national existential anxieties and expansionist ethnic bravado, it is not surprising that the intimate sphere of family, friends and home constitutes an important core of the women directors in particular.[8] Lineage and community weave ideological ties across children, parents and siblings, and beyond them relatives, friends, neighbours, army buddies of parents, parents of army buddies, and more in ever-widening networks of belonging.

Aviad and Cohen, both mothers, posit love of children as an essential 'bottom line', and each of them asks herself the same question that has many Israeli parents, mothers in particular, up at night: Why am I acquiescing in the expectation that I raise my children in this war-torn country? Will we ever be able to bequeath them a heritage of peace? Were our parents right to enlist themselves and therefore us and future generations in the service of this ecstatic project of national revival? Inevitably such questions stir up larger ones about the justice and efficacy of the Zionist project: national identity versus assimilation, co-existence versus partition and separateness, wars of necessity as self-defence versus colonial expansion and wars of choice. That both women work side by side (Cohen produced Aviad's *For My Children*) within that tiny fishbowl of independent Israeli filmmaking makes such affinities all the stronger.

In *For My Children* this questioning occurs against the background of an otherwise carefree life in San Francisco, as Aviad and her husband consider uprooting their nuclear family and returning to Israel. Significantly, while the film's trajectory clearly signals a return 'home', the struggle around that choice remains inconclusive. The return comes across as inevitable but not exactly as willed. Unfolding through a compilation of home-movies, stills, interviews and voiceovers, *For My Children* weaves together a remarkably appealing gathering of disparate individuals who nonetheless constitute 'family': Jew and Catholic, Greek-Italian, Irish-American and British, Holocaust survivor and native Israeli 'sabra', nationalists and disaffected leftists. The meandering retrospective account that Aviad constructs from these imbricated fragments, digressive and ultimately resisting coherence, makes a return to Israel seem inevitable – not a choice but a drift prescribed by a communal imperative. The interwoven life stories, needs and commitments of these people, and the evident warmth with which the camera and voiceovers tell of their diverse journeys toward Israel and into Aviad's children's lives, come together as if inexorably, creating their own apparent necessity.

For My Children qualifies this sense of 'necessity' not only by its portrayal of Aviad and Shimshon's (her husband) personal doubts but, importantly, by its critique of intra-ethnic and class strife among Israel's Jews. It includes footage of Mizrahi Jews ('eastern' but commonly used to name Arab Jews, notably North African) rioting against social and economic injustice, and it registers Shimshon's activism in the far left movement of Matzpen (compass). Still, for all the dismay the film registers quite explicitly regarding the country's political slide to the right on top of the couple's concern for their children's future in it, the sense of belonging lodged so clearly in their extended family propels the family towards a return and the film towards its unresolved conclusion. Intimate attachments become a metonymy for love of country, constructing a semblance of a destined return that is hard to shake.

Yulie Cohen also weaves her role as a mother into the question of living in Israel. After several years in the United States she returned to Israel specifically to give birth to her two daughters and raise them there, and yet she asserts that if she had borne a son she would not have returned, implicitly because of the likelihood of a boy being drafted into combat. This uneasy relationship to Israel's military vocation continues across the next two films as they join *My Terrorist* in a trilogy – *Tzion Sheli* (*My Zion*, 2004) and *Ha'ach Sheli* (*My Brother*, 2007). (*Yisrael Sheli* [*My Israel*], 2008, revisits that trilogy.) In *My Terrorist* we see Cohen's daughters chafing at their mother's protectiveness in face of suicide bombings, while in *My Zion* the focus shifts to the older daughter's impending military service and *My Brother* includes that daughter's effort to get draft exemption.

But Cohen's concerns for the safety of her children are subordinate in the trilogy to the formative issues that haunt Israel's existence: the legacy of Zionism before and during the 1948 War of Independence and subsequent wars; Israel's occupation of Palestinian territories since 1967; the dispossession of European Jews on the one hand and Palestinian Arabs on the other; escalating terrorism and intolerance; and the fierce religious fundamentalism which claimed Cohen's brother. Though these concerns reverse Aviad's priorities in that here communal worries supersede personal ones, the trilogy nonetheless retains the same equation as Aviad's film. In both instances the family and nation mirror one another.

One example of this mirroring is captured in *My Zion* when Cohen's mother refuses to acknowledge war crimes committed by the Palmach.[9] Shortly afterwards, in that same sequence, she also refuses to voice an opinion about whether her granddaughter should try to evade the draft – a step that until recently was considered reprehensibly disloyal. In both instances Cohen's mother categorically refuses to engage in these charged issues. She will not assist the radical questioning that is the film's driving force. It is the director's father who concedes wrongdoing in battle, though even he quickly veers away from this admission once his wife intervenes, stressing the exigencies of warfare. Clearly, then, the lineage of 'fathers' and 'sons' includes mothers and daughters and granddaughters. The relation between the home front and the combat zone rests on resounding silences that count on all to play their parts. While Israel knows many variants of such silence, Cohen's locating the discussion within her own closely scrutinised familial context registers ways in which individuals get sutured into national agendas.

A telling counterpoint to these silences occurs in *My Zion* when Cohen visits her friend Moti Golani's mother, a Hungarian Holocaust survivor now living in Kfar Daniel, previously the Palestinian village Daneel. This aging woman's conversation flows easily between remembering her own life as a refugee at age eleven and an empathetic account of a Palestinian family that periodically visits its abandoned house next door – a house the film shows indexically in several shots. However, in a wry follow-up we see the reverse account as Cohen journeys to Hungary with Moti and their respective daughters. Having located the home Moti's family was forced to abandon, they are awkwardly, almost wordlessly, turned away by the current owners. While the film does not comment specifically on this incident – a near cliché in Holocaust-related documentaries and home movies – the parallel speaks for itself. The notion of a 'return' is a conundrum that has no easy resolution, neither for the Palestinians nor for the Jews.

While these sequences show the range of positions people might take towards violent expulsion and 'return', and implicitly Israel's political options too, their juxtaposition in *My Zion* is also useful as a 'biopsy' of the trilogy's discursive use of its conversation fragments throughout (segments of interviews, short exchanges, direct address, and so on). In Cohen's films such fragments constitute a productive montage that invites the audience to realign its understanding through the dynamic sequencing of disparate and sometimes clashing views. The stitched together spoken texts bring out passionately held yet widely divergent comments through which Cohen weaves her own position as author-narrator. In *My Terrorist*, for example, the soundtrack includes segments of letters read out loud, recorded phone calls, snippets of a televised round-table discussion, home movies, an activist street performance that simulates South Africa's Truth and Reconciliation hearings (and interrupted by abusive passers by), and informal interviews with a bereaved mother, an historian, a journalist and a filmmaker, among others.

Music is more than just an accompaniment in this multi-vocal construction. Most telling and moving (at least to those who know the heritage) is the prelude to *My Zion*, which begins with an Israeli Memorial Day reunion of Palmach veterans singing beloved old-time songs imbued with love of country but also with the mourning that typified that generation of 1948. Spouses, adult children and grandchildren are present, all woven into a history that is also Cohen's, and yet a history she is now questioning. The scene is awash in nostalgic grief for a lost youth and lost lives. Stitched into the film as a whole, the melancholy is for the lost dream of a 'beautiful', almost pre-lapsarian Land of Israel (*Eretz Yisrael hayafa*) – a dream betrayed by its practitioners but also a dream that betrayed its dreamers. Implicit in this short, seemingly 'filler' scene is a challenge to Theodore Herzl's famously inspiring assertion: *Im tirtzu, ein zot agada* ('If you will it [a Jewish homeland], it is not a fable').[10]

In contrast with the dialectical structure that propels the films discussed above, where the practice of juxtaposition calls for audience intervention, Danae Elon's *Another Road Home* unfolds a more tidy quest narrative, where the director's personal story mediates a larger one about Israeli/Palestinian relations. The quest here is for Mussa Obeidallah, a Palestinian resident of the then newly occupied territories, whom her parents hired as her caretaker shortly after Israel's victory in 1967. Now adult, Elon locates Mussa's grown sons in Patterson, New Jersey. She brings him over from Palestine for a moving reunion with her family as well as his own American family, and she then accompanies him back to his West Bank village. On a personal level, this fairly simple narrative trajectory is about 'family' – Elon's, Mussa's and the provisional hybrid family that their respective needs created: his for employment and hers for a surrogate parent. But upon closer examination this notion of family frays. Mussa could not give his sons the love he gave Danae because of his long working hours; Danae's father, an eminent public intellectual (Amos Elon), abruptly leaves the dinner table to which the family invited Mussa because of an 'important meeting'; Mussa's sons evince discomfort with both the young woman (Danae) who entered their American lives uninvited and with the father whom they hardly know; and the women who share these young men's lives have only a shadowy presence in this footage.

Difficult issues fester within this microcosm of Israeli/Palestinian relations. Both Mussa's position as a male servant doing 'women's work' and the family's use of 'Arab labour' – disdained, barred and exploited by both bourgeois and labour Zionism – situate the micro-politics of this household within the larger morass of Palestinian employment and the attendant issues of social class, gender and human dignity. Seen in these terms, Mussa's own divided attachments, notably the love he gave an Israeli girl but could not give his own sons, are wrenching. But beyond the difficult choices that Mussa's family faced are also questions facing the Elons, notably concerning the stance of a privileged liberal household in relation to somebody like Mussa. (Danae's father, was known for his strong support for Jewish/Palestinian co-existence.) Danae does not indulge in self-congratulation. Her need is to probe the accommodation each family devised. She questions her father, talks with her mother, draws out Mussa's sons and, most painfully, wonders what Mussa himself might have felt as he ironed her military uniform.

These questions remain unresolved in *Another Way Home*. The film powerfully exposes the undercurrents of racism and class oppression that seep into all aspects of the Israeli/Palestinian conflict, including the gendered and familial displacements that frequent the colonial condition. At the same time, the film also shies away from addressing these issues squarely. This shying away gets inscribed across the conversations included in the film, where premature editorial cuts leave responses to difficult questions (especially responses by Mussa's sons) suspended, incomplete. In this respect the plot's appreciation of people's capacity to respond to the humanity of the 'other' is undercut by discursive constraints that suppress the very issues that the plot sets out to explore. On the one hand the film comes across as unflinching in its raising difficult questions, but on the other it appears self-protective. Unlike the skeptical self-awareness built into Aviad's and Cohen's soul searching as i-narrators and reflective filters, Elon's acceptance of the documentary genre's truth claims sets one up to expect a closure that her materials do not yield. While Aviad and Cohen use the dynamic structure of compilation documentary to foreground the struggle to construct a whole out of the parts, Elon's use of a filmic discourse that does not question its own operations elides this struggle.

As the above suggests, discursive practices have an active role in how progressive Israeli i-directors articulate their position relative to the dominant ideology. But there are also other determinants at work here, including gender. In this respect the men's i-movies to which we now turn inhabit more explicitly the public sphere than the films by women i-directors discussed so far. While these differences are telling (including issues of social class which are barely touched on here), my own concern is with ways *all* these i-directors challenge a prescriptive national political consensus. At issue is their shared generational chafing against the nation-building project they inherited, a discomfort they re-enact through their discursive practices. This is true of several male i-directors I am not able to include here, including Amit Goren and Dan Katzir, mentioned above, and Ari Folman whom I will discuss only briefly. Rather, the following discussion will focus on Udi Aloni's *Local Angel* and Avi Mograbi's *Happy Birthday, Mr. Mograbi*, selected for their explicit wrestling with their Zionist legacy in the context of increasingly violent Israeli/Palestinian relations.

Aloni's *Local Angel* brings yet another perspective to bear on this wrestling, not least because in this instance the 'father' is a mother and an outstanding woman within the ranks of the secular Israeli 'left': Shulamit Aloni, former

Knesset Member and Minister of Education, founding leader of the liberal-left Meretz party, and an outstanding human rights activist. But at issue is not pedigree. What is significant about *Local Angel* in this discussion is its treatment of the tension between Israel's foundational myth and the activism of a progressive parent who nonetheless cannot deliver change, and the effects of this dynamic on the son who is the i-director of this film. In this instance the son's response is to go into exile, literal and symbolic. His film starts and ends with him living in New York City, where exile and metaphysics push aside the pragmatic politics central to the work of other i-directors. Here the 'son''s struggle with the 'father' – in this instance the phallic mother – looks to a global apocalypse that gives this film its name.

The invocation of the angel, Aloni tells us, was inspired by Walter Benjamin's short passage about the 'Angel of History', written in response to Paul Klee's painting, *Angelus Novus* (1920) (see Benjamin 1969: 257). *Local Angel* opens to a post-9/11 New York cityscape and shots of a hooded drummer (suggestive of currently familiar images of war prisoners, interrogation and torture). Following is Aloni's 'talking head' ruminating about being caught between a Hebrew language that is getting further away from him and an English language he will never master. For him this liminal linguistic condition is a site of chronic existential alienation – an alienation that defines the 'son's quest for spiritual wholeness throughout this i-movie. Fittingly, much of the film takes place in Israel, responding to the framing site of exile with a symbolic 'return' to the point of origin, Israel. But also fittingly, the film ends with Aloni anticipating a renewed exile in an alien New York that will never be his home. Self-exile here is a political act.

Local Angel shows Aloni, who lost his father early on, as an intimate witness to his mother's unswerving fight for peace and human rights, including her warm relationship with her Palestinian counterpart, Hanan Ashrawi, and her companionable ease with Yasser Arafat. (The film documents visits to both.) But though mother and son are spared the stark rifts that are so close to the surface in the preceding films, it is nonetheless haunted by Aloni's discomfort with his mother's position as a Zionist supporter of the two-state solution. It is the core meaning of his Zionist heritage as a birthright to 'the land' that troubles this film, articulated through sequences he calls 'theological-political fragments'. Among them, footage dedicated to Haviva Padai's biblical commentary and poetry constitutes an important *leitmotif*. An observant Jew, theology professor and poet, she brings to the film a metaphysical slant on Zionism, notably through her poem, 'A Man Walks' (concerning Abraham's journey to sacrifice his son at Mount Moriah[11]) as it opens up a wider inquiry into the symbolic meanings of the Zionist project and Jewish identity.

In Aloni's gloss, the journey to sacrifice a 'son' on his 'father''s altar parallels Zionism's symbolic and literal journey back to a place where people's raw desire to possess holiness can end in slaughter. Padai is less troubled: when the temple is absent, she glosses, the whole land becomes a temple, a place of transition from destruction to reconstruction. Though this redemptive view of land ownership is troubling in its Messianic rationale for an expansionist 'greater' Israel, Padai's sense of destiny nonetheless appeals to Aloni, as seen in several other sequences that endow Zionism's physical 'return' with metaphysical implications.

Local Angel is infused with an inchoate sense of longing that springs out of such melding of the tangible and the intangible – the actual trauma he shows as suffered by both sides of this bloody conflict, but also the cathartic and perhaps even redemptive force that can emerge from seeing the connection between opposites. We see such linkage in a montage of anguished Israeli and Palestinian funerals of victims of this enmity, for example, or in footage juxtaposing Israeli and Palestinian street violence, and in musical interludes that move seamlessly between the Hebrew and Arabic languages, fusing both. It is a longing for conciliation, emerging also through footage documenting conversations with scholars and politicians, Palestinian and Israeli, with all speakers situated as the i-director's 'parents' and guides through the morass of the festering politics he inherited.

But ultimately Aloni's 'theological-political fragments' do not yield the coherence for which he strives. The text resists such integration. Its structuring of thematic fragments concern desire more than pragmatic politics. Like Theodore Herzl's dictum, 'If you will it, it is not a fable', Aloni's appeal to willing as action and to imagination as agency highlights the conundrum of his quest. A political resolution remains evanescent. This emerges most explicitly in a sequence where Aloni and his mother, driving through nighttime darkness, allow their disagreement around the question of a Palestinian 'return' to surface. Addressing the camera, Aloni confesses: 'The truth is that I don't know what I think. I'm torn between my mother's Zionism and the bi-nationalism of Nunu' (Prof. Amnon Ras-Grakovsky, interviewed in the film). For Raz-Grakovsky Zionism is a material injustice; for Haviva Patai it is a secular intrusion that delays the building of the temple; for Shulamit Aloni it is a necessity to be guided by secular-humanist values.

Such political-theological fragments refuse to coalesce in *Local Angel*. It is to Walter Benjamin's enigmatic angel, an apocalyptic messenger of both salvation and devastation, that the film turns for succour. Moving from Jaffa's Muslim Cemetery to its Christian counterpart, the camera frames an angel statue 'blessing' the burial ground. Aloni sees that angel as poised to depart backward, into the open blue space of the sea and sky to Israel's west. He is dreaming, Aloni tells us, of Benjamin's angel, who 'sees one single catastrophe that piles up wreckage upon wreckage ... an angel who cannot resist the call of the west' (1969: 257).[12] Rather, it is through the symbolic function of mother – iterated through a resonant rendition of *Stabat Mater* and the figures of Ashrawi and Shulamit Aloni – that the film segues from its catastrophic view of history to protesting rather than acceding to the 'son''s sacrifice. But protest is no protection. A quick transition from that sequence has Aloni preparing to return to a New York that spells exile, not home. *Local Angel* concludes with an enigmatic prophecy: 'The Messiah will come one day after his arrival.' But is this 'he' who will precede the Messiah the angel assigned to see 'wreckage upon wreckage'?

In sharp contrast with Aloni's metaphysical yearnings, Avi Mograbi's *Happy Birthday, Mr. Mograbi* constitutes a pugnacious, satirical, materialist encounter with Israeli realities. Like all the films discussed above, it constructs a fragmented discourse that foregrounds the elusiveness of conciliation, except that this film assaults the viewer. Even its speaking 'I' functions differently. The other i-directors' autobiographical stance is not troubled by the ironies of objectivity and truth, while Mograbi's stance is explicitly performative (see Lebow 2006, 230–1). Seemingly chaotic in structure, refusing to distinguish between fiction and actuality, withholding the comforts of closure, and rejecting appeals to humanist decency and spirituality, his film withholds reassurance. It insists, rather, that resolving the Israeli/Palestinian conflict is the viewers' responsibility.

This shifting of responsibility to viewers occurs here through several discursive strategies that subvert the i-movie genre. Unlike the other i-movies discussed above, *Happy Birthday, Mr. Mograbi* smashes the evidentiary and confessional truth-claims that are the backbone of this genre. Refracting the authorial persona, it puts the i-speaker's multiple performances on show and in this way casts doubt on the evidentiary, confessional and commenting functions ascribed to first person speakers. While Mograbi the i-director comes across as the directorial presence we may take for the living Avi Mograbi, much as we accept all the i-directors mentioned above, the film undermines that authority when it includes a blatantly fictive 'Avi Mograbi' who is the living i-director impersonating himself. This 'Mograbi' is also making a film and looks exactly like his progenitor (they are both acted by the same person – Avi Mograbi himself).

While the film renders the artifice of these dueling, contentious 'Mograbis' as an absurd comedy bordering on farce, there is also something uncanny about these 'twins' as they externalise the dispute within an ostensibly unified *persona* and destabilise the conventions of both the i-movie and documentary genres. Viewers' thinking is put in crisis. Even when Mograbi the i-director addresses the camera frontally and at close range – i.e. from a position coded as direct and therefore engaging and reliable – his performance undermines his credibility as a conversational partner. Instead of the claims to contact and intimacy that make i-movies compelling, here the mediating cinematic apparatus renders direct address discomforting and even confrontational. It prevents rather than coaxes connection to the text. As with döpplegangers and Brechtian *Verfremdungseffect*, the authority of unitary representation and foolproof understanding collapses, replaced by an uncanny confusion and an anarchic erasure of boundaries that threatens reason.[13]

This conundrum extends to other aspects of the film, one of them concerning the futile struggle of both the i-director and 'Mograbi' the fictive director to live up to their respective assignments. The fictive 'Mograbi''s failure to deliver the promised film straddles farce and nightmare as an all-out fight erupts between him and his fictive 'producer'. In contrast, the i-director comes across as the 'real' Avi Mograbi, though he too fails to complete an assignment that is also ultimately fictive. Supposedly he is to make a film celebrating Israel's fiftieth anniversary while his Palestinian journalist friend, the 'real life' Daud Kutab, asks him to locate and film the remains of Palestinian villages depopulated during the *Nakba*. These two assignments, both fictive though the second addressing the generative dilemma of this film, encapsulate the opposing narratives all the directors discussed here face. These opposing narratives are at the core of the Israeli/Palestinian conflict: the narrative of building and that of destruction, the narrative of immigration (known in Hebrew as *aliyah* – which means literally, 'rising' or 'ascending') to the Promised Land and that of expulsion and exile. In the face of this radical incompatibility neither the i-director nor his over-acted 'Mograbi' alter ego is able to produce the requisite footage, let alone complete his assignment. Meanwhile Kutab, who serves as the film's voice of conscience, exists for the audience only as a simulacrum, via mechanical reproduction. Exiled from his homeland, he leaves messages on Mograbi's answering machine that are re-recorded for us. Faint and disembodied, they seem to come from an unspecified 'beyond'.

Though the i-director cannot produce more than one or two of the images Kutab requests, neither can he bring himself to make the imaginary 'celebratory' film commissioned him. The footage he supposedly garnered is a series of false starts, made up of episodes that range from a dim record of homeless people destitute on an urban beachfront to a bleak celebration of multicultural harmony (yet another national myth) signaled by a dismal array of supposedly ethnic foods and celebrants. Most blatantly false in this mirthless sequence is the enthusiasm voiced for the meagre wild *hubeiza* (a tiny legume) promoted during the young state's austerity years. There is no rejoicing in this footage, no chance of a happy anniversary film.

The film's conceit that the state's fiftieth anniversary happens to coincide with the director's birthday also falls apart as the film invents a bogus date for Independence Day, attenuating further the relation between fact and invention. Who is this Mograbi, and indeed, which one of them is meant to be celebrating a birthday? The first two (the fictive one and the i-director one, both within the diegesis) are imagined beings while the third one, Mograbi the director behind the creation of both characters, is obviously toying with his viewers' credulity. Even the appellation of 'Mr.' smacks of ridicule given the i-director's casual self-presentation and the dubious standing of his avatars. With the text freed from the constraints of accountability and reason, at issue is not fact but the signifying function of form; not the lie of the state's fictive anniversary but the conjunction of 'birth' dates as they stamp the 'son' – any one of the film's three directors – with the seal of the 'father'. The co-existent birthdays, together with the Mograbi's evasion of Kutab's *Nakba* assignment and the failure of both directors to produce their assigned films, strand viewers between unacceptable myths, deliberate lies and unwelcome truths.

This frustration is echoed by yet another narrative strand, this one concerning an inadvertent clerical error that gave 'Mograbi' a slice of his abutting neighbour's lot. Since 'Mograbi' has been building what he calls his 'dream house' on this wrongly demarcated lot, he cannot return the usurped land to its owner without tearing down his own new house. When the neighbour demands restitution, 'Mograbi' hides under self pity: the errors was not of his making, it happened in the past, it's now irreversible given the 'facts on the ground,' and so on. Speaking frontally to the camera, he banks on a show of disarming regret to win us over. Here, then, is a parable of a small-scale territorial squabble that points to the larger territorial warfare in which both 'fathers' and 'sons' are implicated. With this fictive conflict over land ownership timed a symbolic half century after the Palestinian *Nakba* and the Jews founding of their 'dream house', 'facts on the ground' is the *shibboleth* that clearly situates this episode at the eye of the storm.

Of all the films discussed here, *Happy Birthday, Mr. Mograbi* is the most condemnatory regarding the corrosive realities that are so hard for Israelis to face. It does so with considerable anger and frustration, irony and doubt, albeit mediated by parody, comedy and satire. Still, these leavening qualities do not subdue the rage. They merely funnel it towards the audience through the tangle of reason and unreason created by the film's 'hall of mirrors' design. The very use here of the assertive 'formal voice' rather than the inquiring 'open voice' (Platinga 1997: 101–11) subverts i-movies' normative claim to introspective authenticity.[14] Placing the i-speaker front and centre, the film nonetheless undermines its speaker's credibility. It shifts the emphasis away from the empathic reception which is so useful in i-movies, including the ones by Aviad, Cohen, Elon and Aloni, discussed above, and foregrounds instead a discomforting reception where the text's destabilising operations force viewers into a particularly active engagement.

It is illuminating at this point to compare, or rather contrast, *Happy Birthday, Mr. Mograbi* with Ari Folman's *Waltz with Bashir* (2008), as both de-personalise their i-speakers but do so to very different effect. Folman's animation lends his i-movie an aura of unreality that meshes seamlessly with its surreal rendition of Israel's invasion of Lebanon in 1982 and with its i-narrator's process of reconstituting his lost memory regarding his presence at the edge of the massacre at the Sabra and Shatila refugee camps. Its animation also strips away the 'thickened, dense sense of the textuality of the viewing experience' that Nichols describes as an aspect of the phenomenology of the film experience (1991: 62). As such, it at once accepts its representation of reality and creates one degree of separation from it, while Mograbi interrogates representation itself. Mograbi probes and parodies the instability of indexical knowledge and the sophistry of avoidance, while Folman tracks the elusiveness of knowledge as trauma-induced and retrievable. Here a young Israeli 'son' confronts an ethical-political crisis initiated and sustained by his 'fathers', gradually emerging from it with a reconstituted sense of self as willing to take responsibility for his actions. Fittingly, by the film's end, once the Freudian 'repressed' has been released, *Waltz with Bashir* shifts from the amplified non-realism of animation to the 'truth' of documentary. Formally and thematically it ends with a reassuring coda: confession has been made, understanding has been restored, and the artifice of animation is now recuperated into 'real' documentary representation.

Yet for all this reassurance (to the 'healed' protagonist, not the victims), the absolution *Waltz with Bashir* proffers is shaky. One can quibble with the film's politics (for example its relatively light treatment of Prime Minister Sharon and some officers – false 'fathers' all – or the unsullied innocence it ascribes to the Israeli soldiers[15]), but most relevant to the present discussion is the film's closure, which ascribes Folman's amnesia to his parents' trauma as Holocaust survivors. On its face this line of thinking makes sense: the trauma of the parents visits the sons. However, while Folman's parents were truly victims, the logic of the analogy falters. Folman and the nation as a whole are indeed marked by these inherited wounds, but they were also perpetrators, aiding the Phalangists in mass slaughter. Further, the Holocaust is hardly the 'repressed' in Israeli culture; retrieving it is possible at every turn. To the extent that *Waltz with Bashir* concerns the retrieving of repressed yet historically grounded memories of trauma, the link may be, rather, to the effects of a prolonged state of war on the souls of its Israeli combatants. The formative elision in *Waltz with Bashir* – its lost memory, if you will – may be the line connecting Sabra and Shatila to the massacre of Palestinians in Deir Yassin in 1948.

I note this link not to wag a finger at *Waltz with Bashir*, which is in many ways a remarkable film, but to highlight my attempt to disentangle the conflicting loyalties that bedevil Israeli i-movies – the self-induced myopia that is the conundrum mapped across this discussion. In the case of *Happy Birthday, Mr. Mograbi* the mutual negations and multiplications of its tangled strands project a sense of manic anarchy that is the opposite of the closure *Waltz with Bashir* attains. 'The centre cannot hold', as William Butler Yeats puts it in his poem, 'The Second Coming' (1920). Aviad's, Cohen's and Elon's i-movies reach for a coherence which reality withholds from them, while Aloni's turn to metaphysics exempts him from it and Folman's resolution protects him. Mograbi, however, enters into the thick of the fray. He stages a crisis of judgement that draws viewers towards a political discourse they might otherwise evade, and evasion is at the core of this discussion.[16] At issue for at least this group of Israeli i-directors is not only the way the nation as a whole lets its eyes glide over what is 'at the roadside', literally and figuratively, but their own struggle between seeing and not seeing.

Notes

1   'Nakba' (catastrophe) names the depopulation of some 400 Palestinian villages (estimated numbers vary) during the war of 1947–49 and its immediate aftermath.

2   S. Yizhar's novella, *Khirbet Khizeh* (2008), and A. B. Yehoshua's story, 'Facing the Forests' (1970) are notable exceptions. Ram Levi's film *Khirbet Khizeh* (1977) was banned for years. Dalia Karpel's documentary, *The Diaries of Yossef Nachmany* (2006) is barely available and short documentaries by Amos Gitai, among others, are rarely screened.

3   Erroneously attributed to Israel Zangwill ('Palestine is a country without people; the Jews are a people without a country', 1901), this aphorism antedates him. Originated by Restorationist clergyman Alexander Keith (1843), it nods in the direction of Britain's imperial stakes in Ottoman territories. Zangwill's own views evolved over time from viewing this land as empty to questioning the Jews' 'historical right' to that land.

4   Though many Palestinians are also Israeli citizens, my focus here is on Jewish-Israeli i-movies. I believe Palestinian-Israeli i-movies deserve full discussion in and of themsleves. Ibtisam Mar'ana's *Fureidis; Lost Paradise* (2002) is a notable Palestinian-Israeli i-movie (see Baram and Amir 2007; Gertz and Khleifi 2008), and of course the work of Kamal Aljafari, discussed by Peter Limbrick in this volume. Elia Suleiman's *Divine Intervention* (2002) and *The Time That Remains* (2010) take the genre further into fictional territory.

5   These films participate in an increasingly visible Israeli questioning of the country's foundational

myths. See Meron Benveniste (2000), Tom Segev (2000), and Benny Morris (2008), among others.

6   Jacqueline Rose's *The Question of Zion* melds psychoanalysis and history in her examination of the origins of Zionism and the Israeli-Palestinian conflict.

7   Performed by the Jewish and Palestinian Acre Theater Group. The slogan *Arbeit Macht Frei* (work makes one free) was posted at the entrance to several Nazi concentration camps.

8   Filmed in a military outpost 'manned' exclusively by men, Aviad's *Did You Ever Shoot Somebody?* (2002) explores gender outside of normative domesticity.

9   An acronym for Plugot Mahatz (roughly, 'Crushing Companies'). Palmach fighters were the elite of the Hagana, the progenitor of the Israel Defence Forces. Like Cohen's mother, Arna Mer Hammis, the Israeli protagonist of *Arna's Children* (2003), also dismisses reports of Palmach violence though research does not support this soft-pedaling.

10 Cf. Uri Barabash's film, *The Dreamers* (*Hacholmim*, 1987). Regarding Herzl's much quoted statement, Rose notes that going 'beyond reason, Herzl makes the creation of Israel something unrepresentable' (2005: 63).

11 Mount *mora yah* (awe of God): Jerusalem's Jewish Temple Mount and Islam's Haram al Sharif.

12 Note also Israeli sculptor Dani Karavan's installation, 'Passages; Homage to Walter Benjamin' (Tel Aviv Museum, 1997–98), and Toni Kushner's *Angels in America* (first performed in 1992). Both Aloni's and Kushner's apocalypse include cemetery angel sculptures. Karavan's memorial is at Portbou, the site of Benjamin's suicide.

13 Döppleganger or 'double': cf Dr Jekyll and Mr Hyde, Dorian Gray and his portrait, Kafka's 'Arthur' in *The Castle*, etc. Brecht's *Verfremdungseffect* is variously translated as 'defamiliarization', 'estrangement' and 'distancing'.

14 This conundrum regarding the authorial voice extends to Mograbi's other films, including *How I Stopped Being Afraid and Learned to Love Arik Sharon* (1997).

15 Cf. Joseph Cedar's soldiers in *Beaufort* (2007) and Samuel Maoz's in *Lebanon* (2009).

16 Mograbi's documentary, *Z32* (2009) confronts the permutations of giving, recording and withholding testimony. Focusing on an Israeli soldier's confession of a war crime, the film asks, re-presents and relocates segments of testimony. As the account trails off, gets recast and is replayed, it imprisons the viewer in a murky, obsessive account, where the difficulty of telling becomes an audiovisual crisis of knowing and resistance to knowledge.

References

Baram, N. and M. Amir (eds) (2007) *Documentally: An Anthology of Essays on Israeli Documentary Film*. Tel Aviv: Am Oved. [Hebrew]

Beatie, K. (2008) *Documentary Display; Re-Viewing Nonfiction Film and Video*. London and New York: Wallflower Press.

Benjamin, W. (1969 [1921]) 'Theses on the Philosophy of History', in H. Arendt (ed.) *Illuminations: Essays and Reflections*. New York: Schocken, 253–64.

Benveniste, M. (2000) *Sacred Landscape: The Buried History of the Holy Land Since 1948*. Berkeley, CA: University of California Press.

Bruzzi, S. (2000) *New Documentary: A Critical Introduction*. London: Routledge.

Butler, J. (1997) *The Psychic Life of Power*. Stanford: Stanford University Press.

____ (2005) *Giving An Account of Oneself*. New York: Fordham University Press.

Caruth, C. (ed.) (1995) *Trauma: Explorations in Memory*. Baltimore, MD: Johns Hopkins University Press.

____ (1996) *Unclaimed Experience: Trauma, Narrative and History*. Baltimore, MD: Johns Hopkins

University Press.

Duvdevani, S. (2010) *First Person Camera*. Jerusalem: Keter Books. [Hebrew]

Felman, S. and D. Laub (1992) *Testimony: Crises of Witnessing in Literature, Psychoanalysis, and History*. New York, NY: Routledge.

Gertz, N. and G. Khleifi (2008) *Palestinian Cinema: Landscape, Trauma, and Memory*. Bloomington, IN: Indiana University Press.

Herzl, T. (1902) *Altneuland* [Old New Land]. Leipzig: Hermann Seemann Nachfolger.

Guerin, F. and R. Hallas (eds) (2007) *The Image and the Witness: Trauma, Memory and Visual Culture*. London: Wallflower Press.

Kadman, N. (2008) *Erased From Space and Consciousness: Depopulated Palestinian Villages in the Israeli-Zionist Discourse*. Jerusalem: November Books. [Hebrew]

Lebow, A. (2006) 'Faking What?: Making a Mockery of Documentary', in A. Juhasz and J. Lerner (eds) *F is for Phony*. Minneapolis, MN: University of Minnesota Press, 223–37.

____ (2008) *First Person Jewish*. Minneapolis: University of Minnesota Press.

Morris, B. (2008) *1948: The First Arab-Israeli War*. New Haven, CT: Yale University Press.

Nichols, B. (1991) *Representing Reality*. Bloomington, IN: Indiana University Press.

Peled, R. (2002) *'The New Man' of the Zionist Revolution; Hashomer Haza'ir and its European Roots*. Tel Aviv: Am Oved. [Hebrew]

Platinga, C. R. (1997) *Rhetoric and Representation in the Nonfiction Film*. Cambridge: Cambridge University Press.

Rascaroli, L. (2009) *The Personal Camera: Subjective Cinema and the Essay Film*. London: Wallflower Press.

Renov, M. (ed.) (1993) *Theorizing Documentary*. New York and London: Routledge.

____ (2004) *The Subject of Documentary*. Minneapolis, MN: University of Minnesota Press.

Ricoeur, P. (2006) *Memory, History, Forgetting*. Chicago, IL: Chicago University Press.

Rose, J. (2005) *The Question of Zion*. Princeton, NJ: Princeton University Press.

Segev, T. (2000) *One Palestine Complete: Jews and Arabs Under the British Mandate*. New York, NY: Henry Holt.

Sontag, S. (2003) *Regarding the Pain of Others*. New York: Picador.

Vaughan, D. (1999) *For Documentary*. Berkeley, CA: University of California Press.

Walker, J. (2005) *Trauma Cinema: Documentary, Incest, and the Holocaust*. Berkeley, CA: University of California Press.

Yehoshua, A. B. (1970 [1963]) *Three Days and a Child*. New York, NY: Doubleday. [Hebrew]

Yizhar, S. (2008 [1949]) *Khirbet Khizeh*. Jerusalem: Ibis. [Hebrew]

Zangwill, I. (1901) 'The Return to Palestine', *The New Liberal Review*, December, 615.

DIASPORIC SUBJECTIVITY

Looking for Home in Home Movies:
The Home Mode in Caribbean Diaspora First Person Film and Video Practice

Elspeth kydd

'SIFTING SAND': FRAGMENTS OF A FAMILY HISTORY

1946: A photograph taken of two family groups, separated by a short distance. There is a corrugated iron wall to one side and a large opening to the other. Both groups are dwarfed by the surroundings. The family on the left includes my mother, grandparents, uncles and aunts. They are at the pier as my Uncle Harold prepares to either arrive from or return to the US on one of his occasional visits to Trinidad. It is

the post-World War II period, people are coming and going; the US army presence is decreasing and Trinidadian servicemen are returning from the war. As far as I can tell, my Uncle Harold is taking the picture. He came back to visit his family in Trinidad after serving in the US army. But is he on the boat or is he standing on the shore? Is he arriving or is he leaving?

Talking to my mother about this photograph I find that, although she doesn't remember seeing it before, she remembers my uncle's visit. She is 22, standing in the front row in a patterned dress. I found this picture in my uncle's collection of photos and films. His collection was large as he was the first son to leave; the family kept in touch using photographs. Many appear with inscriptions and dates written on the back. Later in my research I come across another copy in my grandmother's album in the family home in Trinidad; it was probably sent to her by her son. This exchange of photographs becomes an act of mediated communication, a visual extension to the letters and cards that link a family separated by the process of diaspora. As John DiStefano claims: 'Transnational

kinship is often characterised by the physically absent members of one's family made present through mediated forms [...] More often than not, it is the displaced person who attempts to make tangible what is missing and absent' (2002: 39).

Among my uncle's other photographs from that time, there is one that could be the reverse-shot; he is looking out from the boat at the shore. This picture has an inscription on the back: 'SS Athos II, July 17, 1946.' It is shot with an evocative over-exposure; Harold gazes on a bright, sunlit world that we cannot fully see. Placing these pictures together I can start to construct a story from my family's past: a story of going away and coming back, of separations and reunions, of spaces and locations, not only of homes, but of transitions.

This is only a moment, a fragment, from which this story can emerge, fractions of time captured, secured in a past that can be remoulded into a story, or, better yet, left fragmented, incoherent and partial. This is not a record of the past but an echo from it.

As I look through old family photographs – my uncle's collection, those from my parents, photographs from the family home in Trinidad – the attempt to construct a coherent story or a clear picture of the family through its movements and shifts, reminds me of the words of an old calypso song I learned as a child: 'All day, all night Miss Mary Ann/Down by the seaside sifting sand.' The song comes from that same era, from the calypsonian Roaring Lion (Rafael de Leon), a song for the carnival celebrations of 1945 at the end of the war. I have always been struck by the lyric of this song and the strangeness of what Miss Mary Ann is doing; what, after all, is the purpose of sifting sand? It is a futile activity. Yet sand sifting has become for me a metaphor for the dual processes of theorising and practicing Caribbean family autobiography, a deceptive process, difficult and with no hope of the ultimate goal; there will be no clean beach of sand, and no clear story to recount. But in the best traditions of structural-materialism, the process *is* the goal. Can you sift sand without feeling the joy of the beach and the pleasure/frustration of sand falling between your fingers? Can you search through the images of family history, listen to the memories recounted, and revisit the sites of past lives without experiencing the joy of the search or the pleasure of acknowledging the incoherent, fragmented and unstable narrative that emerges?

I have looked through my uncle's images many times and I often find the photography 'amateur' in style as well as fact; poor exposure and focus, with the clumsy framing capturing action to the side of what I want to see. When I look at my uncle's photographs with an eye for the rules of composition I see failings – a lack of 'professional standards'. But with this image, I do not care. I like this photograph. It is a portrait of family in the process of dispersion at a crisis point for the narrative of arrival and departure, on the pier, waiting to go out, and holding the promise of return. Here, I see the context in which this family moment is captured: one small family on a small island of families on the move. (There is another family adjacent in the picture; what is their story? Who are they waiting to meet or waving goodbye? Is there another family album, commemorating their moment of transition?) Many of the young people pictured here will leave; my mother and uncle will move to Britain in the years that follow and another uncle and aunt to Canada later in their lives. Other family members are missing from the photo, either absent that day or already living abroad. Still others will choose to stay and some will leave to return later. We are a diaspora family; linked visually by these fragments, these images, these memories.

My family photographs are not unlike many others, often documenting ritualistic moments of clan unity: weddings, births and baptisms, birthdays, anniversaries, parties, reunions, holidays, Christmases. They are located in the spaces of these celebrations; homes, churches, tourist sights. Yet this image captures another moment: travel towards and away from a home. It is located on the pier; a liminal space of mobility. The family is surrounded and dwarfed by the context; an image that captures, for me, the ambiguities of departure and return that characterise a Caribbean diaspora experience. There are many images of travel in my uncle's collection, pictures of and from ships in the 1940s and 1950s, planes and airports from the 1960s onward. The only film he has of my immediate family catches us with an unstable shaky camera in the airport in Trinidad, preparing to leave after a holiday in 1973. We are a diaspora family; frozen in still images that evoke mobility.

This photograph was taken twenty years before I was born. I have no memory of the events it presents. For me, this image perhaps marks a 'postmemory', a term that Marianne Hirsch has used to describe this connection with a family past:

> Postmemory is a powerful and very particular form of memory precisely because its connection to its object or source is mediated not through recollection but through an imaginative investment and creation. [...] It characterises the experience of those who grow up dominated by narratives that preceded their birth, whose own belated stories are evacuated by the stories of the previous generation shaped by traumatic events that can be neither understood nor recreated. (1997: 22)

The mobility and transition evident in my uncle's photograph is not the ultimate collective trauma of my family history. Nevertheless, the image of the shore, the ship and the pier in 1946 is reminiscent of traumas from generations earlier than my mother's: of other ships, other landing points, and other (non-voluntary) crossings from ancestors whose memory has faded from our recountings and from whom no images remain. The ship and the journey are a fragment of a family story that reminds us of lives lived before our own and arrivals to a Caribbean destination not greeted by a welcoming family. As Paul Gilroy describes it, the 'images of ships in motion across the spaces between Europe, America, Africa and the Caribbean' is a 'central organising symbol' for the discussion of the 'Black Atlantic'; 'ships immediately focus attention on the middle passage, on the various projects for redemptive return to an African homeland, on the circulation of ideas, activists as well as the movement of key cultural and political artefacts' (1993: 4).

I encounter this photograph, and many others like it, as I go through the research process of creating a documentary based on my family's experience. As I work through the images of the past and elicit recollections from family members of our experiences of home and away, of fixity and dispersion, I also work through the creative and theoretical process of creating a first person film. Here, part of the plurality of the experience is drawn from the nature of my family; they represent a wide range of connections and experiences that cross class, gender, race, generational and cultural lines. This essay forms a part of the critical practice process of creating this film and as such, explores a range of influences that inform first person filmmaking in the context of the Caribbean diaspora.

The culture of the Caribbean as a whole is fragmented on a number of levels. Geographically it is a group of small islands, most of which are now individual nation states, with national identities constituted through their separation from their former colonial powers. This former colonial affiliation does, however, provide another level of identification, one that is based on common languages and shared histories of oppression across the islands and nations. With several languages spoken in the diverse islands, the fragmentation of Caribbean identity is also a function of these linguistic differences as well as the size of the various islands, and the combination of migrant populations. Historically, national identity formation has also depended on the economic structures; the combination of the plantation economy and absentee ownership contributed to a fragmented consciousness. This fragmentation is further compounded by the diversity of cultures brought together through the experience of diaspora, as explained by Sandra Pouchet Paquet in *Caribbean Autobiography*:

> The themes of diaspora in the Caribbean are complicated because the Caribbean writers and scholars have been at great pains to represent the region, historically and culturally, as diasporic space – more commonly in terms of the competing claims of African, Asian and European ethnicities. Diasporic space represents the Caribbean in specific histories of conquest and settlement, population movements, exile and migration. It exists in tension with the concept of community that is inscribed within sites of ancestral dwelling. (2002: 6)

Paquet further explores how this diversity of culture and fragmentation of Caribbean identity is expressed through the process of autobiography: 'the radical instability of the Caribbean as a cultural domain coincides with the radical instability of autobiography as a genre' (2002: 8). The process of written autobiography for the Caribbean subject is part of a tradition of storytelling and of history-making. While this autobiographical writing reclaims a voice for a silenced people – individual voices that enunciate counter narratives to the official versions of history and of fantasy – it also presents a fragmented and disaggregated sense of self and an identity forged through the intricacies of difference and displacement.

On the other hand, Caribbean filmmaking has been limited by cultural, economic and political obstacles that have only rarely been overcome enough to bring fresh perspectives of West Indian experience to different audiences. Often the limited resources available for making films in the Caribbean are deployed to document the immediate social and political problems or the contextual history of the developing nations. As some have argued, autobiography holds a marginalised place in film in general (see Hampl 1996: 54) and in the context of the limited production of film in the Caribbean it has not yet found full expression.

These challenges presented by the dearth of first person visual representation in Caribbean and Caribbean diaspora filmmaking have led me to look at the neglected area of home movies as a key part of first person filmmaking.

Home movies are autobiographical films, limited by genre, technology, their status as amateur work and the heavily coded expectations that surround their viewing. They have long been overlooked as an object of study due to their form, style, authorship and limited access for systematic analysis. Yet these films can articulate as well as any a narrative of familial experience of diaspora and displacement. The films I will be looking at are family films created by my father and uncles. They do not constitute a systematic study so much as a creative reflection on this form.

'WILLED TO ME BY MY FATHER'S HAND': HOME MOVIES AT HOME

I am looking at a sequence from one of my family's films. It is the first reel my parents took of my sister Angela and brother Sandy. It starts with the family life in our home in Leyland, England. Conventional childhood images unfold: Angela and Sandy eating and playing outside in the garden. The images of happy children are balanced with my brother crying and walking towards the camera. Then, there is a time shift, we see the end of the street in Aberdeen, Scotland, where we live a year later, cutting to a shot of our new house. My brother and sister run out toward the camera, talking and laughing. A Scottish-Caribbean family, burdened with over-determined cultural symbols, Angela wears a tartan dress and Sandy carries a 'gollywog'. I have now arrived in the family; the next shot shows my mother, Nora, carrying me out of the house to join the group. She tickles me to make me the laughing baby required of the moment. We are pictured together, the standard happy family at home, captured by the camera in my father's hand, the staple of the home movie genre. The final shot of this sequence, reverses the gaze briefly, as my mother films my father cycling into the driveway, fulfilling the role of the patriarch returning home from the imagined work place. In constructing family life in the simple frozen image of the home movie, what is left out? What don't these flickering frames show? No family film documents the fights these cute little children got into when their Scottish peers and compatriots called them by the 'N' word or any of its unpleasant synonyms. Only a few of the contradictions of mixed heritage are left in the silent film of children wearing tartan and clutching a symbolically ambiguous doll.

The visual style of the images that we do see form part of what Richard Chalfen calls the 'home mode', in some sense easily interchangeable with many other middle-class families in their construction of the imagined ideal of the family (1982: 8–9). I see this idealised middle-class life and recognise in it at least a fragment of my past. I am not 'unsettled' by these images, as Richard Fung is when he finds himself confronting the home movies from his family past, which 'contradicted what [he] remembered' (2008: 32). I acknowledge, as he points out, the similarity of my family films to the others from 'the template of suburban America' (2008: 33) (or Britain, even), but there is a specificity here as well, one to do with not only what we see in family memorabilia but how we see the images of our family: what Hirsch calls the 'affiliative look'; 'recognising an image as *familial* elicits [...] a specific kind of readerly or spectatorial look, an *affiliative* look through which we are sutured into the image and through which we adopt the image into our own familial narrative [...] it is idiosyncratic, untheorisable: it is what moves us because of our memories and our histories, and because of the ways in which we structure our own sense of particularity' (1997: 93). Fung's response to his family movies is no less valid than mine, both are grounded in an experience of family that is on one level universal (our films are similar to other middle-class home mode representations) and specific (they are our films). As Hirsch explains: 'What I see when I look at my family pictures is not what you see when you look at them; only my look is affiliative, only my look enters and extends the network of looks and gazes that have constructed the image in the first place' (ibid.).

Thus, home movies are a specific experience for the in-group viewer and a different experience for the guest or the outside observer. There is a narrative already written into the viewing: through memory, recognition, repetition and ritual. Watching the old films again on a DVD transfer with my brother and sister, we laugh at different scenes, cringe at our moments of youthful nakedness, get nostalgic for favoured bits of clothing, and recount fragments of memory from outside the frame. My clearest memories of childhood may not be in the films, but the films infiltrate my memories of all other parts of my childhood. When others watch this film it is in the company of a family member who projects it and contextualises the images. The last time I showed a friend my family films, we sat on the floor with the projector trained against the wall. She had once met Sandy, but knew no one else in my family. Through the films she encountered the rest of my kin, frozen in the idyllic and idealised scenes of childhood. She laughed hardest at the images of me as a baby, but ultimately shared the projected nostalgia of a happy family past/passed. By the ritual of viewing and the context of my screening, she was sutured temporarily into my familial, affiliative look. Watching these films with the family member present, the guest viewer is given momentary access to another's family and allowed space to project their own memories, stories and fantasies onto the film. Home movies are designed to be viewed by the specific audience that anchors their meaning in the now and the shared experience of viewing. They can be devoid of fictional narrative or documentary factual conventions because they are meant to be seen differently as part of the process of creating and sustaining familial memory, and by extension community ritual formation.

Home movies are conventionally created, ritualistically viewed and simplistic in style; nevertheless they are important cultural documents. The recent interest in the scholarly field attests to this and the incorporation of examples of this form into archives and collections develops this interest. So before I say more about my collection of films, I will explain clearly what they are and how I came by them. My uncle's films came to me first when he moved into a nursing home in Florida in 1994. He had lost his wife, was suffering from dementia and was no longer able to cope with living alone. My parents travelled to Florida to help him with the sale of his house and possessions. My mother put his films and photographs in an old red suitcase and had it shipped to me where I lived in Ohio, with some furniture that I bought from his estate. Looking through this old collection I was fascinated, but did not take the time to sort through or explore the collection for a number of years, until after my uncle had died. There were many boxes, envelopes and albums of photographs. The films were a mixed collection: some edited compilation reels ('My WI trip 1965', 'Our Trip to Canada 1967') of ten minutes or more, mixed in with thirty or so 100ft reels, with occasional information and dates. Attempting to catalogue this work, I combined the written information with edge letter processing dates, and what I can recognise and reconstruct from conversations with various others.

The second part of the collection came to me in 2002. My father, Robbie, asked me to take his old home movies to transfer to video, but it was yet again something I did not accomplish until later, again after his death. Robbie's films were more systematically preserved. With the exception of a few 100ft reels of miscellaneous family visits and outtakes, each reel is a 10–12-minute compilation of an event, holiday or designated time period; with holiday films making up the majority. Among them are one or two reels of short film that my brother or I shot during our teen years (after Dad got the Super 8 camera when we were allowed to mess with the old regular 8). When I was 18, I borrowed the Super 8 camera and made my first full film. Both parts of the collection are visual legacies and come with a responsibility to preserve and share a collective family past. It is out of this that my documentary emerged with the accompanying interest in the role of home movies in the creation and preservation of cultural memory.

'AN EQUAL PLACE': HOME MOVIES IN THE HOMELAND

If home movies exist within the frame of familial consciousness, they are also reflective of other, larger ideological functions in articulating social groupings and a further affiliation to the 'imagined community' of the nation. In her study of memory, culture and the domestic photograph, Annette Kuhn analyses an image of herself, dressed up in a special ceremonial dress for the Coronation in 1953. The photograph, taken in the familial context, becomes part of a larger discourse about national identity (see Kuhn 1995: 59–67). In the ritual of the Coronation the participation of the everyday families binds a complex set of meanings around nationality. Thus, there are records, not only of the official activities of royalty and guests, but families participating in the Coronation as a form of community bonding around a national symbol. In this way we can see how domestic photography and the home movie can be reflective of larger ideas about the imaginings of a nation.

Another example of this relationship between amateur photography/film-making and larger social constructs is Heather Nicholson's exploration of the films of amateur filmmaker Charles Chislett. His domestic holiday films reproduce the discourses of national identity and the construction of 'Englishness' prevalent in the 1930s and 1940s:

> The ideological context within which domestic travelogues were made and shown may be set against much better known voices engaged in diverse attempts to re-imagine national identity. In its own way, showing home movies also helped to construct notions of national unity. Their domestic and unofficial disclosures of the everyday reinforced the more explicit messages, which … came from J. B. Priestley's radio chat shows, Humphrey Jennings' documentaries, and a stream of broadcasts from the British Broadcasting Corporation and Ministry of Information. (2002: 57)

This idea that home movies contribute to an everyday construction and reinforcement of nationalism can be seen in the evidence of my family films. The most well-worn film in my father's collection is of a family holiday on the Scottish island of Colonsay. The film projects an idyllic rural Scottishness: bucolic and pastoral. The highland holiday is a part of my upbringing that is visualised in these images of walking in hills, playing on the beach and participating in the local community sports day. One sequence shows my family out fishing with a local father and son whose labour is framed as rustic spectacle. The film's *mise-en-scène* places the family grouping in woolly jumpers and wellies; it is an imagining of postcard Scottishness, personalised through the family's participation.

In contrast, the first among my parent's films is an unusual home movie, made shortly after their marriage. It looks at their life in the New Heys reception centre for children where my father worked as warden and where both my parents also lived. In this large Victorian house with a group of about thirty children in care, the notion of 'home' in home movies becomes destabilised. On the one hand, for my father the boundaries between home and work are blurred and on the other, it documents the life of children whose experience of conventional home life has been disrupted and undermined. This film also disrupts the national imagining that is part of the home movie project, through its focus on the racial diversity of the home and the tensions of the surrounding community of Liverpool. Early in the film a sequence of shots introduce the location of Liverpool, including a wall with the graffiti 'Keep Britain White' – a shot which is also intercut into a later sequence when a diverse group of children and adults in the home dance the twist together. As a home movie this is an interesting and unconventional example. It is edited into a ten-minute reel, with a type-written commentary included in the box. Structured both narratively and rhetorically, it is more like an amateur documentary than a standard home movie, addressing the intersecting issues of home, community, city and national identity. The undeniable racial and cultural diversity of the children in the home contrasts with the antagonism of the surrounding community and directly relates to the shifting demographic of the nation.

This example shows a complexity within the home movie's representation of Britishness and the encounter of post-colonial diasporic shifts in population. But what about the ways in which the home mode can articulate a Caribbean consciousness in its own right? Images of Trinidad carnival are a staple of how the tourist gaze structures the Caribbean as spectacle for consumption. Yet carnival is simultaneously part of the construction of a national ritual, on which a complex Caribbean identity is written. In my family films, carnival recurs in different places. Robbie's films record the celebrations of 1962, the second film after New Heys, documenting my parents' first visit to the family home in Trinidad as a couple, but before they had children. The carnival part of the longer compilation reel of their holiday, starts with the children's parade, where my cousins are identifiable among the costumed groups. Then the film continues with the exhibition of carnival bands parading across the Savannah (the large park in the centre of Port of Spain). My mother tells the story of how my father used up all his film on the first day of carnival, not realising that the main spectacle occurred on the Tuesday. It is a mistake that speaks to his position as tourist and outsider. Likewise, the film itself has both the flavour of exotic spectacle as well as the potential for reading the images as national spectacle. Within the carnivalesque portrayal we can see a fragmented and hybridised Caribbean identity emerge. For example, my favourite image of this film (and perhaps of all my father's films) is of a carnival band of Trinidadian men marching, dressed in short red kilts with t-shirts and tams, while in the foreground, a man dances with a large map of Africa on his back. This image, with its equal parts syncretism and parody, would have appealed to my father at the time, and echoes the ironies of a cross-cultural family life even as I watch it today.

Among my uncle's collection there are also films of carnival, several 100ft reels of different celebrations and a compilation of the 1964 event. The 1964 film is hypnotic to watch, as repeated scenes of dancing groups cross the screen, with a similar use of long shots, visual framing and takes of equal measure. There is a sequence of children's carnival on one reel as well, but in this case it is hard to distinguish any of my cousins. The camera-work is shaky, taken as if by someone in the middle of the action, rather than viewing from a distance. Also notable among the films that I received from Harold are two 100 ft reels not taken by my Uncle Harold, but by my Uncle James (uncle by marriage). James was a keen photographer and probably shot these reels of film with Harold's borrowed camera. Although James was later to move to Canada, at this point he lived in Trinidad, so the films are not the diasporic documents that Harold's and Robbie's are, but a native Trinidadian's home movie. James' camera style is much more methodical and controlled than either Harold's or my father's. The images of the carnival bands are produced with carefully executed long-shot pans. Although knowing Uncle James, my affiliative gaze sees this style as part of his personality, I also see the care and caution of someone for whom film is a rare luxury, to be consumed with diligence and respect. The boxes these films come in attest to this, as they are labelled with great care, addressed to Kodak in the US where they would have had to be sent for processing as this was not available in Trinidad (see Fung 2008: 30). In this example, the native Trinidadian view of carnival is distanced by the stylistic choices, rather than the involved shooting of Harold, the diaspora son from away, with his shaky camera movements and closer take on the action or my father's more impressionistic participation.

Dare I mention the last carnival film of the collection, when I can hardly bear to look at it? In 1985, I also shot a carnival film. With my father's borrowed camera it was my first attempt at filmmaking (other than the fragments of regular 8 I shot with my brother when I was younger). There is nothing remarkable about these four 100ft reels, unless it is my tendency for short takes and interest in shooting scenes of my extended family enjoying the party, rather than the more conventional images of the costumes and bands. The carnival sequences are surrounded by footage of other events, and the last reel shows the conventional, formal march past of the bands from the viewing stand in the Savannah. But nearly a third of the footage shot is of a group of cousins 'liming' (hanging out) at the corner of Stone Street, near where the family house is situated. We are watching, dancing and drinking. This corner also appears in both Harold's and Robbie's films (Angela and Sandy returned to that spot for carnival 2001, my mother shot a sequence of photographs from that location during carnival 2008 and I returned there with my video camera in 2009). It is a place that speaks to the family's connection to the national spectacle, our participation comes from this spot. It is not our family home itself that is the point of intersection for our diasporic connection to the national ritual, but another liminal space of transition. We are a diaspora family; we gather, dance and lime on the corner of our street.

As a document of a national celebration, the films from the four family members speak to a fragmented and incoherent sense of how carnival expresses the Trinidad and diaspora identity. This identity is spoken through style, the affiliative gaze, but also the acknowledgment that the home movie in the Caribbean context is privileged through the limitations of access. Richard Fung makes this point when he argues for a complexity in the role of the home movie in the Third World context: 'in Third World countries home movies were accessible only to the relatively privileged, and the footage draws attention to social difference rather than commonality. Its use therefore undermines, or at least provides a counterpoint to, the inclination to conflate the 'I' of the Third World autobiographical film or video maker with the 'I' of the nation, to extend Henry Loius Gates formulation about identity and race in African-American autobiographical writing' (2008: 39). It is undeniable that the relationship of home movies taken in Trinidad (and by necessity processed elsewhere) and any project of national or regional imagining would be inevitably overlayed with questions of privilege, access and technology. Yet there are ways in which home movies do speak to a specific national context even as they articulate part of a history defined by questions of privilege. Here the comparison between the Third World autobiographical film and the racial identity exposed in African-American autobiographical writing is valuable. Gates (1985) refers in his article to the development of the slave narrative tradition and the way it grew into a form of articulation of the black American experience. This tradition grew at a time when literacy itself was a privilege not available to all, just as access to home movie technology is limited within Third World contexts. Despite, or in addition to, the privilege these forms evince, they nonetheless also become important cultural and historical referents.

Roger Odin sees the home movie's potential to articulate an experience outside the proscription of official discourses of history:

> Family filmmakers are involuntary endotic anthropologists; they film those moments of life that professionals ignore. Official reports fail to document entire aspects of society. Home movies are sometimes the only records of some racial, ethnic, cultural, social communities marginalised by the official version of history. Even if these films do not recount the entire history and often show what the community sanctions, these films represent important documents. (2008: 263)

HOME MOVIES AS TRAVELOGUE

Home movies expand out beyond the space of the home. Although many of the moments they celebrate are created in that familial space and often it is on a wall or screen at home where they are viewed, they stretch out beyond the house to view the family life outside of the home. A significant subgenre of the home movie is the holiday film, often documenting international travel and the tourist's encounter with another culture. If, as Michelle Citron suggests, 'vacationers take 70 percent of all photographs shot worldwide' (1999: 7) then the way that the amateur photographer, or home moviemaker, views the world is highly relevant to perceptions of cultural difference.

Travel holiday films are derivative of the images perpetuated through tourist travel discourse. They are often framed in terms of the family's journey to the exotic, constructing objects of the tourist gaze. They are films documenting the leisure time activities associated with travel; tourist attractions, beach and relaxation, parties and festivals. As Nicholson points out, the holiday film has a pre-written narrative structure; with preparation, departure, travel, sights and activities of the holiday and ending with the return (2002: 54). Holiday trips, like home movie technology, speak to who has the economic power to travel and make images.

In both my father's and uncle's collection, holiday films are a significant feature. My father's films include three trips to visit family in Trinidad (for carnival in 1962, Christmas in 1969 and the summer of 1973), one trip to family in New York and Toronto and the aforementioned highland holiday to Colonsay. These films, and the Trinidad films in particular, represent a fractured family experience of travel. For my mother, Trinidad was a journey home, reuniting with family in a known and comfortable environment. For my father, it is more clearly a holiday, in the sense of visiting a place that was not home and where he would always be a foreigner and a guest. His position in the process, as filmmaker and outsider, in some ways allows for these images to be created. Yet his presence as a visitor also inflects how Trinidad is seen through the eyes of a non-Trinidadian. This outsider role gives these films a different inflection than home movies that emerge from a native Caribbean context. There is another layer of conflict that can be read into what appear to be simple records of a family holiday. As Robbie operates the camera, he structures the image partially through the tourist gaze and partially through his affiliation as an in-law member of the family. Thus, the films mix visuals of tourist sites and holiday activities with family members congregating. Pictures of carnival, which to the non-affiliated tourist are mere exotic spectacle, to the affiliative gaze involve picking out family members among the costumed crowds and seeing the activities in the context of a participatory national spectacle.

As I watch these films through my own affiliative look, I see the paradox at the heart of the images that resonates with the conflicted nature of these journeys as I experienced them as a child. Visiting from Scotland, away from the home of my childhood, my sister, brother and I are clearly on holiday. But through our mother's connection, we are bound to Trinidad more intimately than the average tourist: it is a return of sorts to a motherland, marked by a feeling of duality. We are and we are not tourists, we are not and we are home. I anticipated these trips as a child as holidays and expected them to be fun, but remember them as more fraught – with family visits rather than time on the beach, heat that I found insufferable and the culture clash of 'aunties' and 'uncles' I could barely remember invading my not-inconsiderable Scottish personal space. My memories are not unique, they are shared by siblings and cousins who felt to varying degrees, similar discomforts of this home/not home.

I re-watch one particular sequence repeatedly, encountering traces and evidence of the conflicted diaspora experience in the film. It is from our 1969 visit to Trinidad, when I was three. I am absent from this short scene, possibly marking the territory of my future life behind the camera. My mother and her sisters are buying fish from a stall in Mayaro, they talk among themselves, occasionally acknowledging the presence of the camera. My mother tries to keep hold of my brother as he pulls away and my sister looks on with interest from the sidelines (she became a marine biologist, so perhaps she was foreseeing her future also). If I were to watch this sequence without the familial context it could appear as exotic spectacle of the market taken by a passing tourist. But the comfort of the three sisters with each other and with the camera binds even the non-affiliative spectator into the family moment. The camera, and with it the viewer, is part of the group. The scene catches for me the diaspora family film, with multiple levels of address visible in the frame and more interpretation accessible in the viewing context of the home mode.

HOME MOVIES AND THE DIASPORA

One of the questions that I seem to be repeatedly asking myself in this research is whether home movies produce or reproduce, familiarise or defamiliarise, critique or undermine conventional images of the Caribbean. As an extension of the tourist impulse, holiday films serve functions supported by the appeal of tourism. Yet I would argue that there is a different set of prerogatives for the home movie produced by the member of the diasporic family, a function linked to the disjuncture of home and separation articulated in the Caribbean first person narrative. The diaspora home movie creates a different view of travel from that of conventional tourist films. Travel here is not the simple narrative structure of the holiday suggested by Nicholson. It is not a going out from the routedness of home and the return, but a constant shifting and migratory relationship between different spaces, locations and familial splits. It is not a search for the exotic or simplistic cross-cultural moment so much as a search for the connection between disparate family members. I am not arguing here for a radical rewriting of the home mode in the diaspora, so much as a shift in the affliative gaze.

What in the images of the home movie articulates this difference? After all, are not my family doing similar things as other home movie families? The images are interpreted by the affiliative gaze in the context of experience: therefore different artists reading and anchoring the home movie image reframe and recontextualise their films in relationship to different forms of experience. In *Capturing the Friedmans* (Andrew Jarecki, 2003), for example, the way the film contextualises the home mode images encourages the viewer to search for evidence of abuse, while in *Tarnation* (Jonathan Caouette, 2003) the viewer is invited to see the effects of mental illness reflected in the home mode. I search my family archive for the visual representations of the stories of diaspora and displacement.

The diaspora home movie does not represent a break or a radical rewriting of the form of home movies, but it does show significant shifts from the convention of the holiday film in its intentions and reception. As the quotation from Di Stefano at the start of this chapter suggests it is often the absent family member who makes the images to create the imagined 'connection' with the space of home or the connection with imagined space of 'home'. This replays certain power relations as suggested by Fung especially if the absent family member accesses resources of economic or social privilege through residence in the first world.

Diaspora home movies function as a social bridge, reaching across physical distances to perform basic familial functions, such as introducing a new baby, inviting the family over to see the new house, or acting as a alternative reunion. Sometimes, as discussed earlier, they document the trip home and the reunion with family moving through the transitory image of arrival or leaving. At other times they are like an animated Christmas card, going beyond the stasis of the still photographs circulated to absent family members, substituting for the presence that holidays demand. Of course they do all this while simultaneously coming up short: silent, two-dimensional images on the wall, flickering to a close, always ending too soon. These diasporic filmic envoys are always intended for an audience beyond the home, structured to address a different audience than that of the usual nuclear family home movie. The shift in the context of reception, points to the diaspora home movie as involving a divergence in the intentions of the family filmmaker, to address family across geographic divides. Here the destabilised notion of home links a variety of spaces where different family members now live into a common shared and imagined space: a virtual home created by home movie.

*

After I had written the initial draft of this essay I came across personal evidence to support this theory that my family's home movies were part of the intricate system of communications between the separated family members. I found a letter written from my maternal grandmother to my father to congratulate my parents on my birth. In this letter my grandmother describes having seen the first part of the reel I mentioned earlier in this essay, my brother and sister in the garden in Leyland. I wonder about the logistics of this ritual viewing; my grandmother probably had to borrow a neighbour's projector to watch the reel of film sent from abroad for viewing. Without a dedicated screen in the house, the images would have been projected against a wall. Home movies were not reproducible as still images and could not be kept in multiple spaces of the dispersed family, it would have to have been returned after viewing. This is a more precious and fragile ritual of image sharing than today's world of endlessly reproducible digital capture. This brings me spiralling around in a circle (although not by any means the proverbial 'full circle') to:

January 2008: I approach the pier in Port of Spain by boat, with a camera in my hand, as my uncle probably did over fifty years earlier. Through the viewfinder, the frame includes my mother in the foreground and the background of approaching new highrises climbing out of the building sites. I am documenting another moment of return. My mother has not been to Trinidad in over twenty years; she is coming back for a six-week break that will include her first sight of carnival since the 1962 celebration documented in the old home movie. The sea journey seems forced, more orchestrated for the video opportunity and its narrative significance than a documenting of a moment of homecoming. Of course we flew over the Atlantic; few people travel across by ship anymore, however poetic the visual metaphor may be for evoking the history of the 'black Atlantic'. The ship is only the short-hop ferry that brings us over from Tobago, where we arrived on the cheap tourist shuttle. We are a  modern diaspora family; our journeys are contingent rather than mythic (or tragic), our wanderings are economic migrations rather than enforced exiles, our homecomings are always tinged with the knowledge that home itself is not a stable space, but a shifting signifier, an uncertain place. Trinidad is no longer my mother's home and it never was mine. If Richard Fung felt discomfort in old family films where I have sought comfort, this is where my discomfort lies: the power of the image, laying over the sheen of professionalism what was once much more organic in the amateur mode.

If this seems like an inconclusive conclusion, it is. It may find some resolution in the documentary that will emerge from this process of research, thinking, writing, listening, looking, recording, filming and editing. Or it may remain the fragmented, incoherent and partial narrative that is the purview of the home movie, the autobiography and the experience of diaspora.

References

Chalfen, R. (1982) *Snapshot Versions of Life*. Bowling Green, OH: Bowling Green State University Popular Press.

Citron, M. (1999) *Home Movies and Other Necessary Fictions*. Minneapolis, MN: University of Minnesota Press.

Di Stefano, J. (2002) 'Moving Images of Home', *Art Journal*, 61, 4, 38–51.

Fung, R. (2008) 'Remaking Home Movies', in K. I. Ishizuka and P. R. Zimmermann (eds) *Mining the Home Movie: Excavations in Histories and Memories*. Berkeley, CA: University of California Press, 29–40.

Gates Jr, H. L. (1985) 'Writing "Race" and the Difference It Makes', in H. L. Gates Jr (ed.) *'Race', Writing and Difference*. Chicago, IL: University of Chicago Press 1–20.

Gilroy, P. (1993) *The Black Atlantic: Modernity and Double Consciousness*. London: Verso.

Glissant, E. (1989) *Caribbean Discourse*. Charlottesville: University of Virginia Press.

Hampl, P. (1996) 'Memories Movies', in C. Warren (ed.) *Beyond Document: Essays in Nonfiction Film*. Middletown, CT: Wesleyan University Press, 51–77.

Hirsch, M. (1997) *Family Frames: Photography, Narrative and Postmemory*. Cambridge, MA: Harvard University Press.

Kuhn, A. (1995) *Family Secrets: Acts of Memory and Imagination*. London: Verso.

Moran, J. M. (2002) *There's No Place Like Home Video*. Minneapolis: University of Minnesota Press.

Nicholson, H. N. (2002) 'Telling Travelers' Tales: The World through Home Movies', in T. Creswell and D. Dixon *Engaging Film: Geographies of Mobility and Identity*. London: Rowman and Littlefield, 47-66.

Odin, R. (2008) 'Reflections on the Family Home Movie as Document: A Semio-Pragmatic Approach', in K. I. Ishizuka and P. R. Zimmermann (eds) *Mining the Home Movie: Excavations in Histories and Memories*. Berkeley, CA: University of California Press, 255–71.

Paquet, S. P. (2002) *Caribbean Autobiography: Cultural Identity and Self-Representation*. Madison, WI: University of Wisconsin Press.

Urry, J. (1990) *The Tourist Gaze: Leisure and Travel in Contemporary Societies*. London: Sage.

Zimmermann, P. R. (1995) *Reel Families: A Social History of Amateur Film*. Bloomington: Indiana University Press.

'If I Am (Not) for Myself': Michelle Citron's Diasporic First Person(s)

Sophie Mayer

'If I am not for myself, who will be for me? If I am only for myself, what am I? If not now, when?'

Rabbi Hillel, Ethics of the Fathers 1:14

Taking its title from the quintessential summation of Jewish ethics by the first-century Babylonian scholar Rabbi Hillel, this essay argues that experimental filmmaker Michelle Citron – as a diasporic (Irish-American secular) Jew, as a feminist, as a lesbian, and as an incest survivor – experiments in order to find a documentary form in which she can be for her self but not only for herself. In an article entitled 'Fleeing from Documentary', she singles out a focal 'dynamic relationship [in her filmmaking] between the media work and the artist's life [...] the ethical dimension dwells' (1999: 273). Her most recent experimental documentary, *Mixed Greens* (2004), examines the ethical dimension occurring between the media work and the artist's life in terms of the relation between biographical self-representation and an autoethnography enlarged by the film-maker's multiple identities or identity positions. This polyvalence challenges the concept of the stable self propounded by first person documentary, but also foregrounds the multiple roles, responsibilities and communities attendant on such a diffused – or diasporic – identity. Moreover, the film investigates spe-cifically where this ethical dimension *dwells*, positing a series of interlocking and intersectional relations between the filmmaker's various identities (includ-ing as a filmmaker) and the domestic, erotic and political spaces in which they play out.

Specifically locating the definition of the self or selves in domestic space (and revealing domestic space as a microcosm of familial, institutional and national spaces), *Mixed Greens* asks how and whether first person documentary can put the 'I' in home by investigating how 'home' is constructed through home movies: as an overdetermined space; as an essentialised identity; and as a political category. Morevoer, it charts and counterpoints the development of the home movie and its (un)homely technologies from slide shows to digital. The ethics of border-crossing and refusal of the centre can be seen in Citron's choice to move across, and develop a multistrand media from, film and video in her early works via film theory (collected in *Home Movies and Other Necessary Fictions*, 1998) to Flash animation in order to articulate the unique intersection she represents and, through that articulation, to document the stories of familial, political and erotic others in such a way that they are not Other.

Distributed as a CD-ROM available from Citron's website, *Mixed Greens* consists of eight films moving from 1920s Dublin to twenty-first-century New York, which include 'straight' autobiographical documentary, fictionalised autobiography, staged video diaries and archive footage with narrative voice-over. Each film is broken down into eight chapters given thematic titles such as 'Heartbreak'. Chronologically, the first three films comprise a conventional documentary about Citron's father's Irish-Jewish family (archival documents and travel film with the filmmaker's voiceover combined with 'talking heads' interviews), while the last four present a history of lesbian America from 1950s butch to a twenty-first-century boi[1] through vignettes of fictional characters that use still photographs, Super 8 film, digital video and digital editing. The section that follows Citron's movement from Jewish working-class childhood to her discovery of feminist and lesbian identity acts as a transition, thematically and materially, drawing on Citron's own experience growing up and coming out, documented through home movies shot by her father and friends.

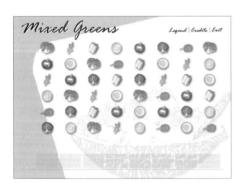

The CD-ROM's main menu (the 'Home' screen to which the viewer returns on each viewing, and from which she sets out) presents a matrix of vegetables: each vegetable represents one of the film strands, and a roll of the cursor reveals a thematic title beneath each vegetable icon. It is possible to watch a single film thread straight through, or to compose a 'film' structured around a single thematic, or to generate any number of 'films' based around randomly juxtaposed chapters. Discussing current 'feminist digital aesthetics', Caitlin Fisher notes the absence of projects that are invested in dismantling, in order to rethink, the potential for coherent, embodied first person identities: 'What is striking, given current feminist projects aimed at deconstructing identities and challenging even the building of narratives or bodies to inhabit, is the lack of critical framework offered by women constructing these [digital] archives' (2007: 151). Fisher suggests that the problem is that contemporary digital artists are unaware of second-wave feminist histories because they have not entered mainstream digital archives, or are insufficiently contextualised (2007: 156). Citron's *survey* of lesbian feminist life in America, which attests through its fragmentary form to its own subjective incompleteness, reinstates a context. By using performers, disembodied voiceovers, and witty pastiches of era-appropriate documentary forms, from the faded photographs tinted with the lurid colours of pulp novel covers for the 1950s to the screen-within-a-screen of the iPod video-like 'developing' Polaroid photographs for twenty-first century, Citron de-essentialises both female and lesbian identity.

Kurt Heintz notes in his review of the project that 'while a few of the clips were simple to compose, it's clear that such a disc requires mastery of production techniques and artistry in several genres and media. The scale of *Mixed Greens* is impressive in and of itself. *Mixed Greens* is thus a *tour de force* in new media, a masterwork that opens the many potentials of video, film and new media working in unison' (2005). The digital dimension of the project, conceived by Citron and created in collaboration with technical advisors, is fascinating in its implications for first person distribution as much as filmmaking. The digital matrix (never quite) containing photographs, film, video and text engages the ethical dimension between media and lived experience, between documentary as representation and critique. Mixing media acts reflexively to draw the viewer-user's attention to the project as a (composite) text, one in which she can intervene by ordering the narrative segments and switching on and off the textual commentary that appears in a frame onscreen. Bill Nichols' description of Frederick Wiseman's films applies equally to Citron's structuring paradigms, which 'imply a theory of the events they describe [that] assumes that social events have multiple causes and must be analysed as webs of interconnecting influences and patterns' (1981: 211–12). *Mixed Greens*' theoretical underpinnings may relate to digitality, but as in earlier documentary experiments, they are material and medium-specific.

Each viewing of the project can be different, destabilising documentary's (and home movies') association with singular identity and authentic memory. In *Shadows, Specters, Shards* (2005), Jeffrey Skoller considers the complex relations between identity, memory and history in avant-garde documentary, with a particular focus on documentaries redefining Jewish diasporic identities. He argues that the form has engaged in 'primary cultural studies research' and in so doing 'has extended the notion of personal expression as a form of modernist mythopoetic universalism toward the investigation of personal identity as socially constructed and historically situated' (2005: xxv). Following his study, I offer a close textual and material reading of the identity being 'socially constructed and historically situated' in *Mixed Greens*, rather than a biographical or psychoanalytic approach: Citron amply details her own negotiations with a psychoanalytic crasis of recovering memories of sexual abuse and teaching feminist film theory in her memoir *Home Movies and Other Necessary Fictions*. Through her obsession with role-playing a character called Dora (scenarios that become a screenplay for an unmade film called *Pandora*), Citron implies that psychoanalytic narratives of lack, castration and dissociation are 'necessary fictions'. She substitutes them with an imbrication of filmmaking and self-fashioning as processual and mutually constitutive. Watching a reel of film shot by her father, which appears in her film *Daughter Rite* (1979), Citron describes herself as a child performing for the camera, and instructing her sister to do the same. 'I am already a director', she comments, an identity that aligns her with the Father (1998: 4). Film, problematically, is by extension a home where, because of her femininity, she cannot be (for) herself on either side of the camera.

As Daniel Boyarin, Daniel Itzkovitz and Ann Pellegrini note in their introduction to *Queer Theory and the Jewish Question* (2003), femininity was doubly complicated by Jewish ethnicity in nineteenth-century Europe. The more demure a Jewish woman, the more she was seen to be performing to cover her excessive, depraved nature. Associated with the Orient's sensuality, 'the Jewess and the female sexual invert both shared ... their alleged excess; both types went beyond the bounds of female virtue and sexual propriety. [...] The manliness and self-promotion with which the female sexual invert was charged also featured in some of the stereotypes of the "Jewess", who was sometimes portrayed as pushy, unladylike in her entry into and activity in the world of paid labour' (Boyarin *et al.* 2003: 5). As the anthology indicates, these stereotypes persist (with a difference) into the twentieth century, most paradigmatically in the figure of Barbra Streisand. Cinema, like paid work, excludes the Jewess and female invert as agents: as performers, both figures must adopt an excessive femininity that is 'all show, a cover for femininity's failure', while taking on the role of the director clearly summons accusations of 'manliness and self-promotion' (2003: 6).

In taking on the role of filmmaker, Citron also makes visible the equivalence of Jewess and lesbian as being manly and excessive. In the most directly auto-biographical section of *Mixed Greens*, which repeats some material from *Home Movies*, there is only one segment in which Citron speaks directly about film-making: she remembers using the women's bathroom at her faculty in 1970, and seeing that someone has graffiti'd a poster for a forthcoming screening that includes her films. The poster is entitled 'Women's Films' but the graffitist has crossed out 'Women's' and supplemented 'Kike's' [*sic*], noting beneath that '*Playboy*'s unabashed dictionary defines Jewish lesbian as Kyke Dyke [*sic*].' The graffitist implies that all women filmmakers are Jews and/because all Jewish women are (rhymingly) lesbian. 'Kike' and 'dyke' imply each other.

The camera tracks slowly up the poster (which Citron must have taken down and kept as a souvenir) as Citron drily narrates the story in voiceover. She does not, however, read what has been written in purple caps, simply pausing both narration and camera movement to let the viewer read. In that moment, the viewer is interpellated into Citron's experience of reading the words, confronted with the charge of 'Kyke Dyke' that *Mixed Greens* turns from fearful dismissal into critical thinking. The poster acts proleptically as a poster for *Mixed Greens* itself as the film of a kike dyke that asks: if a Jewish lesbian cannot make a film about herself, then who can? And if she makes a film only about her self (those selves, as they interconnect and/or cancel each other out), then what is she? *Mixed Greens* turns the slippery, unstable, masculine, emasculating quandary of the invert Jewess into home territory. Rather than seeking to separate the terms in order to protest the graffitist's condemnation, Citron's work disentangles the implications of their pairing by interweaving them.

Mixed Greens suggests that it might be more appropriate to speak of 'first persons' documentary, as the format both integrates and dis-integrates claims to holistic identity. It fulfils Citron's own precept that the 'honest autobiographical film or video publicly speaks about the socially hidden. [...] This is the implicit threat that autobiography poses to the status quo. As a culture, we have been little able to tolerate the truth of the variety of lived experience: that truth threatens the social order' (1999: 272). Even as it does so, it suggests further that the 'implicit threat that autobiography poses', in intersectional feminist terms, is the instability and/or multiplicity of identity, exactly 'the variety of lived experience' as it accrues to the idea of 'first person'. When Judith Butler revoked her conception of the performative in *Undoing Gender*, she argued that 'gender undoes the "I" who is supposed to be or bear its gender, and that undoing is part of the very meaning and comprehensibility of that "I"' (2004: 16). *Mixed Greens* works along axes of gender, sexuality, ethnicity, nationality and age to undo, and thus give 'meaning and comprehensibility' to the 'I'.

The first person of the documentarist is embedded in each section: diegetically present as an interviewing voice or as voiceover and non-diegetically as a teasing, sardonic series of footnotes that appear in a text screen below the image screen. These notes, which often offer playfully politicised definitions of terms mentioned in the voice track, such as 'feminist' and 'gender', can be switched off; optional and contradictory, they act as neither anchor nor relay, in Roland Barthes' terms, but as *supplément*, in Jacques Derrida's. Figured as an excess that defines lack, this supplemental commentary – which could perhaps be seen as echoing Mishnaic practice, albeit with a sardonic twist – also figures the problematic first person in Citron's first person documentary as *supplément*, the author/auteur whose existence we are supposed to do without, the constructed subject whose authenticity guarantees the film. The idea of the supplemental also resonates with Trinh T. Minh-Ha's concept of the interval as a productive model for reading claims to authenticity, which accounts for the fact that 'what is put forward as truth is often nothing more than a meaning. And what persists between the meaning of something and its truth is the interval, a break without which meaning would be fixed and truth congealed' (1990: 77).

Mixed Greens takes place in the space between kike and dyke, questioning both terms' definitional stability by placing them in a relation that generates polyvalence. The film shifts the definition of lesbian through multiple media that make lesbian history visible while refusing mainstream lesbian visibility, in tune with Amy Villarejo's figuration of the lesbian as excess in visual culture. Villarejo asserts that *lesbian*, as an adjective, operates as a catachresis, and focuses her study on the lesbian *in*-visibility in documentaries such as Ulrike Ottinger's *Exile, Shanghai* (1997), another documentary in which Jewish diasporic and lesbian feminist identities are held in tense relation. Writing about the apparent absence of Ottinger's lesbian identity in her exploration of the Jewish community in Shanghai, Villarejo notes that the 'lesbian filmmaker encounters this fabric [of larger discourses of nation and religion] as her archive and records her impression of its texture. The history this lesbian filmmaker confronts is, moreover, inextricable from the *politics* of memory, the ethical necessity for witness' (2003: 97). Villarejo argues that one aspect of the adjectival or catachrestic lesbian is an attention to what is obscured or absented, and to the necessity of witnessing. Drawing on Derrida's work on archives, she further suggests 'the particularly pressing link between Jewishness and memory' in light of the *Shoah* (2003: 98).

Citron's project is not only committed to a medium-specific redefinition of what is obscured by 'lesbian visibility'. It mingles archival documentation, interviews and poetic travelogues to recover the absent history of Irish work-ing-class Jewishness associated with her father. As an amateur filmmaker, he is Citron's model for her self-definition, but *Mixed Greens* both relocates him from behind the home movie camera, and negates the necessity of the film-maker as structuring absence. In *Mixed Greens* the relation is reversed, with Citron's father and surviving relatives appearing onscreen to weave a memorial to an absent figure: a relative who was Michael Collins' only Jewish lieutenant. It is an alternate, and often-forgotten, micro-history of European (and later, Euro-American) Jews whose involvement in a history of violence and self-determination distinct from the *Shoah* 'work[s] to cast a side-shadow on the dominant narrative of twentieth-century Jewish life as catastrophe' (Skoller 2005: xl). Its difference is dual: according to Cecil Roth, the 'Dublin [Jewish] community is in a category by itself geographically, chronologically and eth-nographically, for – alone in the British Isles, outside London – it dates back to the seventeenth century and the major share in its early history was taken by Sephardim' (1950). Citron's alter-ego Dora states that her grandmother's grandparents were Sephardic, and thus distinct from the primarily Ashkenazi Eastern European immigrants to the United States, and particularly the North-East where Citron grew up, where her family was culturally positioned between – and excluded by – both the working-class Irish community and the upwardly-mobile Ashkenazis (1998: 55). In the context of post-9/11 politics, the Citrons' story also challenges definitions of the terms 'activist', 'freedom fighter' and 'terrorist' within both anti-colonial and Jewish contexts. To be a Jew fighting, in solidarity with Catholics, against the colonial power suggests productive affinities with Jewish groups working in solidarity with Palestinians for peace in the Middle East today.

Jewish anti-racist campaigner Melanie Kaye/Kantrowitz identifies the possibility of such affinities, created by recognising the diversity of Jewish experience and identity – particularly embracing Jews of colour and queer Jews – as 'Radical Diasporism', which 'rep-resents tension, resistance to both assimilation and nostalgia, to both corporate globalisation ... and to nationalism' (Kaye/Kantrowitz 2007: xii). Such a radical resistance runs in parallel with Villarejo's lesbian catachresis, as an alternate form of visibility through affinity and intersectionality. Kaye/Kantrowitz projects a history produced by such a politics that is suggestive of both Citron's canny title – calling up the idea of the American 'melting pot'-cum-'salad bowl' – for *Mixed Greens*, and the way in which her interface supports and is informed by feminist calls for non-linear, non-singular histories, through which a 'different pattern of Jewish history emerges. Mix, separate, mix, separate. Each mixing a change so that when time for separation comes around, what separates out is not the same. [...] Or in the language of Jewish aspiration, ingather, wander, ingather, wander' (2007: 98–9). Citron's film follows both her family, and her renewed attention to family history, through its non-linear wandering and ingathering. Her ingathering, which posits two simultaneous 'family' structures between which she is the slash – Irish-Jewish/American-lesbian – concurs with Kaye/Kantrowitz's claim that 'Radical Diasporism ... meshes well with feminism ... and suits queerness, in rejecting the constraints of traditional gendered existence' (2007: xiii).

John Durham Peters, considering 'the stakes of mobility in the Western canon', cites Daniel and Jonathan Boyarin's radical argument for diaspora as a 'mission' (in Gershom Scholem's term), an invitation to hybridity that undermines essentialised identities related to home (1999: 38). For Peters, 'diaspora teaches the perpetual postponement of homecoming and the necessity, in the meanwhile, of living among strange lands and strange peoples' (1999: 39). He associates this with cinema's utopian potential for fantasies of meeting and moving on. The CD-ROM creates a diasporic form of both active spectatorship and first person documentary, in which the filmmaker's self is constantly moving in response to the viewer's input. This suggests a productive redefinition of the problematic of home as a space associated with familial hierarchies and screened narratives: as film becomes diasporic (non-linear, co-authored), it opens a space for the feminist lesbian filmmaker; through such a movie, home itself can be rendered diasporic, encompassing lesbian parents, polyamorous households and mixed-race couples.

In the final section of *Home Movies*, Citron offers just such a spatial metaphor for her experiments in home-making movies:

This also is a story of my love of film. Of images that spoke in the absence of words, and celluloid that storehoused feelings as long as the emotions surrounding the incest ... contaminated all feelings. Unable to penetrate the wall of amnesia, I constructed images from the elements of my craft – actors, spaces, and light – and projected them onto a wall, *the* wall, to hint at what it obscured. And slowly the beam of light burned peepholes through that wall to reveal what lurked behind it, although I sometimes suspect that the secrets were merely the motivation, while the films, themselves, were the real thing revealed. (1998: 137–8)

The metaphor that she uses to describe filmmaking is equally revealing. It conflates production and projection, and locates both of them within a series of suggestive spaces: a storehouse, a walled room with peepholes. These architectural metaphors run through the book: the storehouse with its walls inscribes a filmic architecture of self that is modelled on, through and against the family home. This resonates with Annette Kuhn's reading of 'films in the autobiographical' as 'memory-texts' in *Family Secrets: Acts of Memory and Imagination* (1995) as well as Frances Yates' argument in *The Art of Memory* from 1966 for the architecturality of personal and cultural memory. Citron's films *are* homes, mnemonic architectures, in which she locates her self through intersecting gendered, ethnic, national and sexual identities.

Home, the politically-overdetermined site of the conservative family and the cinematically-overdetermined site of linear narratives of that same family, is reconceived in Citron's experimental practice as formally and narratively queer; this is 'the real thing revealed'. In its interlocking architectural and political senses, home is, and is used representationally as, a technology for the production of self, particularly for women. Home is also a resistant site of amateur and artisanal production, as in the title of *The Home Movie Maker's Handbook*. These movies, as Chuck Kleinhans argues in 'My Aunt Alice's Home Movies' (1986) both reference and refute dominant formal and narrative models. Patricia Zimmermann, in the same 'Home Movies' special issue of *Journal of Film and Video* draws attention to the similarities and disparities between films authored within the family for family viewing and another group of 'home made movies', as J. Hoberman entitles his influential study of the artisanal products of the American avant-garde. Zimmermann goes on specifically to critique Citron's *Daughter Rite* as an avant-garde film using home movies, arguing that 'one is asked by the structure of [the film] to fit the parts together', as if it were flat-pack furniture rather than ready-assembled (1986: 91). She is further troubled by the lack of 'a silent space in which the reworked home footage is in itself articulate and suggestive' (ibid.). Citron's film is, in Zimmermann's reading, neither an amateur home movie nor an avant-garde blueprint for a new kind of home.

By grouping Citron's film with work by Maya Deren and Stan Brakhage, Zimmermann misses the distinction by which home *cannot* be a 'silent space' in which *Citron herself* cannot be 'articulate and suggestive', for reasons of gender, class, ethnicity and personal history. *Home Movies and Other Necessary Fictions* sets out to explore the necessary noise generated by the (dis)assembly of *Daughter Rite*. It begins as a critical study of Citron's father's home movies, and of the patriarchal project (an angle missing from Zimmermann's account) of home cinematography, particularly the paradoxical and polyvalent nature of 'home movies' as they elide public and private, production and reception, event and memory. Home, as she describes in *Home Movies*, both screens and is screened in her family's home movies. 'Screening' is dual: on the one hand, a cinematic material practice in which family gathers to observe and re-narrate itself, focusing on generating memories, implicitly setting the generation of memories of an American life against the vacuum of pre-emigration documentation, and the larger memory vacuum of the *Shoah*. On the other, 'screening' creates and perpetuates such a memory vacuum through the selection of events shot, projected and incorporated into the family's self-defining repertoire of cultural memories. As Citron details movingly, the movies themselves build a home; one that, reflecting dominant media images, displays normative gendered behaviours. The movie camera edits out not only a generational history of sexual abuse, but also poverty, illness and domestic violence.

Mary Ann Doane reads exactly these elisions in the home as a trope of spectatorship and/as *mise-en-scène* in the woman's film, suggesting that 'one could formulate a veritable topography of spaces within the home' depicted in the woman's film, as the female character and domestic space are mapped onto one another (1987: 287). Doane is particularly interested in the 'places which elude the eye', the locked rooms that recur in what she terms 'the paranoid woman's film' in which the husband's house is always Bluebeard's Castle (ibid.). She implies that these elusive places are metonymic for the way in which dominant cinema denies both vision and representation to women, with the house taking the place of the self. The 'paranoid woman's film', while a minor genre most famously exemplified in *Rebecca* (Alfred Hitchcock, 1940) and elaborated in a sequence of postwar American films that Mark Jancovich (2007) argues includes *The Heiress* (William Wyler, 1949), is read as paradigmatic of the operations of classical narrative cinema in which, to quote Doane, 'the house becomes an analogue of the human body, its parts fetishised by textual operations' (1987: 288).

Citron's family history and the films discussed by Doane coincide historically and geographically in postwar America. In *Homeward Bound*, Elaine Tyler May writes that the 'legendary family of the 1950s ... was the first wholehearted effort to create a home that would fulfil virtually all its members' personal needs through an energised and expressive personal life' (1990: 11). Paula Rabinowitz quotes May's insight apropos her reading of television documentary *An American Family* (1973), in which 'the residents of [the family home] are what give it meaning' (1994: 143). The socio-political ideology of the nuclear family haunts the family/house that Citron builds and explodes through her work. Yet it would be possible to invert Rabinowitz's claim: the family is defined, as Mark Wigley (1992) has argued, by the architectural space that they inhabit. Likewise, Citron's cinematic and digital experimentation provides an alternative 'house' shaping both identity and relationality differently, for filmmaker and spectator.

Citron's critical memoir engages with the concentric yet interlocking circles of home as they move outwards from the self through the family to the nation-state and beyond. For Citron, home is triply problematic and unstable, and destabilising of the self: for her as a woman, as a diasporic Jew and as an incest survivor. Home is precisely the spatial and conceptual point at which readings of immigrant narratives and incest narratives can be laid over one another, as home is both the literal and symbolic space being defined and deconstructed (see Levy 2002). This raises the question of whether the filmmaker's eye can be inside as well as looking inside. The question of the observer as insider/outsider has been widely addressed in anthropology and in studies of ethnographic film, but Citron's stance is unique in that she brings together not only the diasporic and domestic, as well as the aesthetic and the critical, but also the amateur and the experimental – reasserting the avant-garde home movie practice to which Hoberman attests in *Home Made Movies* (1981).

Citron writes that 'home movies offer a fiction of the family that reinforces what they want to know about themselves and sanctions a public view of a most private space: the home' (1998: 14). Describing the house where she grew up, she overlays the tension of public and private onto the house itself: 'The backstairs were a passage, used by no one but us, that linked the two apartments in both space and secrets' (1998: 130). In her topography, Doane identifies the staircase as 'the passageway to "the image of the worst" or "screen of the worst"' (1987: 288). This is literalised in Citron's account, although her topography is differently inflected by class than the grand staircase of *Rebecca*. In Citron's apartment building in a working-class suburb of Boston, the backstairs are supposedly a public space, but they are coded by use as private, used only by the family, and enabling Citron's grandfather to commit incest unseen. The connection of secrets and spaces alludes to the ways in which Citron's project is to *spatialise*, and thus visualise, these secrets as a 'home movie', in the sense of a film that lays bare the home, could render secret spaces visible. *Home Movies* has its own unique textual architecture, which includes an image track of single frames from the father's home movies, sometimes running parallel to the text and sometimes in page corners creating a 'flick book'. This works similarly to the optical printing in *Daughter Rite*, and is very different from the traditional use of stills to illustrate specific points in a theoretical book or essay. The 'flick book' film becomes a text on a par with the essay, rather than being its subject.

Through the inclusion of these images, the book also explores a milieu of 1950s domesticity that representationally and affectively resonates with the domestic melodramas discussed in *Home is Where the Heart Is*. Domestic space is strongly gendered – not least in its role as profilmic space for Citron's father's home movies. She describes the space behind the camera occupied by her father as a kind of space 'off', an outside to representation and an escape from a home dominated by women. Throughout *Home Movies*, she investigates her own compulsion to take up the father's position behind the lens. She describes a moment in which, rewatching the home movie footage, she observes her father filming the family, and reads a complicity with the camera/Father in her filmed behaviour: 'do I want to become him [her father] simply because I desire to stand outside the scene – in the space of safety behind the glass wall of the lens, where I can't be touched?' (1998: 6) Writing in Dora's persona, Citron later notes that 'By cutting I hoped to carve a small keyhole between the inside and the outside' (1998: 32). In context, 'cutting' is the delicate cutting of self-harm that designates the body as an architecture of apertures. When isolated from the narrative, the reference to 'cutting' enacts a triangulation in which each term can stand for the other: body, house, film. 'Cutting' film therefore becomes a psychic cry, a way of opening the locked doors in the house and body. Citron names the glass wall behind which she hides, and that which had been hidden behind the glass wall, when she says that: 'Incest gives us a window onto experiences we all have' (1998: 30). In translating the experience of dissociation – being behind the window – into filmmaking, Citron turns the symptom into a cure. Home, in its condensation of meanings, acts as an optic for Citron: a window or keyhole with a view into the self.

Doane writes that in the woman's film, 'the window is the interface between inside and outside, the feminine space of the family and reproduction and the masculine space of production. [...] That interface becomes a potential point of violence, intrusion and aggression' (1987: 288). Mapped onto the act of making home movies, the window or keyhole as aperture or lens is both the site of the violence of sexual difference and a potential point of its reversal. *Home Movies* causes the viewer to look again at *Daughter Rite* and see in it the triangulation

of body/house/film, and to see the formal play as a series of 'cutting' strategies
leaving marks on the surface of the text
that allude to struggle beneath. Citron
writes that '*Daughter Rite* is a movie of
my family's home that incorporates my
family's home movies,' including several movies her father made showing
'private and banal domestic events: my
sister and I cleaning house', for example (1998: 16). *Daughter Rite* draws on

these images of domesticity in order to challenge their production of a gendered self, in which the Father controls the means of production.

Despite *Daughter Rite*'s formal radicalism, critics such as B. Ruby Rich have
noted the willingness, and even desire, of female viewers to read the film's three
strands – the *vérité* documentary about the sisters clearing out their mother's
house; the optically printed, looped home movies; and the voiceover recounting
dreams and conversations about and with the narrator's mother – as forming a
single narrative. Viewers often located it strictly within the confessional mode
that organises the triangle of woman, house, body as authenticators, perhaps
not least because the *vérité*'s maternal domestic *mise-en-scène* seems to correspond to the narrator's repeated anxiety over her mother's impractical housing
choices. Running under this narration, several of the reels of 8mm home movies show the mother and daughters moving outside the home: in the street, in
a park, on a boating lake. The camera domesticates these spaces, as if the presence of the central figures – mother and daughters – linked all the locations
through the trace of home that they carry in their bodies, and through their
connection to the observing camera.

This domestication is partially produced by the implicit domestic site of
original exhibition. Citron persuasively argues that, far from there being a
crasis of meaning produced by the mirroring of home as *mise-en-scène* and
screen, the producing/exhibiting home is a site for the production of complex
and multiple readings of the films: 'The meaning of home images is in constant
flux. This is due, in part, to the fact that we provide a second track, either stories
or memories, at the moment of viewing. By doing so we fuse the present tense
of viewing to the past tense of recording. Time folds back on itself. Two places
on the timeline of our life meet. In this moment of superimposition, a space is
created from which insight can arise. This is the latent hope in all home movies' (1998: 23). *Daughter Rite* creates this fold through the dual relationships
between the two image tracks, and between the image and voice tracks.

Mixed Greens' interactive CD-ROM multiplies the dualities but also the available identities meeting between past and present, and thus the spaces 'from which insight can arise'. In particular, it develops *Home Movies'* enunciation of Citron's lesbian identity and goes beyond it. Unfolding the changing history of lesbian America, it destabilises the heteronormative family home and also the idea of a 'home' identity in which a person resides. Both formally and narratively, it acts to queer home and to show queer homes, specifically producing these spaces through digital technology to offer a new home for an emergent self. The use of Flash extends the formal experimentation of *Daughter Rite's* optical printing and *Home Movie's* textualised filmstrips. This is underlined by the way in which the family history segments remediate documentary images

from nineteenth-century etchings and photographs of Jewish Dublin through 8mm home movies to twenty-first-century digital video.

Each of the lesbian histories is presented in a quasi- or faux documentary form that recalls home movie practices of the 1950s, 1960s to 1970s, 1990s and right up to today. These pastiches reflexively situate visual technology in women's hands, and make them crucial to the production of not only lesbian selves, but a virtual lesbian community. Beginning with still images of a secret butch/femme gathering outside a clapboard house in the 1950s, the sequences move through a series of spatial relations that brings lesbianism close(r) to home. In the 1960s, two women write love letters to each other, one eventually leaving her husband to set up home with her girlfriend. Super 8-style films give impressionistic glimpses of the emergent lesbian home, from babysitting through all-female parties, ending when one woman enjoys erotic encounters without her partner in the tents of a womyn's music festival.[2] The 1990s are heralded by digital video diaries, in which a lesbian couple (one of whom is the daughter of the 1960s couple) record their lives as a gift for their adoptive daughter, who is about to enter their lives. The camera has become a member of the family within a specifically lesbian, urban middle-class but mixed-race domestic space; in fact, it stands in apostrophically for the adoptive child. The camera is placed before the sofa in the traditional site of the television, mapping home production onto exhibition but also critically remarking the televisual familiarity of images of lesbian mothering, post-*Queer as Folk* (UK 1999–2000; US 2000–05).

The final sequence enacts Citron's loving critique of parents-to-be Isabel and Sara. A cute boi holds up images to the screen, including the couple's newspaper wedding announcement. The boi, who has been kicked out of the house by her father, speaks approvingly of Isabel and Sara's partnership, but with resentment of their bourgeois lifestyle. In other segments of her story, she holds up Polaroids that develop to show images of her previous partners. In one of these, a long-haired woman sits up in bed, blinking softly. The moment's poignant reference to Chris Marker's *La Jetée* (1962) underlines the lack of visible domestic *mise-en-scène* in the boi's film. The genderqueer teen's domestic displacement is briefly tinged with the temporal displacement of Marker's anti-hero. While her familial exclusion suggests the circle has turned back to the repressive fear of the 1950s, her facility with technology as the production of subjectivity (rather than being subject to it) suggests emergent identities very different from the 'passing' and married femmes of the 1950s. The Polaroids not only bring home within the frame (rather than home being the frame) by depicting her partners' domestic spaces, but imply that cinematic technology

is the space in which she locates her identity. Movies (and attendant digital visual media) have become home.

Technology also provides the link between the familial documentary and the lesbian histories as Citron reflects on her own lesbian trajectory in the hinge section. The woman on whom Citron had an unspoken crush (Z.), and who re-introduces Citron to filmmaking, films Citron and her fiancé (C.) shortly before their wedding. It is an intertextual moment, also described in *Home Movies*: 'Z. stands behind a spring-wound Bolex shooting her final project for the film course she's taking … in one shot, Z., now behind my father's home movie camera, captures C. and me in a lovey-dovey kiss' (1998: 126). Citron describes this playful day of filmmaking in which the camera passes from being the father's, to being Michelle's as she shoots her first-ever footage, to being used by Z., the woman she has a crush on. Finally, she remediates the clip in *Mixed Greens* – and situates the shot of her kissing C., her fiancé, in the context of her developing erotic interest in women. Through the use of home movies to bridge diasporic family history and a lesbian genealogy, this remediation argues that more than an appropriation of the master's tools, there is an inscription of filmic technology itself as inherently domestic, emphasising the *home* in home movies.

Indeed, each strand is organised around homes, beginning historically with Citron's archival research in Dublin as a locus of authenticity and origin. This ancestral site, whose economic instability is reflected in the increas-

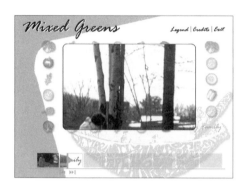

ingly secularised names of her father's family (from Zitron to Citron, the Z. reincorporated in the initial by which she refers to her lost/first love), is connected to her childhood home. Rather than using her father's footage here, Citron returns to the Boston home with her camera (and specifically looks for the shared staircase), thus formally linking this segment in which she documents her own history with her footage of a research trip to Dublin.

The identification of woman as home is subverted here by the historical negotiation of diasporic identity which is set in the political context of Home Rule and Irish self-determination – the home of 'homeland' – a subtext portending both to the *Shoah* and to the Israel/Palestine conflict. This section, particularly through highly critical text screens defining diasporic identities and critiquing racism, intersects the personal and political meanings of home.

By inserting film into the home through exhibition and production, the 'I' in film finds itself in home, making a new word – perhaps the Yiddish *haim*. Movies become homes, with an architecture grounded in Citron's spatialised

poetics. These homes are conceived through a command of technology that parallels the feminist appropriation of labour and space which Citron documented through women working in traditionally male jobs in her documentary *What You Take For Granted...* (1983). Citron writes: 'I create melodramatic films that put the audiences into their bodies, memories and lives. [...] Where the audience and I meet in the emotional space shaped by the film, a kind of intimacy lives' (1998: 70). As in melodrama, that emotional space is a homely one, one that is located in 'bodies, memories and lives' by its femininity and its feminism, by being working class and middle class, by being Irish *and* Jewish *and* American. Citron thus works like the essayists collected in

Annette Kuhn and Kirsten Emiko McAllister's *Locating Memory*, to 'literally locate – *place* – the images in the social world, bringing them "to life" … [tracing] the movement of the images across time as they pass between family and community members and between different audiences, accruing meaning and affect even as details of names and places begin to fade' (Kuhn and McAllister 2007: 1).

Bringing images from her own life (in several senses) 'to life', Citron also allows them 'to work' in the double sense of making them do the kind of critical work described by Kuhn and McAllister, and foregrounding them as signifiers of the intersection of her life/works. Choosing to provide the voiceover, Citron apparently defers her on-screen first person (lesbian) presence while the co-incident construction of sections of any Irish-Jewish storyline next to any lesbian-American storyline will reveal otherwise, paralleling 'Jewish' and 'lesbian' as excessive, destabilising identities. What does it mean to mix, and remix, your greens? In a playful word jumble, Citron exhorts us to engage in the mixed *genres* that allow for the multi-valent articulation of a self that is simultaneously multiple – for herself and not only for herself. First person singular documentary, through its summoning and (de)con-structuring of the pluralities that constitute the 'I', intersects both historical and contemporary communities, opening them out towards each other.

Acknowledgement

All images are from Michelle Citron, *Mixed Greens* (2004), by kind permission of the filmmaker.

Note

1 'Boi' is a contemporary variant on and beyond butch, used to refer to – among other identities – a younger, non-femme identified lesbian; a young transman; and/or a female-born or female-bodied person who does not identify wholly as female or feminine.
2 'Womyn' was the preferred spelling by some second-wave feminists so as to indicate a status independent rather than derivative of men.

References

Boyarin, D., D. Itzkovitz and A. Pellegrini (2003) 'Strange Bedfellows: An Introduction', in D. Boyarin, D. Itzkovitz and A. Pellegrini (eds) *Queer Theory and the Jewish Question*. New York, NY: Columbia University Press, 1–18.
Butler, J. (2004) *Undoing Gender*. London: Routledge.

Citron, M. (1998) *Home Movies and Other Necessary Fictions*. Minneapolis, MN: University of Minnesota Press.

___ (1999) 'Fleeing from Documentary: Autobiographical Film/Video and the "Ethics of Responsibility"', in D. Waldman and J. Walker (eds) *Feminism and Documentary*. Minneapolis, MN: University of Minnesota Press, 271–86.

Doane, M. A. (1987) 'The "Woman's Film": Possession and Address', in C. Gledhill (ed.) *Home Is Where the Heart Is: Studies in Melodrama and the Woman's Film*. London: British Film Institute, 283–98.

Fisher, C. (2007) 'Feminist Digital Aesthetics: The Everyday and Yesterday', in J. Marchessault and S. Lord (eds) *Fluid Screens, Expanded Cinema*. Toronto: University of Toronto Press, 145–59.

Heintz, K. (2005) 'Citron's *Mixed Greens* Premieres at the Chicago Siskel Center', *E-Poets Network*. On-line. Available: www.e-poets.net/newswire/news-2005-06.shtml (21 November 2010).

Hoberman, J. (1981) *Home Made Movies: Twenty Years of 8mm and Super 8 Film*. New York, NY: Anthology Film Archives.

Jancovich, Mark (2007) 'Crack-Up: Psychological Realism, Generic Transformation and the Demise of the Paranoid Woman's Film', *Irish Journal of Gothic and Horror Studies*, 3. Online. Available: http://irishgothichorrorjournal.homestead.com/Crack-upJancovich.html (21 November 2010).

Kaye/Kantrowitz, M. (2007) *The Colors of Jews: Racial Politics and Radical Diasporism*. Bloomington, IN: Indiana University Press.

Kleinhans, C. (1986) 'My Aunt Alice's Home Movies', *Journal of Film and Video*, 38, 3/4, 25–35.

Kuhn, A. (1995) *Family Secrets: Acts of Memory and Imagination*. London: Verso.

Kuhn, A., and K. E. McAllister (2007) 'Locating Memory: An Introduction', in A. Kuhn and K. E. McAllister (eds) *Locating Memory: Photographic Acts*. Oxford: Berghahn, 1–17.

Levy, S. (2002) '"This dark echo calls him home": Reading father-daughter incest narratives in Canadian immigrant fiction', *University of Toronto Quarterly*, 77, 4, 864–80.

May, E. T. (1990) *Homeward Bound: American Families in the Cold War Era*. New York, NY: Basic Books.

Nichols, B. (1981) *Ideology and the Image: Social Representation in the Cinema and Other Media*. Bloomington, IN: Indiana University Press.

Peters, J. D. (1999) 'Exile, Nomadism, and Diaspora: The Stakes of Mobility in the Western Canon', in H. Naficy (ed.) *Home, Exile, Homeland: Film, Media, and the Politics of Place*. London: Routledge, 17–41.

Rabinowitz, P. (1994) *They Must Be Represented: The Politics of Documentary*. London: Verso.

Roth, C. (1950) *The Rise of Provincial Jewry*. The Susser Archive. On-line. Available: www.jewish-gen.org/jcr-uk/susser/provincialjewry/index.htm (21 November 2010).

Skoller, J. (2005) *Shadows, Specters, Shards: Making History in Avant-Garde Film*. Minneapolis, MN: University of Minnesota Press.

Trinh T. M. (1990) 'Documentary Is/Not a Name', *October*, 52, 76–98.

Villarejo, A. (2003) *Lesbian Rule: Cultural Criticism and the Value of Desire*. Durham, NC: Duke University Press.

Wigley, M. (1992) 'Untitled: The Housing of Gender', in B. Colomina (ed.) *Sexuality and Space*. Princeton, NJ: Princeton Architectural Press, 327–89.

Yates, Frances (2001 [1966]) *The Art of Memory*. Chicago, IL: University of Chicago Press.

Zimmermann, Patricia (1986) 'The Amateur, the Avant-Garde, and Ideologies of Art', *Journal of Film and Video*, 38, 3/4, 63–92.

The Camera as Peripatetic Migration Machine

Alisa Lebow

El gusanito va paseando
y en el pastito va dibujando un dibujito
que es igualito al gusanito.

– Jorge de la Vega[1]

When UCLA film professor Teshome Gabriel went back to his native Ethiopia, after a 32-year absence, he armed himself with all manner of 'memory aids' – a video camera, a still camera and a miniature tape recorder – none of which he could bear to use once he actually arrived at his mother's home. For him the technology, or rather the urge to use it, required a kind of outsiderness, a distanced vantage point from which to document – something he felt sure he had acquired in his years in the US, but when the time came to put his detached positionality to the test, he realised it had not been fully achieved. His self-professed lack of critical distance coupled with his desire to experience the full range of emotion available, translated into an inability to shoot. Moreover, the camera was deemed 'superfluous' – an unnecessary supplement, or as he calls it, 'a prosthesis' – which was incapable of capturing the nuances of the interactions or the mood; too inflexible to perceive the shifting parameters of the situation (Gabriel 1999: 76–7).

Argentine filmmaker Andrés Di Tella also arms himself with a camera, complete with crew, for his much-postponed visit to his mother's native India. In his film, *Fotografías* (2007, see Di Tella's own discussion of his film in this volume), he seems eager to have the camera serve as a kind of shield, a defence against the onslaught of emotions sure to arise in the encounter with his departed mother's family and culture, about which he knew precious little prior to his visit. The outsiderness that Gabriel insists would be necessary in order to document the scene is something Di Tella has in abundance. He confesses in the film that he is not only utterly uninformed about his Indian heritage, but that he is unsure whether he wants to know more. This is, of course, a dissimulation, the first of many in this complex film, which goes on to explore his Indian heritage in some detail. Nevertheless, and despite the camera crew and their requisite 'outsiderness', Di Tella's camera still manages to miss the salient details and meaningful encounters, or so claims the filmmaker in voiceover. Everything relevant seems to be happening when the camera is not rolling, a common enough frustration, but one that also points to the inflexibility or superfluity of the camera indicated in Gabriel's account.

For Gabriel, the urge to record the encounter via the filmic apparatus was a sign of his Westernisation and thus the inability to do so in the moment of encounter served as welcome evidence for him of the incomplete project of that identity formation. It was with great relief that this well-known Third World intellectual found that he had not been utterly subsumed by the cultural values he had spent a career critiquing. However, his inability to shoot is a highly atypical response. The three filmmakers whose work I discuss in this essay do not by any means experience the same paralysis with regard to the filmic apparatus. They all shoot, sometimes prodigiously, though to varying degrees the camera may indeed prove itself inadequate, as Gabriel warned, and may even serve as a kind of prosthesis at moments. Prosthesis or otherwise, it nonetheless emerges as a necessary accessory to the treatment of the subject at hand: family diaspora and migration.

The film camera and other related recording devices have been used by individuals and families to document the massive cultural and geographical shifts experienced around the world for decades. This is not to say that all migrations are documented. There are, of course, millions upon millions of undocumented migrations, even more than undocumented migrants. It is, relatively speaking, still a privilege to have the means to document one's journeys across borders – both legally and economically – and not coincidentally, those with the privilege to document are usually also those privileged with documents. Uncommon and class-based as the phenomenon may be, in those cases where motion picture self-documentation accompanies the movement of bodies across borders, that very act of videotaping (or filming as the case may be) has come to be thoroughly integrated into the migratory experience.[2] In fact it is my contention that this act of cine-documentation has particular effects of its own, even propelling some of these seismic geographcal shifts as it appears to simply record them. I am inspired by the image conjured by the epigraph to this piece, which suggests that the movement or flow of life leaves a visible trace that is art, and that art simultaneously propels the movement of life. The lyric is from a famous, semi-hallucinogenic Argentinian children's song (much like the English-language song *Puff the Magic Dragon*) from the 1960s, featured prominently in Di Tella's film. In essence it reminds us that the trail left by life's movements is not only artifact but art; and that the image is not a mere reflection of life but also gives momentum to and is catalytic of that life.

The three films discussed in this essay, *Fotografías* (Andres Di Tella, Argentina/India, 2007), *I for India* (Sandhya Suri, UK/India, 2005), and *Grandma Has a Video Camera* (Tania Cypriano, US/Brazil, 2007) form a subset, not only within the practice of first person filmmaking but of what has become known as transnational documentary. All three films foreground the cinematic apparatus, where the camera does not simply record, but actually enacts aspects of these family displacements, whether standing in as a sign of cultural destabilisation, a symbol of migration or indeed catalysing and/or miming a perpetual state of mobility.

To return to Gabriel briefly, he asserts in his essay that the camera is the quintessential sign of modernity, it is the very thing 'that allows the West to imagine itself as modern, and as different from its "premodern", "non-technological" others' (1999: 77). Of course Gabriel is not the only theorist to link Western notions of modernity to the cinematic apparatus. Much was made of it in the early twentieth century,[3] and more recently, Anton Kaes wrote compellingly about it, associating the cinematic apparatus not only with modernism *per se* but more specifically with the modern phenomenon of urban migration. As we know, the advent of cinema is roughly coincident with the first wave of mass urban migration in the West. The force of momentum, literally the engine-propelled movement of mass in time, can be said to have urged on a new sensibility, a new way of perceiving, that was equally well expressed in the scenery of a landscape as seen from a speeding train window as it was in the imagery screened through the rapid shutter of a projector (Kaes 1998: 182). In considering the imagery of trains and scenery seen from trains in the opening scenes of Walter Ruttmann's *Die Sinfonie der Großstadt* (*Berlin, Symphony of a Great City*, 1927) Kaes notes that motion pictures are an apt metaphor for migration and modernity (1998: 179).

It is not modernity *per se* that my attention is drawn to here, but rather the movement and migration ushered in by the modern era; the wheels it set in motion, as it were. There are many potential avenues of analysis here, and scholars have considered, for instance, the interpenetration between cinema and colonialism, documentary and empire, and so on. But the direction I will take is to look at some recent first person films that gain momentum, you might say, from the transformations in terms of travel, transnational capitalism and cinematic technologies of the intervening years.

MIGRATION AND TRANSMIGRATION

Early on in Di Tella's feature-length documentary, he looks at photos of his mother, recently given to him by his father. She is something of a cipher for him, having died when he was still a teenager. The photos are from the time of his own childhood and before. The same night that he looks at the photos, he tells us, he dreams of his mother. She is on a train, passing rapidly in one direction as the train he is on passes in the other. They are moving in opposite directions. The dream goes uninterpreted in the film but the contradictory forces, the back and forth momentum, the return to the place from which the mother comes, and the potent image of the train itself as a metaphor for migration and modernity, not to mention the resonances with the cinematic image, are all pertinent here. The modern (and postmodern) migrant finds her analogue in the first person journey film (though they do not always move in the same direction). The films themselves soon become, we shall see later, a catalyst for migration as well.

By way of background, Di Tella's mother, Kamala Apparao, the daughter of a noble family, met Torcuato Di Tella, the son of a wealthy Italian-Argentinian industrialist, in India, where both were active in socialist politics. When Torcuato found himself expelled from the country, he left with Kamala, who despite their rocky relationship, was then pregnant with their first son. They moved to London, and eventually to Buenos Aires, where Di Tella imagines his mother to have been the only Indian ever to grace the Patagonian shores. The family was to migrate several more times, to the United States during the military *junta*, and once more to London, where Di Tella learns that his mother's difference is neither unique nor a mere curiosity, but rather a cause for considerable derision.[4] It is in London that he encounters discrimination for the first time on account of his Indian heritage – he is called a wog – and in his young mind, it is all his mother's fault. From then on he distances himself from all things Indian until well after his mother dies. The film is part of a process of reconciliation through discovery of '*la India*', as India is called in Spanish – a term that applies equally well to the country and to the Indian woman who was his mother. The film provides the pretence for the journey, not an uncommon trope for a documentary, first person or otherwise. Yet this journey is far from conventional in many respects. At moments it resembles something closer to a 'trip' of the hallucinogenic variety, both because his mother was very involved in the 'counterculture' of the 1960s[5] and because increasingly it ventures into semi-occult territory.

There are hints of this inclination in the first half of the film, where there is a great deal of talk of Ricardo Güiraldes, the famous Argentine author of *Don Segundo Sombra* (1926), a gaucho novel that every Argentinian school child will have read, whose character's journeys were heavily influenced by Güiraldes' Indian guru. Later, when Di Tella finds his way to India, his panic is such that he suffers first vertigo at the thought of going, and then severe insomnia upon his arrival, rendering his impressions 'dreamlike' – rather like hallucinations. And indeed, this is precisely the state the film eventually induces, with its elusive subject, Kamala, 'played' by herself and an actress, its slippages between archival and contemporary footage (often using Super 8 for present-day shots), and

its multiple false endings that take us unsuspectingly back and forth between India and Argentina, all creating a disorienting effect.

Several times the film slips into a near dream state, as when unexplained, the filmmaker depicts his young son running off into the busy streets of an unspecified Indian metropolis, or when an actress, playing his mother, careens down a hill, in vertiginous close-up, a random memory that comes to the filmmaker towards the end of his journey. But never is the film so completely immersed in the irrational and hallucinogenic as when it takes us to a Hindu séance where a medium communes with Kamala's spirit from beyond the grave. Of all the migrations depicted in this journey of a film, this is without a doubt, the most 'far out'. In this transcendental moment, all is made clear: the mother, via the medium, tells her son that 'the whole concept of this movie was initiated by me. I am instrumental in your making this film and coming to India.' The woman who migrated so far away from her home eventually losing her way to the point of suicide, comes back from the spirit world to incite

her filmmaking son to return to her homeland, camera in hand. From the migration of bodies to the transmigration of souls, the camera is recording device, catalyst and even in part conduit across time and space.

Coming down from these hallucinatory heights, we find a somewhat more sober manifestation of the relationship between movie making and migration in Sandhya Suri's impressive intergenerational, multi-format first person film, *I for India*.

FILM AS DIASPORIC APPARATUS

I for India is a film resonant with generations of voices and images that have travelled countless miles forming a celluloid link between continents, years and cultures. A small wonder of a film, *I for India* deftly integrates forty years of family home movie footage, audio letters and a deep well of family pathos into a broader consideration of socio-cultural phenomena. Suri's parents took part in the Indian mass-migration to England – the so-called 'Brain Drain' of the 1960s. We see the family's struggle to adapt to their adopted land alongside footage that reveals the highly ambivalent British response to its new residents. The clips from BBC programmes of the time are particularly hairraising, ranging from the extreme condescension of *Make Yourself at Home*, a

 show broadcast in the 1960s targeting Britain's Indian and Pakistani immigrants (the unabashedly patronising English host explains: 'This is a switch on the wall, a switch. This is a light, a light. If I press the switch on the wall, the light will come on') to the explicitly racist and xenophobic displays in shows with titles such as *The Dark Million* (BBC 1966). One particularly revealing clip features Margaret Thatcher in an early 1980s interview on a current affairs show, saying: 'people are really rather afraid that this country might be rather swamped by people of a different culture'. She pauses almost imperceptibly over the word 'culture' just long enough to allow it to resonate with the other 'c' word just uttered by the TV presenter, David Jessel: 'colour'. 'And you know, the British character', she intones imperiously, 'has done so much for democracy, for law, and done so much throughout the world that if there's any fear that it might be swamped, people are going to react and be rather hostile to those coming in.' Who counts as 'people' in this tacit approval of such demonstrations of hostility is fairly self-evident.

At the heart of *I for India* is the family archive, unusual for two key reasons: its sheer magnitude (hundreds of hours of Super 8 footage and reel-to-reel audio letters recorded over the course of forty years), and the dual archive. Realising the inadequacy of the written word to convey all of the distinct registers of this new situation, not to mention the unreliability of the postal system, Suri's father bought two Super 8 cameras, two projectors, two microphones and two reel-to-reel audio recorders and sent one full set of equipment to his family in India.

The Super 8 films are phenomenal, of course, but they are also inevitably conventional. The technology was famously marketed and promoted with very specific cultural and social, not to mention technical, conventions in mind, as Patricia Zimmermann, Richard Fung and Elspeth kydd, among others have duly noted (Zimmermann 1995; Fung 2008; kydd, in this volume). When, for instance, Fung describes the uncanny resemblance of his Chinese Trinidadian family's home movies to the white suburban American model as seen on the packaging, he recognises that his 'family's desire to inscribe themselves into the conventions of the technology, and all that this was associated with, means that the films are not always what they seem; their familiarity can be deceptive' (2008: 39). The situation is fairly similar with the Suri family treasure, but with a few notable differences.

The first difference is that the films sent to the family in India provide a kind of ethnographic record of the strange and unfathomable customs, climates and cretins to be found in England. This is 'reverse ethnography' at its best, when we see, for instance, the nurses with whom Yash Suri works, dancing some kind of jig at a holiday party. There is a very satisfying shift of address that these images effect, made all the more enjoyable for Sandhya Suri's audience, with the knowledge that the originally intended audience is the 'family back home'. There is an interest in the material shared by the family on both sides of the migratory divide, a mutuality of edification and emotional enrichment, augmented by the pleasures, surely not lost on the family in India, of occasionally poking fun at the supercilious yet easily lampooned British.

One can also imagine the satisfactions those audiovisual artifacts provided as they momentarily filled the gaping emotional holes left by the family members abroad. Film famously provides an illusion of presence unparalleled in other media, the motion picture far surpassing that of a static image or the written word in perpetuating a potent reality effect. Sound, of course, especially that of the human voice, adds something akin to 'dimension' to that image, despite the fact that neither image nor sound, nor their combined effect, can ever approximate the full dimensionality of the elusive human form. But that doesn't stop people from fantasising otherwise. The films coming from India are in fact taken up with documenting family events for the missing members – the Super 8 camera lens standing in, synecdochically, for the eyes of those who are absent, recording in effect what they would have seen, lived, been a part of, had they been there; filling their 'place'.

The second major and related departure from the conventions that Fung identifies is the epistolary character of this audio/visual material. Sent back and forth between Meerut in northern India and Darlington in northern England, they were meant as envoys, or as Derrida would say *envois* – which also always involves a debt, like an invoice to be paid (see Derrida 1987). And indeed there is revealed in these films, as re-contextualised and re-presented by Suri, a formidable debt felt to be owed to the family back home, simply for having left. It is a debt that at first is promised to be paid by a return of the family to India, something they attempt but ultimately fail at, and in the end this debt can be only partially ameliorated through the effects of these audio-visual letters.

The letters cross a divide, speaking in voices – not written words – that people the void in strange and impossible ways. They speak of and through the gap, unbridgeable in theory, but with the play of light and waves, create this illusion of presence (see Naficy 2001: 103). We see a distinct disavowal in operation, intimated in Di Tella's film, but further developed here. Disavowal in psychoanalytic terms, as is well known, is a defence mechanism in which the subject refuses to acknowledge the reality of a traumatic perception, what might be called in Freudian parlance, the missing 'member'. It can result in the production of a fetish to help to gloss over the unwanted facts of the situation by performing a substitution or 're-placement' always inadequate, but nonetheless psychically effective. In this first person film and others, we see the disavowal of the absent family *member*, gone missing due to diasporic migration, a disavowal enabled by the technological fetish of the cinematic apparatus, used to make films to send back and forth, like emissaries, surrogates, envoys.

The epistolary film is a common trope in diasporic or so-called 'accented' cinema. Hamid Naficy writes about three types of such films, 'film-letters, telephonic epistles, and letter-films' (2001: 5), the first two of which appear in *I for India*. That film also deploys audio letters, not mentioned by Naficy, where they often displace the primacy of the Super 8 films. If the films can never fully overcome the dictated conventions of their use, then it is in the aural register that such conventions are upended. While the images show a happy, growing suburban family, rose gardens, seaside holidays and amusement parks, the audio, cleverly edited by the daughter, produces a powerful counterpoint – where the nagging ambivalences, ambitions, identity crises, longings, doubts and regrets are all expressed. One can imagine the more sombre of the recordings to have been made late at night, when the rest of the family is asleep, and the surroundings must have seemed at their most estranged. Unseen, often whispered or spoken in hushed tones as if issuing directly from the unconscious, these aural *communiqués* subvert the bright illusions of suburban bliss cutting to the core of the trauma and drama of displacement.

In one heart-wrenching scene in particular, the audio virtually rips through the attendant visuals to reveal the extent of the identity crisis that this experience of migration has wrought. Yash, Sandhya's father and the amateur filmmaker responsible for this entire family archive, confides to his father and mother, at first in English, then in Hindi, ashamedly switching back to English when he cannot find the words

to express his feelings in his own mother tongue. He is essentially admitting that he will not be returning home in the near future, his linguistic slide indicating a shift also in his centre of geographical gravity. His distress is palpable, as he babbles on about an equivalency crisis, unable to find commensurability between his longed-for native land, and his economically viable newly adopted one. He speaks with great sorrow of leaving his extended family and not being able to find his way back to them, while the images tell a somewhat rosier story.

The two modes of recording, audio and film, stand in contradiction to one another. Yet they are both part of a larger 'picture' wherein the cinematic apparatus not only records but forms a constitutive aspect of the migratory experience: the disconnect, the veritable cultural dysphoria is revealed in the interval between aural and visual register.

A broad array of visual recording and telecommunicative devices are represented in this film: Super 8, reel to reel, digital video cameras and toward the end of the film, even webcams and internet video-telephony. In the penultimate scene there is yet another migration in the family and

it tellingly ushers in new modes of recording and communicating across the absences acrued. As the middle daughter, the filmmaker's older sister, emigrates from England to Australia, diasporic dispersal is re-enacted by the next generation, making it seem almost habitual, a repetition with no end in sight, the only difference being the audiovisual envoys lose their delay. The audiovisual recording devices here become the very prosthesis Gabriel warns about

– necessary appendages for the mass migration and ceaseless hypermobility of the actors performing in the 'theatre' of global capitalism.

We return inevitably to questions of motion and migration – watching in awe as people swiftly adapt these changing technologies to their needs. To borrow and modify a phrase coined by Barbara Kirshenblatt-Gimblett in her article 'Spaces of Dispersa', I will call this phenomena 'the shifting technologies of connection'. When the film adjusts its register from Super 8 to webcam, we see an escalation of the 'presence' already implied in the film's earlier epistles. As Kirshenblatt-Gimblett notes, the 'instantaneity of telecommunications produces a vivid sense of hereness and interactivity the feeling of presence' (1994: 342). Here, ever more effectively, the audiovisual technologies mask a disavowal of that which is nonetheless operating upon the actors (or should we call them 'users'?) namely: distance and separation. The medium is used even more efficiently than before as a force to condense time and space, and consequently to minimise the role of memory as constitutive of the migrating subject. Memory's vicissitudes are traded in for the fragile fibre-optics that allow the virtual presence of our missing loved ones on our computer screens.

Once upon a time, not that long ago, diasporic memory was implicitly cut off from its origins – as Andreas Huyssen claims (2003: 152). Generations of migrants, like my grandparents, never saw their homelands again once they had left. Leaving was final, permanent, irreversible. Home became a memory and a metaphor, awash in unchecked nostalgia or obscured by terror, depending on the terms of departure. Letters and still photographs were the only link to the past, and these, though perhaps fiercely cherished, could not as effectively engender the vivid technicolour disavowals enabled by the moving image and related recording technologies. What has changed in the contemporary experience of migration is the heightened – and reversible – mobility. Tellingly, the recorded images themselves are no longer static but 'on the move', an almost bionic enhancement. And as diasporic experience becomes less a matter of resettlement and more a matter of transnational transience, the back and forth movement itself has become not only a central theme of migration, but the subject of several first person films.

With the '*shuttling* of whole migrant populations between host nation and homeland', the notion of diaspora requires 'some new conceptual language' (Huyssen 2003: 151; emphasis added). It clearly also mobilises a whole host of new visual and aural devices to simulate presence and thus give a semblance of unity to emphatically fractured identities. Diaspora, it seems, can no longer be imagined without its attendant cinematic technologies. The shuttling back and forth of these contemporary migrations could easily bring to mind, in a kind of Vertovian visual analogy, the shutter of a camera, constantly in motion.

But if hypermobility and technologies of connection are inextricably linked in *I for India*, I want to conclude by looking at an even more itinerant diasporic first person film to see the near-total interpenetration of the human shuttle and the cinematic shutter. Remember, the shared etymological roots of the words 'shuttle' and 'shutter', both deriving from the Old Germanic *skeutanan* (and later the Anglo-Saxon *sceotan*), which also means to shoot. In Tanya Cypriano's *Grandma Has a Video Camera* the eponymous Grandma Elda is perennially shooting her camera, as she shuttles back and forth between São Paolo and San Francisco. Her video camera serves a veritable peripatetic migration machine.

PRESS PLAY TO START

In Cypriano's film, the grandmother – the *vovó* – anchors the story, though she turns out to be quite an unmoored character herself. The film essentially begins and ends with the grandmother leaving her city of residence, but in the intervening fifty-plus minutes, we see her videotaping her migrant life as she makes her way back and forth – seemingly inadvertently and with the pretence of permanence each time – between Bahia and California. These are not your average tourist visits. Cypriano's grandmother, Elda Rosa de Jesus, migrates to San Francisco to take care of her latest grandchild, stays on with only a tourist visa for ten years, goes back to São Paolo reluctantly with her daughter and granddaughter, and then both together with them and alone proceeds to migrate back and forth for another ten years.

Grandma Elda is an inveterate videographer, taping all manner of events and non-events, including a virtual catalogue of apartments they lived in and various household consumer items they bought. The camera moves from hand to hand, in a new kind of 'shared textual authority' (Renov 2004: 222) that we might call *immigrantitis*: the mania to document one's first impressions of a new place in which one intends to live. Beyond documenting immigration of the family, as they come one by one and in pairs, Grandma's camera practices are a vehicle, a kind of shuttle mechanism – by granddaughter Tania's reckoning – bridging the distance between her two homes, neither of which she ever fully privileges. 'Back and forth we live, back and forth images are recorded', Cypriano tells us in voiceover, with a tinge of weariness. It is not merely a matter of sending video letters back and forth, which Grandma does with alacrity, nor just documenting others' comings and goings. Grandma herself is in seemingly constant motion. The continuous filming becomes an obvious metaphor for continuous migration. It is as if once the process of migration was set in motion, once the motion picture camera was switched on, and once Grandma hit the record button, there was no stopping the movement either of Elda or her camera.

Admittedly, Cypriano's own movements tend to follow a more linear pat-

I'm always filming. Wherever I go, I film.

tern both in life (she migrated from São Paolo to San Francisco and from there to New York, where she has settled permanently) and in her shooting style. Her more 'professional' camera work serves as a visual reminder of another, steadier, more predictable, path. Yet it is not Tania's trajectory which propels the overarching narrative of the film, nor is it her ironically old-fashioned migratory pattern that reflects the new 'shuttle/shutter' migration.

Grandma's camera is witness to, and perpetrator of, a repetition compulsion that brings grandma migrating back and forth between Brazil and the US no less than seven times. Though the editing of this personal documentary does not detail every upheaval, it does indicate that each move was duly documented. As suggested, Grandma's camera becomes not just synecdoche for migration, it becomes a veritable migration machine itself, without which Grandma's migratory exploits would no doubt have to come to an end. In fact, this is precisely what occurs. The trauma of migration is relived, re-experienced, and re-imaged over and over again via the video camera until what we are led to believe is Grandma's final migration back to Brazil. As Grandma's aging body can no longer take the wear and tear of shuttle migration, she determines to go home to São Paolo, essentially to die. And how do we know this is the final chapter? Grandma leaves her beloved video camera behind. The migration machine is thus disabled, and Grandma can finally rest in peace; her shuttle mechanism switched off for the last time. In truth there is one more round of migration, but it is more like a last gasp than a forthright act.

Of course, not all films are quite this explicit about the relationship between migration and the moving image, but this documentary forcefully articulates that which many transnational diasporic first person films merely imply: the camera is not simply a recording device that captures the experiences of the displacement, it can be a symptom of that very displacement. Here the process of documenting a displaced subjectivity via the cinematic apparatus, or as it used to be called, the motion picture camera, reveals within it the seeds of its own destabilisation. And in some way, the camera in this film and in the previous two discussed here, resonates with the little worm, the *gusanito*, in the Jorge de la Vega song in Di Tella's film: like the *gusanito*, the camera is simultaneously the trace of the movement that it records.

Notes

1 This lyric is from a very well known Argentinian song from the 1960s and translates roughly as follows: 'The little worm draws a little drawing as he worms through the grass and the little drawing is identical to the little worm' (translation my own). The song goes on to reverse the image in the next stanza by saying, 'the little drawing worms its way along and in its worming it makes a little worm that is identical to the little drawing'. The little worm asks itself later in the song whether the whole world isn't a drawing in reverse.

2 I am clearly asserting here that it is a class privilege to document one's migration and indeed all three films discussed here benefit from some measure of this privilege. Despite any possible claims to the contrary, video has not yet become the great democratising medium for most migrants, still less for undocumented ones. A notable exception to this rule is the work of the Palestinian refugee filmmaker, Osama Qashoo, who's trilogy *A Palestinian Journey* (2006) includes a segment on the exploits of an undocumented political refugee, attempting with difficulty to gain residency in the United Kingdom.

3 I refer here to studies within the Frankfurt School, by Sigfried Kracauer and also Wilhelm Stapel, though their writings refer strictly to intra-national migration, as industrialisation created a magnetic urban forcefield to which the peasantry of the countryside seemed irresistibly attracted. There is a high degree of cultural homogeneity in their somewhat agitated accounts that generally dwelt upon the incompatibilities between the urban cultural elite and the uneducated rural masses descending on the modern cities with little in the way of preparation for the new cosmopolitan lifestyle. These studies are, of course, not infinitely adaptable to the various and polysemic post-colonial, post-industrial and post-modern migrations and transitions enacted in the century to come.

4 The migrations of the Di Tella family in relation to the political events in Argentine history is the subject of his impressive prior film, *La televisión y yo* (*Television and Me*, 2002).

5 Kamala appears to have been very involved with the avant garde artists of the Instituto Di Tella (for a time the leading centre for contemporary art in Buenos Aires, closed in 1970) as well as having been heavily influenced by her friend and mentor R. D. Laing, an early experimenter with hallucinogens as therapeutic aids.

References

Derrida, J. (1987) *The Post Card: From Socrates to Freud and Beyond*, trans. A. Bass. Chicago, IL: University of Chicago Press.

Fung, R. (2008) 'Remaking Home Movies', in K. Ishizuka and P. Zimmermann (eds) *Mining the Home Movies*. Berkeley, CA: University of California Press, 29–40.

Gabriel, T. (1999) 'The Intolerable Gift: Residues and Traces of a Journey', in H. Naficy (ed.) *Home, Exile, Homeland*. London: Routledge, 75–84.

Huyssen, A. (2003) 'Diaspora and Nation: Migration Into Other Pasts,' *New German Critique*, 88, 147–64.

Kaes, A. (1998) 'Leaving Home: Film, Migration, and the Urban Experience', *New German Critique*, 74, 179–92.

Kirshenblatt-Gimblett, B. (1994) 'Spaces of Dispersal', *Cultural Anthropology*, 9, 3, 339–44.

Naficy, H. (2001) *Accented Cinema: Exilic and Diasporic Filmmaking*. Princeton, NJ: Princeton University Press.

Renov, M. (2004) *The Subject of Documentary*. Minneapolis, MN: University of Minnesota Press.

Zimmermann, P. (1995) *Reel Families: A Social History of Amateur Film*. Indianapolis, IN: Indiana University Press.

VIRTUAL SUBJECTIVITY

Blogging Identity.com

Peter Hughes

One of the most important changes in media, especially since the invention of the internet, has been the trend towards a post-broadcast environment characterised by increasing fragmentation and individualisation. Jupiter Research, Pew Research, Gartner and Technorati have all released regular reports on the growth and influence of blogging, particularly in relation to politics (see Rainie 2005; Regan 2006). More recently attention has turned to 'social networking technologies' sometimes also called Web 2.0, or 'sociable media' (see Donath 2004). Web 2.0 is claimed to be more 'interactive' than the original world wide web using design features that enhance creativity, information sharing and collaboration, and includes blogging, social networking sites (such as MySpace and Facebook), media sharing sites (such as YouTube and Flikr) and wikis (the best known of which is Wikipedia). One popular claim about social networking has it that while the original internet connected people to information, Web 2.0 connects people to people. The development of Web 2.0 is symptomatic of a significant change in media structures and cultures away from a broadcast-based mass communication model (the model that has underpinned television and radio, large circulation newspapers and mass market models of cinema exhibition and film distribution) to a much more fragmented model of media in which audiences are more fluid and able to access a wider range of media forms at a time and place of their choosing: a 'post-broadcast' model. Broadcast media which addressed audiences as unified, stable (and usually as citizens of 'the nation') are being replaced by a fragmenting global culture of more heterogenous identities based on privatised modes of consumption. *The Future of Media Report* of 2008 (Future Exploration Network 2008) points to seven developments driving change in the media in general, three of which are:

participation, personalisation and fragmentation, concepts central to much of the discourse around Web 2.0. It is this culture of participation, personalisation and fragmentation which increasingly provides the contexts of production and reception for documentary.

I want to examine the assumption inherent in this discourse that blogs and social networking technologies open up new, demotic and democratic spaces within which ordinary people are able to reflect on their everyday experience and tell their own stories. This is not a new claim to make about developing media technologies, indeed, similar utopian claims attend the emergence of each new media technology. Such claims go back to the marketing of Kodak's Box Brownie, and have been repeated for audiovisual media from 16mm and 8mm film, portapak video, right up to DV cameras, each of which was promoted as providing cheap and accessible technology which would enable democratisation of the media (see, for example, Weiner 1973; Lipton 1974; Sorenson 2008). In the past, such opportunities have actually been confined to small sections of the population leaving the mass media to continue as before. However, with the convergence of a number of new and continuing media forms such utopian hopes have returned with the promise of more widespread accessibility regardless of geographic location or personal expertise (see Jenkins 2002).

It is not my argument that blogs and social networking, in themselves, provide new spaces for documentary. To do so would require a drastic redefinition of 'documentary', which, as a noun, is largely construed as an audiovisual project (based on film and/or video). However, computer-mediated sociable media are symptomatic of a major cultural shift towards increasing sociability, personalisation and fragmentation. Web 2.0 technologies have the potential to disrupt 'top down' models of discourse through their potential to foster collaboration between individuals (see Funnell 2008), in contradiction to the linear, centralised model of communication of older broadcast media. John Hiler, for example, argues that blogs have 'the capacity to engage people in collaborative activity, knowledge sharing, reflection and debate' (quoted in Williams and Jacobs 2004). It is no longer the case (if it ever actually was) that the positions of producer and audience are mutually exclusive, as these positions converge into what Axel Bruns has called the 'produser' (2005, 2008).

However, it is evident that a number of contradictory trends co-exist in contemporary cultural contexts. While blogs and wikis provide technologies facilitating the collaborative production of knowledge; they also open up spaces for identity production and self-presentation. So, paradoxically, the development of Web 2.0 also coincides with an increasing emphasis on neo-liberal notions of individuality (see Giddens 1991; Rose 1991, 1996; Beck and Beck-Gernsheim 2002). Secondly, at least at this stage (and in contrast to documentary, which commonly seeks to develop an analysis in depth), blogs, YouTube videos and other manifestations of sociable media tend to be relatively brief and fragmentary.

This is in contrast to another paradoxical development: parallel to the increasing individuality, personalisation and fragmentation of much of the media, in specialised cinemas and on DVD there has also been a return to 'long form documentaries' which have attracted large audiences and significant box office returns for their producers. However, while this is true, a full discussion of the implications of this is beyond the scope of this chapter, and it is nevertheless the case that the existence of a strong cinema and DVD audience for documentary does not negate the trends to which I am pointing. It may be that both the development of sociable media and the return to long form documentaries reflect some dissatisfaction with 'mass media'. Nevertheless, it is notable that a number of the successful long form documentaries are built around narratives from a first person perspective (see *Bowling for Columbine* (Michael Moore, USA, 2003), *Fahrenheit 9/11* (Michael Moore, USA, 2004), *Sicko* (Michael Moore, USA, 2007), *Born into Brothels* (Zana Briski and Ross Kaufman, USA, 2005) and *An Inconvenient Truth* (Davis Guggenheim, USA, 2006) as examples). Furthermore, I have argued elsewhere that the packaging of DVD boxed sets of documentaries (Hughes 2008; see also Kompare 2006) is symptomatic of the personalisation of the media.

The first form of Web 2.0 to come to popular notice was the weblog, or blog, of which the earliest examples were simply lists of links to interesting websites compiled by enthusiasts. Quickly the compilers of these sites began interpolating comments into these lists so that they quickly became link-driven websites incorporating 'unique proportions of links, commentary, and personal thoughts and essays' (Blood 2000). With the development of simple, readily available software which made the production of weblogs feasible for individuals without web markup skills, increasing numbers of weblogs emphasised the elements of personal reflection in the form of a 'sort of short form journal' (ibid.).

Rebecca Blood points to two major forms of the weblog: initially, 'the filter site' and later 'the short form journal'. The filter site 'reveals glimpses of an unimagined web to those who have no time to surf. [On such sites] an intelligent human being filters through the mass of information packaged daily for our consumption and picks out the interesting, the important, the overlooked, the unexpected'. In the process, a 'distinctive voice and personality' begins to emerge on these sites, leading some bloggers to become celebrities (within the blogging community) based on their reputation for accuracy, or for the particular tone of voice they adopt. Karen McCullagh argues that 'regular readers [of blogs] can get a sense of the identifying "voice" or "persona" behind the posts' (2008: 8). Nevertheless this personal voice remains, for Blood, in the service of information. In this discourse the value of the blog is as a site for information beyond that available in the media itself. The dominant perspective on blogs in popular and critical discourses is concerned with the blog as an alternative form of journalism, or a threat to journalism as it has come to be practiced (see Cooper 2006).

Cornfield *et al.* conclude that it would be a good thing if the 'blogosphere' became a fifth estate: 'the national discourse could benefit from a sector favouring transparency over opacity, conversation over presentation, small pieces over big works, flexibility over anchorage, incompleteness over conclusiveness, documentation over description and, paradoxically, individuality over institutionalisation' (2005: 31). This quotation points to the utopian possibilities raised by blogging as an alternative to mainstream journalism. Jay Rosen, for example, has an extensive website devoted to proselytising in favour of citizen journalism and sees blogging as an essential element to this democratising development in journalism. 'Joey' of 'UrbanJacksonville' in his 'Urban manifesto' proclaims: 'this city needs to wake up and realise that WE ARE THE NEW MEDIA. [...] I am talking about all of us, the citizens of this community' ('Joey' 2006; emphasis in original), while Lev Grossman and Anita Hamilton (2004) argue that 'blogs represent everything the Web was always supposed to be: a mass medium controlled by the masses, in which getting heard depends solely on having something to say and the moxie to say it'.

A variation on this debate is the degree to which blogs have the potential to finally realise the ideal 'public sphere' usually associated with Habermas (see Poster 1995; Dahlberg 2001; Hiler 2002; O'Baoill 2004; Abrash 2006; Kellner n.d.). Much of the revisionist debate around the notion of the public sphere has pointed to the limitations of Habermas' early conceptions. It has been often argued that the Habermasian notion of the public sphere tends to make too rigid a distinction between public and private spheres, and excludes the concerns of a number of groups who were marginalised by the public sphere – most notably women (see Fraser 1985; Poster 1995; Dahlberg 2001; O'Baoill 2004; Kellner n.d.). Blogs and social networking technologies can be interesting for the potential space they provide for the marginalised to tell their stories and provide their analyses, including those with limited technologies or developed literary skills at their disposal.

Within this part of the debate blogs are either praised or criticised for qualities they are perceived to have which distinguish them from conventional journalism: personal perspective and a multiplicity of voices. This personal perspective is the basis for both Cornfield *et al.*'s optimism, and Leslie Cannold's

(2006) concern about 'misinformation'. Such comments about 'misinformation' position the debate within a positivist paradigm and 'communication model' still common in much academic study of journalism, where discussions centre on whether blogging as 'citizen journalism' provides legitimate, alternative spaces for public information and debate, albeit beyond the control of institutional gatekeepers, or whether concerns about questions of accuracy and fact checking undermine the value of citizen journalism (see Grossmann and Hamilton 2004). From this perspective blogs are valued or criticised for their ability to provide 'information' about the world, supplemented by reasoned opinion, well supported by evidence and a proper sense of journalistic balance.

However, an alternative perspective on blogs (consistent with Blood's second model of blogging as short form journal) sees them as sites for questions about identity and performances of the self shifting the terrain from positivist concerns with objectivity to the acceptance of subjectivity. Such a shift from information to identity is familiar in the development of documentary theory. Brian Winston (1993, 1995) has pointed to the empiricist emphasis in much documentary; however, a range of documentary theorists have pointed to the development of new subjectivities in documentary as alternatives to that empiricist discourse (see Nichols 1994; Renov 1995, 2004). Michael Renov noted that, by the 1990s,

> the documentative stance that had previously been valorized as informed but objective, was now being replaced by a more personalist perspective in which the maker's stake and commitment to the subject matter was foregrounded. (1995)

This shift was evident in a number of developments eschewing 'objectivity', including (but not restricted to) essays in film theory such as *Serious Undertakings* (Grace and Addis, Australia, 1983), *Camera Natura* (Gibson, Australia, 1985) and *Landslides* (Gibson and Lambert, Australia, 1986); documentaries in which a central figure (often male) anguishes over his epistemological uncertainty, including *Waiting for Fidel* (Rubbo, Canada, 1974), *Sherman's March* (McElwee, USA, 1985) and *The Leader, His Driver and the Driver's Wife* (Broomfield, UK, 1991); and, most relevant to this argument, the many autobiographical documentaries in which identity is constructed on screen such as *A Song of Air* (Bennett, Australia, 1988), *Nobody's Business* (Berliner, USA, 1996) and *Tarnation* (Caouette, USA, 2003). A number of writers have theorised such developments in the context of performativity in documentary and the foregrounding of the position of the enunciation (see Nichols 1994; Bruzzi 2006).

Renov went on to argue that

the cultural climate of this period, at least in the West, has been characterized by the displacement of the politics of social movements … by the politics of 'identity'. (Ibid.)

Renov's point is that this represents a shift away from the politics of the social towards a politics of identity. He goes on to quote Stanley Aronowitz arguing for a notion of identity which is multiple and fluid, and makes the point that

If we now live in an age of intensified and shifting psycho-social identities, it should surprise no one that the documentation of this cultural scene should be deeply suffused with the performance of subjectivities. (Ibid.)

If Renov was concerned with the position of the subject in documentary, I am concerned with the position of the subject in blogs and social networking sites, where, it seems to me, this shift towards the politics of identity has already slid precariously into an obsession with the self, with political implications entirely consistent with the current dominance of neo-liberalism. So, I am pointing to a shift from 'information' to a discourse of 'identity' and 'the self' in relation to blogs; one instance of an intense fascination with the self in Western culture, equally evident in a range of forms of popular factual entertainment, such as some forms of 'reality television'. Indeed, a case can be made that the trajectory of media development from mass media to personalised, fragmentary media, is consistent with an increasing sense of individualisation and concern with identity in late modernity (see Giddens 1991; Bauman 1992; Beck and Beck-Gernsheim 2002).

Whereas Renov argues that in 'current documentary self inscription' remains 'fully embroiled with public discourses' (1995), it seems to me that the obsession with the self is consistent with a significant shift in public discourses toward an increasing privatisation of the economy, and of the individual (see Bauman 1992; Dovey 2000). Paul Hodkinson argues that 'in recent times there has been a significant shift among internet users towards the use of individual web logs ("blogs") and, in particular interactive online journals … the vast majority of blogs are created, maintained and centred upon a single individual rather than a group' (2007: 626). Like Blood, Hodkinson sees a shift in the blogosphere since the development of 'user-friendly blog platforms' such as Blogger and LiveJournal 'combining the individual-centredness of the personal home page with the frequency of update and multi-directional communication previously associated with group discussion forums' (ibid.). He asks 'to what extent increasing use of the person-centred online journal is liable to encourage individualistic patterns of interaction and identity' and places this question in the context of existing social theory (in particular Bauman 1992, 2001; Beck and Beck-Gernsheim 2002) which argues that 'individuals have become increasingly detached from traditional structural, institutional and communal sources of collective identity' producing 'short-lived and superficial affiliations of convenience'; in the society of the 'do it yourself biography ... the detached, insecure, floating individual is deemed to have become the prime social unit at the centre of a plethora of "until further notice" forms of interest and attachment' (2007: 626–7, citing Beck and Beck-Gernsheim 2002).

So far I have been arguing that the development of sociable media, in particular blogs, can be understood as evidence of a cultural and social shift towards personalisation and fragmentation of the media, and towards an increasing emphasis upon the individual and the expression of individual identity, or selfhood. Hence, the concept of identity and selfhood needs to be considered in more detail in this context.

In Western conceptions of the self, one dominant assumption sees the self ontologically, as an entity amenable to empirical study (see Gergen 1971: 14; Potter and Wetherell 1987: 95). In the twentieth century a number of theories of the self, within the framework of social psychology, made this assumption. The first of these was trait theory, which saw the self as 'an honest soul' (Potter and Wetherell 1987: 96) with a number of traits possessed by the individual which remained stable regardless of context. This conception of the 'honest soul' rejects any conception of the self as performative. Alternatively, role theory understands the self as context dependent, seeking to reconcile self-expression with social determinism. The self derives, in this view, from the performance of social roles, suggesting the possibility of a fragmented self, sometimes seen as an actor performing a role (Erving Goffman cited by Potter and Wetherell 1987: 98). Role theory opens up the possibility of an insincere, inauthentic self responding to social awareness, potentially as a 'social dope' or victim of society (Potter and Wetherell 1987: 99).

Humanistic, as opposed to psychological, conceptions of the self, have a provenance going back at least to the Romantic era. Phenomenologically, the Western individual tends to experience herself as having agency – as a 'richer character' than the self of social psychology. Humanism sees a space for a 'double consciousness' in which the metaphor of the actor becomes, once again, apposite. The self is both the role and the real person who is performing. Humanistic therapy, then, tends to see therapy as the search for 'the authentic true self': 'an individual's life is seen as a process of searching to establish this true self, as a quest for self-fulfilment and self-actualisation' (Potter and

Wetherell 1987: 100). As Jonathan Potter and Margaret Wetherell point out, two views of this quest have developed. In the first the pre-existing, authentic self has been lost and needs to be recovered while in the second the authentic self needs to be willed into existence. In this latter view the self is a 'project' in the process of being constructed (see Gergen 1971: 18).

Social psychological and humanistic conceptions of self 'do not call attention to themselves as constructions or discursive articulations but present themselves as representations of the real object' (Potter and Wetherell 1987: 101) the subject which is assumed to be the centre of experience, initiator of action, coherent whole, autonomous and unitary. On the other hand, the self can be understood not as an entity but a discursive construct. Here, the emphasis is how the self is imagined – trait theory, role theory and humanistic notions of 'character types' are merely 'possible methods of making sense that someone might draw upon to describe themselves' (Potter and Wetherell 1987: 102).

It is productive, then, to understand personal blogs and other forms of social media as discursive practices by which people seek to construct themselves 'in public' – to understand themselves, will themselves into existence and to perform themselves. For example, current research by Alison Horbury and myself has noted people posting on a range of social media sites constructing themselves as caring and ethical selves able to imagine solidarity (however momentary and ephemeral) with distant others effected by the 'Black Saturday bushfires' (wildfires) in the Australian state of Victoria in February 2009 (in which 173 people died). Zygmunt Bauman argues that 'our present, postmodern habitat ... construes life as a process of self-constitution' (1992: 21), while for Anthony Giddens 'the self is a reflexive project for which the individual is responsible' (1991: 6). One of the strands evident in blogging is a range of personal sites which have analogues to various forms of 'life writing' or 'self-representational' writing.

Viviane Serfaty understands 'self-representational writing' (including diaries, as the precursors of personal blogs) to have its origins in Western cultures: Catholicism, English Puritanism and the diaries of Libertines (2004: 5).[1] The first two of these place the diary in a religious context. For the Puritans the diary is a record of the spiritual journey towards personal salvation, and a mode of religious self-discipline. For the Libertines the diary is produced in a framework of reason, as befits the Enlightenment context of their production. While both of these impulses are relevant to the blog, social psychological and humanistic conceptions of the self are consistent with the Enlightenment project, rather than the religious. The model of the self evident in this discourse remains an entity which precedes its representation, and is imagined as autonomous.

One further conception of the self seems particularly relevant to the study of blogs and sociable media: the dialogical self. Role theory sees the self in social contexts, imagining the individual and society engaged in a struggle over identity, in which the individual may be forced to assume certain 'roles' as camouflage over the real self. Alternatively, however, the self may be imagined as entirely relational (see Aronowitz 1992; Eakin 1999). Paul Eakin is concerned with 'literary' autobiographies in which the self is narrativised (as in documentaries about the self), rather than the more fragmentary performances of the self which are available on some personal home pages and blog sites, but nevertheless the conception of the self as relational is valuable. More recently Alisa Lebow (2008), building on work by Renov (1995, for example) has productively taken up the question of relational identity with specific reference to first person documentary. Taking this notion one step further, if the self is constructed in relation to others, both real and embodied, and imaginary and disembodied (as in memory and in autobiography) then it might be possible to think of some forms of personal home pages and blog sites as spaces within which the individual can explore the self in (imaginary and sometimes real) relation to others. Eakin points out that the subject is structured as a conversation (1999: 64). Indeed, one notable aspect of the blog is its potential to provide a space for dialogue, through the comments feature which allows others to post replies to the original blog (a potential even more evident in social networking technologies such as MySpace and Facebook). As a form, blogs are particularly amenable spaces for personal reflection (like the earlier book-based diary) including reflection on the self. Serfaty sees such self-reflexivity as one of the defining characteristics of the personal blog; this dialogical, conversational aspect of the self may be explicitly articulated through the comments feature of the blog.

As we have noted, the weblog began as a word-based form, initially as lists of links, and then with the addition of commentary, self-reflection and opinion. However, since its inception the blog has also served, a perhaps truncated a form, as an index of the personality of its creator, through the use of design elements (colour, shape, font choice) as well as through literary factors such as linguistic tropes. With increases in bandwidth it has become possible to include photos, as well as audio and video files on blogs; and social networking sites such as Facebook provide the interface to make the uploading and sharing of images and sounds as simple as the sharing of words, producing a textually richer form of media. The result, for many users, is the construction of a performance of identity, drawing, bricolage fashion, from a series of pre-existing tools and applications on the site, resulting in something related, though perhaps not identical to the audiovisual elements of the documentary.

At this point my argument runs something like this: new cultural (and, it must be admitted, commercial) technologies such as blogging, MySpace, Flickr and YouTube all provide spaces in which ordinary people may tell their own stories or present their own reflections on individualised, personal experience. Frequently these are manifest in highly fragmented and highly conventionalised forms; fragmented because they are produced in the brief moments in their lives when they have time, and conventionalised because they use the templates available for free to all users. However, as these technologies develop they provide the potential for ordinary people to document their lives, and their identities, in ways which are much more public than the diaries, scrapbooks and photo albums of previous generations; and without the limitations of institutionalised structures of documentary, as they are available to anyone who has access to a computer, a high speed internet connection, a digital camera (or camera phone), and perhaps a mini DV camera.

The result is, at this stage in the development of new configurations of the web, we find the technologies to be increasingly personalised, individualised and fragmentary, in complete contrast to the social and cultural contexts in which the documentary as a social and epistemological project developed.

In 2006, in order to test some ideas we had been exploring in a class on digital media I set my students the assignment of producing a weekly blog. In doing a relatively crude analysis of the resultant blogs I noted a number of recurring discursive features, including a more personal writing style than would normally be expected in formal assessment items, a significant use of rhetorical questions, and, importantly for this argument, a heavy reliance on first person direct address, as if imagining the writer was engaged in a dialogue with readers. I am arguing that the blog provides a space for a relational or dialogic understanding of identity, and that this is the case as long as the blogger imagines that there is some (potential) reader of their work (and because a blog is publicly accessible, this is a reasonable assumption). This imagined dialogue with the audience is evident in many of my students' blogs.

For example Kevin [all names have been changed for ethical reasons] engages in a moment of direct address to his imagined audience when he interpolates: 'At this point, if you so desire, you may skip these paragraphs to avoid the pop-culture references and get right to the academia, but I feel that often fiction manages to stir up just as much thought.' This example points to another interesting pattern in a number of postings. While much of the critical discourse on blogging sees it as a form of, or alternative to, print journalism, some students seem to be imagining their blog and its audience in oral rather than, or as well as, written terms. For example Gavin finishes his final posting with 'That's all for now. Thank you' – as if ending a radio broadcast.

Diane concludes her final posting with '...this will be my final blog entry. I hope that all my loyal readers have enjoyed the past few months and that you have gained something from my thoughts on the digital media'. Although she imagines her audience as 'readers' one of the features of this comment is a somewhat archaic, naïve structure, rather like a radio announcer from a by-gone era 'signing off'.

Olivia demonstrates the use of first person direct address when she says in her final posting 'I hope my blogs have been interesting to read, and you have enjoyed hearing about my thoughts', but equally interesting here is her language. She speaks of her blogs as an interesting 'read', and equally of 'hear-ing about' her thoughts – as if she has spoken her thoughts rather than, or in addition to, writing them.

Although the students were to use the blogs to reflect on classroom reading they did not merely present 'information'. They could not help but construct a sense of self, of identity, through their writing style. Joshua constructs a style which is highly ironic. In his reflection on the process he comments: 'Also, actually using a new media tool in the study of new media! How clever!' The irony is even more evident in a posting on identity which begins: 'Defining the self: (Besides being an arduous academic exercise); a life-long struggle and process of invention and re-invention, soul searching, sacrifice and spiritual reward OR just plain philosophical wank?' Later, self-deprecatingly, he contin-ues: 'Ahh, the self, a topic I contemplate possibly too much (to the consequence of myself and anyone unfortunate to know me).'

The irony in these posts was evidence of a side to Joshua's personality which was not apparent in face-to-face classroom interactions. Joshua was very quiet in class and had to be pushed quite hard to participate in discussion at all. In his blog he was 'voluble' and expressed his opinions strongly and in a very articu-late manner. In this case the postings seem to serve as evidence for some of the claims we sought to examine in class: that blogs provide a space for individuals to construct and perform an identity, and furthermore that identities online might well be different from those performed in face-to-face interactions. In a constructivist model of education, in which the subject is presumed to be constructed by the learning process such 'personal development' as students reported occurring through their experience of blogging is crucial.

In her final posting Olivia makes some comments about her own writing style: 'As you would probably have noticed, my blogs started out as academic reflections on the required readings ... my writing style started to change towards the final few weeks. Although I was inconsistent with my writing styles, I decided that I felt much more comfortable with a more laid-back, personal approach to the weekly topics. From trialling both an academic and a personal format for my blogs, I feel that the personal writing is much more suited for blogs. It gives the readers inkling into the personality of the writer, as well as their personal thoughts and interests.' Such self-reflection is an important aspect of identity construction. This sort of self-reflection might be available in any medium, especially in a personal journal or diary, but the significant element here is that students are aware that they are doing so in public. There is a sense of performance here – they are performing the self in a public space.

In common with all the examples of first person direct address noted in the student blogs, the addressee is not specified, nor it is entirely clear. Some clues exist in individual postings, and no doubt at some level it was me as coordinator of the subject. However, there is some sense, from phrases such as 'Dear reader' that the imagined audience is a more amorphous group of people including but not limited to the teacher and fellow students. It is also likely that the imagined audience may involve complete strangers who come across the blog by chance. Evidence for this latter possibility is in the designation of one blog by a journalism student as 'the Virtual Press' and the announcement of its project as if a new publishing venture.

These are minor examples but they do point to the dialogic nature of the blog, which invites (and in many cases receives) a response, especially in those blogs with a comment button. If, as Zygmunt Baumann has argued, the postmodern self is a 'project' (1998) this dialogue (imagined or real) is central to a project of building a relational understanding of self, an understanding in which the self is performatively constructed through a real or imagined dialogue, conducted in the first person.

The writing style and mode of address of the blog implicitly constructs the voice or persona, to which Blood and McCullagh refer. Another feature of the blog is the use of links; one of the ways in which 'identity' is constructed on the site is through the accumulation of links which serve as indices of the personality and interests of the blogger. However these links may well do more than act as an index of the self of the blogger, they may serve to establish an imagined (or actual) dialogue between bloggers, through which conversation the subject continues to be constructed and performed. They also serve as a collection of 'virtual' possessions, or commodities. Just as in the real world individuals use material goods to construct a public self, on web pages, blogs and social networking sites, links can construct the accoutrements and accessories associated with a virtual public self.

To summarise my argument, blogs provide a space in which aspects of the 'documentary project' are made available in a demotic and potentially democratic form. Because of the ways in which new cultural technologies allow for forms of interaction, they place an emphasis on the performative, relational self.

A paradox of this development is that this turn to the self represents the current victory of individualist discourses over the collectivist, social discourses which informed the documentary project in its earlier incarnations. This argument is also relevant to 'social networking' sites such as MySpace, video sharing sites such as YouTube and photosharing sites such as Flickr; however, it is quite possible that the collaborative aspects of Web 2.0 will increasingly be used to move away from such an individualist project, and, along with such movements as the 'creative commons', 'open source' and 'open access' movements might all represent moves toward a new form of collectivist, social discourse.

Note

1 This European perspective, of course, does not account for the popularity of blogging in places like Japan and Korea.

References

Abrash, B. (2006) 'Digital Media and the Public Sphere: Rapporteur's Report', Proceedings of *Digital Media and the Public Sphere* Conference. Charles F. Kettering Foundation. New York. Available: www.centerforsocialmedia.org/future/docs/blogs_convening2.pdf.

Aronowitz, S. (1992) 'Reflections on Identity', *October*, 61, 91–103. Available: www.jstor.org/stable/778789.

Bauman, Z. (1992) 'Survival as a Social Construct', *Theory, Culture and Society*, 9, 1–36.

―――― (1998) 'Is There Life after the Panopticon?, in Z. Bauman, *Globalization: The Human Consequences*. Cambridge: Polity Press, 48–54.

―――― (2001) *The Individualized Society*. Cambridge: Polity Press.

Beck, U. and E. Beck-Gernsheim (2002) *Individualization: Institutionalized Individualism and Its Social and Political Consequences*. London: Sage.

Blood, R. (2000) 'Weblogs: A History and a Perspective', *rebecca's pocket* [website]. Available: www.rebeccablood.net/essays/weblog_history.html [23 April 2012].

Bruns, A. (2005) 'Anyone Can Edit': *Understanding the Produser* — Guest Lecture at SUNY, www.slideshare.net/Snurb/anyone-can-edit-understanding-the-produser [23 April 2012].

―――― (2008) *Blogs, Wikipedia, Second Life, and Beyond: From Production to Produsage*. New York, NY: Peter Lang.

Bruzzi, S. (2006) *New Documentary*. Second edition. London: Routledge.

Cannold, L. (2006, August 10) 'Net a Window on the World, but Not Always the Facts', *The Age*. Available: www.theage.com.au/news/opinion/net-a-window-on-the-world-but-not-always-the-facts/2006/08/09/1154802957759.html.

Cooper, S. D. (2006) *Watching the Watchdog: Bloggers as the Fifth Estate*. Spokane, WA: Marquette Books.

Cornfield, M., J. Carson, A. Kalis and E. Simon (2005) 'Buzz, Blogs and Beyond: The internet and the National Discourse in the Fall of 2004', *Pew internet Research*. Available: www.pewinternet.org/ppt/BUZZ_BLOGS__BEYOND_Final05-16-05.pdf.

Dahlberg, L. (2001) 'Computer-Mediated Communication and the Public Sphere: A Critical Analysis', *Journal of Computer Mediated Communication*, 7, 1. Available: http://jcmc.indiana.

edu/vol7/issue1/dahlberg.html.

Donath, J. S. (2004) 'Sociable Media', in W. Bainbridge (ed.) *The Encyclopedia of Human-Computer Interaction*. Great Barrington, MA: Berkshire. Available: http://smg.media.mit.edu.

Dovey, J. (2000) *Freakshow: First Person Media and Factual Television*. London: Pluto Press.

Eakin, P. J. (1999) 'Relational Selves, Relational Lives: Autobiography and the Myth of Autonomy', in P. J. Eakin (ed.) *How Our Lives Become Stories: Making Selves*. Ithaca, NY: Cornell University Press, 43–98.

Fraser, N. (1985) 'What's Critical about Critical Theory? The Case of Habermas and Gender', *New German Critique*, 35, 97–131. Available: (stable URL) www.jstor.org/stable/488202.

Funnell, A (2008) 'Networking for Good', *The Media Report*. Radio National Australia.

Future Exploration Network (2008) *Future of Media Report: 2008*. Available: www.futureexploration.net.

Gergen, K. J. (1971) *The Concept of Self*. New York: Holt, Rinehart and Winston.

Giddens, A. (1991) *Modernity and Self-Identity: Self and Society in the Late Modern Age*. Cambridge: Polity Press.

Grossmann, L. and A. Hamilton (2004) 'Meet Joe Blog', *Time*, January 13.

Hiler, J. (2002) 'Blogosphere: The Emerging Media Ecosystem: How Weblogs and Journalists Work Together to Report, Filter and Break the News'. Available: www.microcontentnews.com/articles/blogosphere.htm [accessed 21 October 2010].

Hodkinson, P. (2007) 'Interactive Online Journals and Individualization', *New Media and Society*, 9, 4, 625–50.

Hughes, P. (2008) 'Individualisation of the Documentary: Documentary on New Media', paper presented at the Society for Cinema and Media Studies Conference, Philadelphia, USA. 6 March.

Jenkins, H. (2002, March 2002) 'Blog This: Online Diarists Rule an internet Strewn with Failed Dot Coms', *Technology Review*. Available: www.technologyreview.com/printer_friendly_article.aspx?id=12768 [accessed 26 June 2007].

'Joey' (2006) 'Urban Manifesto', *Urban Jacksonville*. Available: www.urbanjacksonville.info/2006/04/05/urban-manifesto [accessed 20 March 2007].

Kellner, D. (n.d.) 'Habermas, the Public Sphere, and Democracy: A Critical Intervention'. Available: www.gseis.ucla.edu/faculty/kellner/papers/habermas.htm [accessed 23 April 2012].

Kompare, D. (2006) 'Publishing Flow: DVD Box Sets and the Reconception of Television', *Television and New Media*, 7, 4, 335–60.

Lebow, A. (2008) *First Person Jewish*. Minneapolis, MN: University of Minnesota Press.

Lipton, L. (1974) *Independent Filmmaking*. London: Studio Vista.

McCullagh, K. (2008) 'Blogging: Self Presentation and Privacy', *Information and Communications Technology Law*, 17, 1, 3–23. Available: http://dx.doi.org/10.1080/13600830801886984.

Nichols, B. (1994) *Blurred Boundaries: Questions of Meaning in Contemporary Culture*. Bloomington, IN: Indiana University Press.

O'Baoill, A. (2004) 'Weblogs and the Public Sphere', *Into the blogosphere: rhetoric, community, and the culture of weblogs*. Available: http://blog.lib.umn.edu/blogosphere/weblogs_and_the_public_sphere.html [accessed 4 October 2004].

Poster, M. (1995) 'The Net as a Public Sphere?', *Wired*, November. Available: www.wired.com/wired/archive/3.11/poster.if_pr.html.

Potter, J. and M. Wetherell (1987) 'Speaking Subjects', in J. Potter and M. Wetherell (eds) *Discourse and Social Psychology: Beyond Attitudes and Behaviour*. London: Sage, 95–115.

Rainie, L. (2005) 'Data Memo: The State of Blogging', *Pew internet and American Life Project*. Available: www.pewinternet.org/.

Regan, T. (2006) 'Blogs Now Have a World of Influence', *The Christian Science Monitor*. Available: www.csmonitor.com/2006/0517/p14s01-cogn.html.

Renov, M. (1995) 'New Subjectivities: Documentary and Self-Representation in the Post-Verite

Age', *Documentary Box*, 7. Available: www.yidff.jp/docbox/7/box7-1-e.html.

____ (2004) *The Subject of Documentary*. Minneapolis, MN: University of Minnesota Press.

Rose, N. S. (1991) *Governing the Soul: The Shaping of the Private Self*. London: Routledge.

____ (1996) *Inventing Our Selves : Psychology, Power, and Personhood*. Cambridge: Cambridge University Press.

Serfaty, V. (2004) *The Mirror and the Veil: An Overview of American Online Diaries and Blogs*, Amsterdam Monographs in American Studies; 011. Amsterdam: Rodopi.

Sorenson, B. (2008) 'Digital Video and Alexandre Astruc's Camera-Stylo: The New Avant Garde in Documentary Realized?', *Studies in Documentary Film*, 2, 1, 47–59.

Weiner, P. (1973) *Making the Media Revolution: A Handbook for Video Production*. New York, NY: Macmillan.

Williams, J. B. and J. Jacobs (2004) 'Exploring the Use of Blogs as Learning Spaces in the Higher Education Sector', *Australasian Journal of Educational Technology*, 20, 2, 232–47. Available: http://ascilite.org.au/ajet/ajet20/williams.html.

Winston, B. (1993) 'The Documentary Film as Scientific Prescription', in M. Renov (ed.) *Theorizing Documentary*. New York, NY: Routledge, 37–57.

____ (1995) *Claiming the Real*. London: British Film Institute.

The ME and the WE:
A First Person Meditation on
Media Translation in Three Acts

Alexandra Juhasz

ACT 1: <u>Mp:me, Variant of a Manifesta</u> (After Dziga Vertov, 'WE: Variant of a Manifesto, Vertov [1922] 1984)

In which the intrepid feminist media professor revisits the 1922 manifesto of a respected master (Vertov [1922] 1984) *to demonstrate what changes when the heralded machines and ideas of his 'modern' adapt over history, across gender, through the shifting strategies and demands of radical art and politics, and through digital technologies.*

I call myself MP:me (MediaPraxis:AlexandraJuhasz) – as opposed to 'cinematographer', one of a herd of machomen doing rather well peddling slick clean wares.

I see no connection between true femi-digi-praxis and the cunning and calculation of the cine-profiteers.

I consider manipulated corporate reality television – weighed down with music and narrative and childhood games – an absurdity.

To the American victim documentary with its showy dynamism and power disparities and to YouTube's direct-to-camera dramatisations of so many individuals' personal pain or pleasure, this femi-digi-practitioner says thanks for the return to real people, the hand-held look, and the close-up. Good ... but disorderly, not based on a precise study of Media Praxis (the hundred-year history of theoretical writing and related political media production).[1] A cut above the psychological drama, but still lacking in foundation. A Cliché. A copy of a copy.

I proclaim the stuff of YouTube, all based on the slogan (pithy, precise, rousing calls to action or consumption, or action as consumption), to be leprous.[2]

– Keep your mouse from them!

– Keep your eyes off those bite-sized wonders!

– They're morally dangerous!

– Contagious!

I affirm the future of digital art by hacking its present and learning from its past.[3]

I am MP:me. I build connections to history and theory and inter-relations between individuals and committed communities. With my small cheap camcorder, my laptop and internet connection, I make messy, irregular feminist video committed to depth and complexity.

'Cinematography', the earliest male tradition built on sizeable machines, stylish form and solo cine-adventures must die so that the communal art of femi-digi-praxis may live. I call for its death to be hastened.

I protest against the smooth operator and call for a rough synthesis of history, politics, theory, real people and their chaotic, mundane desires and knowledge.

I invite you:

– to flee –

the sweet embrace of America's *Next Top Model*

the poison of the commercial send-up

the clutches of technophilia, the allure of boys' toys

to turn your back on music, effects, gizmos

– to flee – out into the open with camcorder in hand, into four dimensions (history, politics, theory + practice), in search of our own material, from our own experiences, relationships and commitments to social justice.

Mp:me is made visible through a camcorder femi-digi-praxis: a small, hand-held, retro video aesthetic connected to a lengthy history of communal, low-budget, political and theoretical media production.

Author's Note 1: Since the mid-1980s, I have been making community-based, activist video about social issues to which I am committed – AIDS, feminism, queer pride and families, war, representation. Building on past theories and practices of political filmmaking, engaging within modern-day communities of activist practitioners, I have attempted to model a theoretically and ethically aware communally-produced media practice making the most of affordable consumer technologies. Last year, I attempted to move this media praxis to YouTube and was disappointed to find that the mere expansion of access to production and dissemination does not a media revolution make. My manifesta conjures the cynicism of our era, while maintaining a commitment to the thrill of conviction and the relevance of history and theory for today's new media forms.

ACT 2: The Me & the We Move to YouTube

In which the humble, bumbling amateur – the very same bombastic Mp:me introduced in ACT 1, the self-same 'I' of the 'Author's Note 1', the 'director' called 'SCALEthedoc' on YouTube – gets cut down to size as a result of translating her manifesta into short YouTube videos. In this Act, our professor attempts to describe, using words alone, how she hacked the new media of YouTube to inter-cut her short Mp:me videos with other Vertov homages, and related digital sundries, to create a veritable Vertovian internationale through the clunky 'Playlist' function, itself demonstrating what is bettered and lost by transformations in technology, time, place, politics and technique.

1. I Call Myself Mp:me

In a bedroom, on a bureau. A round mirror.
Feminine space cluttered with photos, knick-knacks, papers.
The stuff of women and home.

We hear: 'I call myself MP:me (MediaPraxis:AlexandraJuhasz)...'
(We remember: 'WE call ourselves *Cine-Eyes*...' (Vertov 1988: 69)

Slow (but shaky) zoom into mirror. The first of many (circles, mirrors).
The female videomaker's reflection, camcorder in hand, comes into focus.
She is all women filmmakers. She is Mp:me, not WE.
Media feminists quickly claimed the first person I, eschewing authorial
    distance and artistic mastery. An I towards the WE.
At home with technology. Alone with her consumer camera. On her bed.
She's dressed (none of this prurient eye-blinking-bra-on-shit).
Her seated figure slowly fills the frame as she speaks her manifesta.
Dialogue stilted. Poorly performed. She's no actress.
But he didn't use actors either. The WE he caught was unaware, and she is very
    aware, hyper-aware. She's quoting nearly hundred-year-old film theory for
    God's sake.

'THE MOST UNPROFITABLE, THE MOST UNECONOMIC WAY OF
COMMUNICATING A SCENE IS THROUGH **THEATRICAL COMMUNI-
CATION.**' (Vertov 1988: 92)

Different reals. New truths. Changing theatricals.
She continues: '...as opposed to "cinematographer", one of a herd of machomen
    doing rather well peddling slick clean wares.'
(It conjures: 'as distinct from 'cinematographer' – that flock of junk dealers
    who do rather well peddling their rags' (Vertov 1988: 69).)

And she's no cinematographer. No machoman junk dealer.
Just a postmodern feminist inserting her words into what's left behind.
    Repeating. Ripping. Fan-girl.
A Cliché. A copy of a copy.
He invented a world seen newly. She clicks Command-C and corrupts.
He never filmed himself, although the rest of the WE, his brother and wife,
    were characters in the movie, playing themselves, cameraman and editor.
She's all alone at home like so many present-day mediamakers.

Reaching out through the wires, but isolated even so.

We wanted the personal to become the political. A different move toward the communal.

But YouTube is premised upon the isolated masses.

Still zooming: the eye of the camera fills the frame. Beyond self-referential into the endlessly reflective digital domain.

Using the Playlist function, which allows YouTube to present a series of pre-selected videos in one's tiny desktop video screen in the order of the 'director's' selection, we cut to:

2. *The Man with the Movie Camera, 1929, by Dziga Vertov*[5]

Discordant electronica matched to a stream of the fastest cuts imaginable. Faster than the master.

'THE ELECTRIC YOUTH' (Vertov 1988: 92)

Ripped Vertovian iconography on steroids. On Final Cut Pro.

'MAKE WAY FOR THE MACHINE!' (Vertov 1988: 91)

No need for scissors. Or hands. Or a camera. We see his stolen:
Eyes. Crowds. Eyes. Trains. Eyes. Projector in a crowded cinema.

'I, a machine, am showing you a world the likes of which only I can see' (Vertov 1984: 5).

Modern adventurer giving it all for the project of enhanced vision,
    new knowledge.

'The Eye, disputing the visual concept of the world by the human eye and offering its own "I see"' (Vertov 1984: 7).

Postmodern couch potato taking from the original 'I' to build a new sort of
    we/I see.
Double vision. Then and now. His and mine. It's all become ours. Zeros and
    ones.

'Fragments of actual energy [...] condensed into a cumulative whole by the great mastery of an editing technique' (Vertov 1984: 6–7).

Extended final shot: the signature extreme close-up, again, of camera eye.
Shutters close.

After clunky playlist transition that includes suggestions for random videos that YouTube suggests you might want to see (and you often might, thus beginning an aimless, mapless trip to unrelated sounds and images, the opposite of montage – driven as it should be by cuts of meaning). Cut to:

3. Corporate Reality TV: A Cliché (Mp:me part 3)[6]

A messy sink. Home again.
Inescapable digital clarity. Too crisp, really.
I want to make a video about women, a woman.

You hear my manifesta: 'I consider manipulated corporate reality television – weighed down with music and narrative and childhood games – an absurdity.'

This everyday kitchen is mine. A place for women where the common stuff of life is made, cleaned, remade. Reality TV stripped of dramatic effects. The plain mundane detritus of daily life.

'Life is so complex and contradictory in everyday situations that it continuously creates dramatic conflicts and resolves them unexpectedly in the most extraordinary way. My idea is to select and connect different episodes and facts in a manner which will create a new narrative whole as a unique dramatic event' (Shub 1933: 449).

Camera begins slow continuous circular pan to the left.
Not a place for *Desperate Housewives*. Too dirty; too funky.
You can tell it belongs to the woman shooting it, not some man with
    a camera.
The images lack expertise and distance. Stuff's drying in the sink.

I say: 'To the American victim documentary with its shown dynamism and power disparities and to YouTube's direct-to-camera dramatisations of so many individuals' personal pain or pleasure...'

Shub again: 'For a long time I have wanted to make a cinematic document about Soviet women. Now, everybody can judge the result of this endeavour. Nothing in this film is supposed to be invented. There will be no actors in it. All the individuals seen on the screen will have their personal names, families and addresses. Perhaps they will turn out to be your acquaintances, friends or enemies' (1933: 451).

Camera continues to circle.
Of course there's real, and then, real again. Styles change. And reality with it?
Stove with spices and teapot. Can we go somewhere neat?
Can we hear this chick talk about herself? Her abusive husband?
    Her anorexia?

'...this femi-digi-practioner says thanks for the return to real people...'

'If in 1914 the citizens of Imperial Russia had wanted to know what woman is
    like, the art of the period could have provided them with a precise answer.'
The thunder of circus music. Marches and fanfares.
A blue and pink woman with a golden wreath around her head emerges on the
    screen.

An infant lies in her arms.

She changes into a full nude woman with red cheeks, lying on green grass.

She becomes Leonardo da Vinci's beauty with the egoistic smile.

She changes into the woman painted by Beardsley. [...] Throughout this
pageant, the circus music repeats marches and fanfares' (Shub 1933: 451).

Circling. 'Real' kitchen: knives. Refrigerator. No fanfare.

Here's Vertov: 'It is necessary to get out of the circle of ordinary human vision:
reality must be recorded not by imitating it, but by broadening the circle ordi-
narily encompassed by the human eye' (1984: 10).

'...the hand-held look, and the close-up. Good ... but disorderly...'

Oh, it's disorderly. Camera keeps moving. This kitchen, and the machine that
records it, are a mess. She needs some training. And a vision.

'The sound of the motor dominates.

1934.

A field. A pasture. A tractor is working...

We continue to move through the field. Apparently, we are on an invisible car
which takes us from the field on the bridge over a small river.

The village opens up before us.

We jump out of the invisible car. Everything swings and shakes. The sound of
the motor is cut off. We are now firmly on the ground.

We realise that the car which brought us here is, in fact, a mobile sound-movie
theatre' (Shub 1978: 454).

'Not based on a precise study of Media Praxis (the hundred-year history of
theoretical writing and related political media production). A cut above the
psychological drama...'

Wires crossing on the counter, crossed wires. Coffee pot. Mixed machines,
mixed metaphors.

'...but still lacking in foundation. A Cliché. A copy of a copy.'

Circle's complete.

My teacher did it first. A 'woman's way of seeing.' A 'Riddle'.

What do women want? See?

'Very slow 360-degree panning shots encompassing different environments, from the domestic to the professional...' This could be seen as a formal development of the Lacanian analyses that Mulvey had applied to the female image in film in essays such as 1975's 'Visual Pleasure and Narrative Cinema'.

Camera pans up. And there's the camerawoman, again. Me. The voice. In my little kitchen mirror. No community here. Still alone in the house. Moving from room to room, mirror to mirror. Shooting herself with commitment if not expertise. A broken tautology built on references, opposed to cinematic beauty, disappointed in all that is not delivered.

'As we look at the artist sighting along his outstretched arm and forefinger towards the centre of the screen we are watching, what we see is a sustained tautology: a line of sight that begins at Acconci's plane of vision and ends at the eyes of his projected double. In that image of self-regard is configured a narcissism so endemic to works of video that I find myself wanting to generalise it as the condition of the entire genre. Yet, what would it mean to say, "The medium of video is narcissism?"' (Krauss 1976: 50)

Her eyes move rapidly up and down. From direct gaze at the viewer, to quick glances at the viewfinder, the new kind that is itself a stand-alone private screen.

'DON'T COPY THE EYES' (Vertov 1988, 91)

'[We] reveal both the real life and the psychology of a typical woman working in the Soviet village. If we succeeded, it will be the first direct film-interview with the new woman farmer in the USSR. Therefore it has to be done in a such a way that the conversation does not look contrived... One day in Khlevyansky Selsoviet, to be filmed on the specific day, month and year of 1934' (Shub 1978: 456).

CRASH! Something's fallen and the woman with the camera starts. No control. A specific day, month, year, and room, 2008. Cut to:

4. *Rails*[7]

A shot from below of a train endlessly elongated with invisible edits (tinyscissors, computercuts).
Vertov refracted. Machines extending durations.

'DOWN WITH 16 FRAMES A SECOND!' (Vertov 1988: 91)

Looping moving forward on straight dynamic lines.
Massive metal beast roaring above. WE are its power.
A machine. One man.
Man with a movie camera.
All weight and might and moving stillness.

Ghostleg superimposes computer-generated spirals on to linear perspective
   of yore.
Things change, they stay the same.
Things move, they stay still.

Celebration of ancient modern digital vision machine.
Perennial masculine emphasis on kinetic linear forceful machine aided vision.

*'Our path leads through the poetry of machines, from the bungling citizen to the
perfect electric man'* (Vertov 1984: 8).

YouTube cuts to:

5. *I am MP:me Part 5*[8]

Camera starts on polka-dot shoes. As she pans up we see that while she is still
inside, she's now in an artist's studio cluttered with paints, brushes, and the
portrait of a young black girl (her daughter). Of course, the long take (no cutting for her!). Of course it ends with herself framed in a portrait-like if messy
mirror shot. She's no master and her images are frustrating. They do not well
reflect the ideas of her manifesto (where is the community? The interaction?
Who is her we? YouTube viewers? Feminists? Women? Why is she always
alone?)

[Author's Note 2: *It's hard to get together a crew, not to mention the expense,
and who wants to be the boss anyway? Let's face it, some things don't deserve a
fancy-pants camera and its associated cinematographer, some things just want
to be said, and why can't I say them, and show them, and if people want to see
them, all the better, and if they don't, who cares? I'm not trying to be some kind
of genius. An electric man. An international art star. Is that the only reason to
make art?! To speak? Real people make messy, regular things and God bless
'em. I'm not saying I'm a bungling citizen but I'm no machoman either*]: 'I am

MP:me. I build connections to history and theory and inter-relations between individuals and committed communities. With my small cheap camcorder, my laptop and internet connection, I make messy, collaborative, irregular feminist video committed to depth, interaction and complexity.'

Over the past twenty years, I have made experimental, personal, political documentaries about and within communities I am already engaged: AIDS activists; media feminists; queer, feminist and leftist families; the peace movement. My scholarly work on activist media has pushed me to engage in an ethical practice, veering from the tradition and tactics of the victim documentary (taking pleasure in another's pain), and instead imagining community-bound, communally-produced feminist visions of radical, political subjectivity. My politics, which are theoretically informed and consider the relations between power, subjectivity, community and control of representation, are communicated through the way I organise the documents I produce about my own lived experiences and ideas about the historical world: my femi-digi-praxis.

7. Alex on intimacy, tension & beauty of small scale video[9]

I made my documentary *SCALE: Measuring Might in the Media Age* (2007) with and about my sister Antonia, an anti-war activist and self-declared policy wonk, as she engaged in a 'scale-shift', leaving her grassroots community behind to pursue a corporate book-tour.[10] In the documentary, we consider how the stress and connection between sisters, and across the Left, mirror larger stories of power and intimacy.

In this longish, five-minute clip of footage from the documentary (YouTube is at its best at two minutes or less), we face the camera, sitting next to each other on a train. I hold a large microphone, and a pad of paper with notes. I appear to be interviewing my sister. We are looking at each other, not the camera. Our bodies face each other. Our body language easy and interactive. She asks me if it will look weird that my documentary cuts footage from my 'small hand-camera' with that of the professional cameraman (who is clearly shooting this interview). 'It will remind viewers about my SCALE', I answer. 'Maybe they'll think it's an artistic choice', Antonia suggests. I reply that it is, in fact, an artistic and a practical choice, to shoot small. The cameraman is expensive! 'There's an artistic and formal beauty to me in something that looks like one person made it by themselves [...] there's an artistic decision to see my hand. To see that I am not a television station. I'm not even like my cameraman, whose independent work moves at a higher level than does my own. That's an idea of the piece that will be said visually.'

Antonia wants to talk about the intimacy and tension created by being sisters engaged in a documentary project. The cameraman pushes in. The sisters agree it has been hard to be together 24/7. It comes with its own 'drama'. The interaction loosens and the sisters become more demonstrative: eye rolls, laughs. We say we'd treat each other differently if we were random human beings, filling the typical roles for documentary making. 'But, all of my work has been made about people I have intimate relationships with. There's something in the intimacy and tension that is vital to my work, and it's why I work on a small scale. [...] Now you're a spokesperson, not my sister. So when I make an intimate documentary about you it tells a very big story.'

8. *I call for the death of Cinematography (MP:me part 6)*[11]

I'm in a makeup mirror. Circled by an oval of light. On a vanity.

'LEGITIMISED MYOPIA' (Vertov 1988: 91).

First person work. Multiplied. Fragmented. What am I fighting for?
Our movement was to be from the I to the we. This technology gets in
    the way.

'I am a film writer. A cinepoet. I do not write on paper, but on film. [...] Now I am working on films about the woman. This is not one subject, but a series of themes. These films will be about a school-girl, about a girl at home, about a mother and child, about abortion, about the creative female youth, about the differences between our girls and those abroad ... about the infant girl, about the mature woman and the old woman...' (Vertov 1944: 369).

Watching myself. Listening to myself speak. Mature woman. Girl at home.
Gaining and losing self, authority, mastery and community.
Vertov and his boys shot the people.
He let his brother play himself, the lead in a film about no one, everyone.
Authority was put onto others, diffused, to be reclaimed. Cemented for the
    man.

I declare: 'Cinematography, the modernist male tradition built on sizeable machines, stylish form, and solo cine-adventures must die so that the communal art of femi-digi-praxis may live. I call for its death to be hastened.'

YouTube cuts to:

9. *Man with a Movie Camera: The Participatory Remake*[12]

Split screen.

Old on the left. New on the right.

Media connects the world.

'You are walking down a street in Chicago now, in 1923, but I force you to bow
    to the late Comrade Volodarsky, who is walking along a street in Petrograd
    in 1918 and who responds to you with a bow.' (Vertov 1988: 92)

Interactive, state (and art world) funded local/global exchanges.

'The impending *revolution through newsreel film.*' (Vertov 1988: 91)

Access opened. Just as he anticipated.

Some things change. Some stay the same.

On the left and right: pretty girls wake and get dressed, each lovely lady
    puts her bra on, as before.

Intercut with the cameraman on the move.

You are invited to upload. Participate.

Coda: Vertov's signature eye in the lens (left), a man's unmediated eye (right), with a corner of a smile.

Credits: Commissioned and Produced by Cornerhouse, the bigger Picture; Enter_; Lumen Gallery in association with the BBC, Funded by the Arts Council of England.

'THE MACHINE & ITS CAREER' (Vertov 1988: 91).

YouTube cuts to:

10. *On activism versus the movement of ideas*[13]

My sister is being interviewed by me in medium close-up. She's on a couch in her apartment, looking at the camera eye (me).

'Do you consider yourself an activist?'

'Yeah' (she laughs).

'How do you define that?'

Antonia answers: 'For me being an activist is putting ideas I have into some form of action which means some form of organizing. It's not just protest and it's not just articulating problems, but trying to change them.'

'So your book [*The BUSH AGENDA: Invading the World One Economy at a Time*] is not activism, but a preliminary step towards activism. It will become activism if...'

'I organize around the ideas of the book.'

'One of the issues for me', continues Alex, 'as someone who works in the movement of ideas... Well, we both create ideas. We're intellectuals. We both move ideas through writing or video... is that I debate this: is that itself activism – probably not – when it hits up against another human being and creates a new way of knowing.'

'I think it's about what you do with the item.'

'You can't have one without the other. You can't have activism without the ideas moving, But activism means a related action and change in the world, not just the world of ideas.'

'I agree', concludes my sister.

ACT 3: My iManifesta

In which I try to justify ACT 2.

YouTube lets me effortlessly make and share my messy wares. The man with a movie camera had to ride motorcars, climb smokestacks, and crawl beneath rails while I access his ancient footage at home with one click. The woman with the editing machine had to line up celluloid strips on hooks on the wall which she cut with scissors and sealed again with glue while I link with another click. While artistry counts for a lot – genius, beauty – it is not the only reason to make or watch media, and it is hard for real people to muster or master. DIY (and contemporary feminism) were beyond Vertov's vision, even as his subject was the people/women. The 'bad' video of YouTube, mine included, heralds a new form of communication, built from old and new machines. For instance, using the (new) clunky YouTube Playlist function, I intercut between the simple video chapters of my (new) manifesta and some of the ubiquitous (old and new) YouTube versions of *Man with a Movie Camera*, always at my reach. On-line, making easy use of the new technologies and forms of YouTube, I believe I effectively demonstrate sustaining tensions and connections (but that's been harder to accomplish here): between modernist/post-modernist form, male and female approaches to media, the home and the city, the private and public, the personal and the social, going solo and communal, the self and the group, the self and the other, film and video, the analog and the digital, the expert and the amateur, the communist and the feminist, and how the powers of new media undo or redo many of Vertov's claims about cinema (linking, montage, the unscripted and scripted real), including the changing processes of production, participation, and collaboration.

Author's Note 3: Trained as an academic and a video artist, it has not been easy for me to depart from the tried and true methods that give our work its place. Or perhaps it's been too easy: my feminist inclinations have meant that I've almost always written in the 'I' voice, disavowing jargon, affecting the pretence of the loosening of authority. And I've always insisted on also making personal/political videos, too, whatever my bosses say is the norm. In any case, I have attempted here to model the possibility for play, experimentation, drafting – the waning of expertise – that YouTube, at its best, creates for anyone with access to an increasingly inexpensive set of home digital tools. For this essay, I tried to creatively translate into writing a uniquely YouTube movement (and moment) linking images and sounds easily created and/or gathered from across the history of cinema only then to be equalised on a digital screen. I mimicked the poetic (and perhaps bombastic) writing style of Vertov (and also Esther Shub) to create 'scripts' of videos that can never be seen on paper, but are easily accessible on YouTube. The Soviets anticipated a visual Esperanto, beyond the word, whose time is upon us. And yet it is not. For here, I write, and feel better heard. More people can see these 'films' on YouTube than ever saw them on Vertov's agit-trains or in cinema studies classrooms. More people will hear me rant on YouTube than will ever read these pages. Yet, on YouTube, isolated from their context of production, and embedded within corporate frames, these videos flow interchangeably and without the necessary shock of the new. Made by newly liberated consumers, many of them look like, are, or pay homage to corporate media. They fall outside a community of believers, or even learners, as they are produced and consumed by individual eyes alone in their private home-media-palaces. These three Acts attempt a translation and re-translation – from Vertov to contemporary feminist to video to page – pointing to specificities of access, language, medium and expertise that are becoming confused, due to YouTube's power of cross-media – but which are always at the heart of making, understanding and writing about first person media work.

Notes

1   See my website: www.mediapraxis.com.
2   See my blog on things YouTube: www.aljean.wordpress.com.
3   See my experiment in digital education, Learning from YouTube: www.youtube.com/mediapraxisme.
4   http://www.youtube.com/watch?v=i7ZVHQC6RUY&feature=PlayList&p=4D3B25B7DBECDCD5&index=0. **From:** SCALEthedoc. **Added:** February 28, 2008. 29 seconds.
    Description: I call myself MP:me — as opposed to 'cinematographer,' one of a herd of machomen doing rather well peddling slick clean wares. (After 'WE: Variant of a Mainfesto,' Dziga Vertov, 1922). **Category:** Film & Animation. **Tags:** MPme Alexandra Juhasz Dziga Vertov Manifesto video camcorder feminist media documentary experimental theory politics
5   http://www.youtube.com/watch?v=brVO2I4bONc&feature=PlayList&p=4D3B25B7DBECDCD5&index=3. **From:** prlosolvidados. **Added:** July 01, 2007. 13 seconds.
    Description: How many plans Vertov can show in just 13 seconds? **Category:** People & Blogs. **Tags:** Dziga Vertov Kino Glaz
6   http://www.youtube.com/watch?v=bor6x1_kl8k&feature=PlayList&p=4D3B25B7DBECDCD5&index=4. **From:** SCALEthedoc. **Added:** February 28, 2008. 1:00.
    Description: I consider manipulated corporate reality television — weighed down with music and narrative and childhood games — an absurdity. To the American victim documentary with its shown dynamism and power disparities and to YouTube's direct-to-camera dramatizations of so many individuals' personal pain or pleasure this femi-digi-practioner says thanks for the return to real people, the hand-held look, and the close-up. Good...but disorderly, not based on a precise study of Media Praxis (the hundred year history of theoretical writing and related political media production). A cut above the psychological drama, but still lacking in foundation. A Cliché. A copy of a copy. **Category:** Film & Animation. **Tags:** MPme Alexandra Juhasz Dziga Vertov Manifesto video camcorder feminist reality TV documentary experimental politics
7   http://www.youtube.com/watch?v=9XZzk0UnjrM&feature=PlayList&p=4D3B25B7DBECDCD

5&index=5. **From:** Ghostleg. **Added:** February 17, 2008. 1:13 minutes.

Description: remix of dziga vertov recorded live at funkworthy fm, bowery poetry club, November 30, 2007. **Category:** Film & Animation. **Tags:** vj ghostleg vertov soviet monotreme tinyscissors

8 http://www.youtube.com/watch?v=LpcKOi9My8A&feature=PlayList&p=4D3B25B7DBECDC D5&index=8. **From:** SCALEthe doc. **Added:** Feburary 28, 2008. 20 seconds.

Description: I am MP:me. I build connections to history and theory and inter-relations between individuals and committed communities. With my small cheap camcorder, my laptop, and internet connection, I make messy, collaborative, irregular feminist video committed to depth, interaction and complexity. (After 'WE: Variant of a Manifesto,' Dziga Vertov, 1922). **Category:** Nonprofits & Activism. **Tags:** MPme Alexandra Juhasz Dziga Vertov Manifesto video camcorder feminist YouTube documentary experimental theory politics

9 http://www.youtube.com/watch?v=zM6RtfRDz8g&feature=PlayList&p=4D3B25B7DBECDCD 5&index=9. **From:** SCALEthe doc. **Added:** February 11, 2008. 5:08 minutes.

Description: Alex discusses her feminist analysis of small scale video: the difference in style, tone, and effect of small cameras and production, working with people you know, and using small stories to tell big ones. **Category:** Film & Animation. **Tags:** SCALEthedocumentary SCALE Antonia Alexandra Juhasz independent small feminist alternative grassroots video media

10 See www.snagfilms.com and www.scalethedocumentary.com.

11 http://www.youtube.com/watch?v=_Eno4Rk7Xqc&feature=PlayList&p=4D3B25B7DBECDCD 5&index=10. **From:** SCALEthe doc. **Added:** February 28, 2008. 30 seconds.

Description: 'Cinematography,' the earliest male tradition built on sizeable machines, stylish form, and solo cine-adventures must die so that the communal art of femi-digi-praxis may live. I call for its death to be hastened. I protest against the smooth operator and call for a rough synthesis of history, politics, theory, real people and their chaotic, mundane desires and knowledge. (After 'WE: Variant of a Manifesto,' Dziga Vertov, 1922). **Category:** Science & Technology. **Tags:** MPme Alexandra Juhasz Dziga Vertov Manifesto video camcorder feminist YouTube documentary experimental cinematography

12 http://www.youtube.com/watch?v=IrZjqmrSFdY&feature=PlayList&p=4D3B25B7DBECDCD5 &index=11. **From:** perrybard. **Added:** November 18, 2007. 2:17 minutes.

Description: Based on Dziga Vertov's 1929 film by the same name, people around the world are invited to log onto the website http://dziga.perrybard.net and upload footage interpreting Vertov for the 21st century. This short segment contains uploads by 15 people from 8 countries. Log on now! **Category:** Film & Animation. **Tags:** animation art documentary experimental short film

13 http://www.youtube.com/watch?v=TSGvsdB89Uc&feature=PlayList&p=4D3B25B7DBECDC D5&index=13. **From:** SCALE thedoc. **Added:** January 31, 2008. 2:38 minutes.

Description: Antonia and her sister, Alex, debate the relationship between ideas and activism...theory and practice. **Category:** News & Politics. **Tags:** SCALEthedocumentary SCALE activism change organizing protest Antonia Juhasz anti-war anti-globalization

References

Juhasz, A. (2007) *The BUSH AGENDA: Invading the World One Economy at a Time*. New York, NY: HarperCollins.

Krauss, R. (1976) 'Video: The Aesthetics of Narcissism', *October*, 1, 50–64.

Mulvey, L. (1977) Screenonline, *Riddles of the Sphinx*. http://www.screenonline.org.uk/film/ id/567526/

Shub, E. (1978 [1933]) 'I Want to Make a Film About Women', In V. Petric (ed.) 'Esther Shub's

Unrealized Project', *Quarterly Review of Film Studies*, 3, 4, 449–56.

Vertov, D. (1944) 'Films About Women', trans. V. Telber, The Writings of Drigo [Sic] Vertov, www.vasulka.org/archive/Writings/From_the_Manifesto.rtf : 369.

____ (1984) 'WE: Variant of a Manifesto,' in *Kino-Eye: The Writings of Dziga Vertov*, ed. A. Michelson, trans. K. O'Brien. Berkeley, CA: University of California Press, 5–9.

____ (1988 [1923]) 'We. A Version of a Manifesto' [1922] and 'The Cine-Eyes. A Revolution,' in R. Taylor and I. Christie (eds) *The Film Factory: Russian and Soviet Cinema in Documents*. New York, NY: Routledge: 69–71 and 89–93.

FILMOGRAPHY

This filmography includes first person films, videos, interactive media and web content discussed in the chapters of this volume. It is not meant to be an exhaustive list of first person documentary.

The American Who Electrified Russia (Michael Chanan, 2009, UK)

Amor Sanjuan (Luis Misis, 2006, Spain)

Another Shot (Daniel Singelenberg, 1973, US)

Autoportrait (Olivier Fouchard, 1997, France)

Autoportrait refilmé (Olivier Fouchard, 1998, France)

Bare (Santana Issar, 2006, India)

Berlin 10/90 (Robert Kramer, 1993, US)

Born into Brothels (Zana Briski and Ross Kaufman, 2005, US)

Bowling for Columbine (Michael Moore, 2003, US)

Bucarest, la memoria perdida (*Bucharest, Memory Lost*) (Albert Solé, 2008, Spain)

Camera Natura (Sarah Gibson, 1985, Australia)

Caro diario (*Dear Diary*) (Nanni Moretti, 1993, Italy)

Chantal Akerman par Chantal Akerman (*Chantal Akerman by Chantal Akerman*) Chantal Akerman, 1997, France)

Chelovek s kino-apparatom (*Man with a Movie Camera*) (Dziga Vertov 1929, USSR)

Chronique d'un été (*Chronicle of a Summer*) (Jean Rouch and Edgar Morin, 1960, France)

El cielo gira (*The Sky Turns*) (Mercedes Álvarez, 2004, Spain)

Claro (Glauber Rocha, 1975, Brazil)

Coffee Break (Gail Camhi, 1976, US)

Daggueréotypes (Agnés Varda, 1976, France)

Daughter Rite (Michelle Citron, 1979, US)

David Holzman's Diary (Jim McBride, 1967, US)

Demain et encore demain (*Tomorrow and Tomorrow*) (Dominique Cabrera 1995–97, France)

Desperately Seeking Helen (Eisha Marjara, 1998, Canada)

Detroit: Ruin of a City (Michael Chanan and George Steinmetz, 2005, UK)

Diario argentino (*Argentinian Diary*) (Lupe Pérez, 2006, Spain/Argentina)

Di-Glauber (alt title: *Di Cavalcanti*) (Glauber Rocha, 1977 Brazil)

Emak Bakia (Man Ray, 1926, France)

Eyes of Stone (Nilita Vacchani, 1990, India)

Extreme Private Eros: Love Song (Kazuo Hara, 1974, Japan)

Fahrenheit 9/11 (Michael Moore, 2004, US)

Family Portrait Sittings (Alfred Guzzetti, 1975, US)

Familystrip (Lluis Miñarro, 2009, Spain)

Un film, autoportrait (A Film, Self Portrait)
(Marcel Hanoun, 1985, France)

Film Portrait (Jerome Hill, 1972, US)

Flying: Confessions of a Free Woman (Jennifer
Fox, 2007, US)

Forget Me Not (Unglee, 1979, France)

For Maya (Vasudha Joshi, 1998, India)

For My Children (Michal Aviad, 2002, Israel)

Fotografías (Andrés Di Tella, 2007, Argentina/
India)

Fuente Alamo (Alamo Fountain) (Pablo García,
2001, Spain)

Les glaneur et la glaneuse (The Gleaners and I)
(Agnès Varda, 2001)

De Grand Evenements et des gens ordinaire
(Of Great Events and Ordinary People)
(Raúl Ruiz, 1978, France)

Grandma Has a Video Camera (Tania Cypriano,
2007, US/Brazil)

Guest (José Luis Guerín, 2010, Spain)

Haciendo memoria (Making Memory) (Sandra
Ruesga, 2005, Spain)

The Hidden Story (Ranjani Mazumdar and
Shikha Jhingan, 1995, India)

El horizonte artificial (The Artificial Horizon)
(José Irigoyen, 2005, Spain)

The House on Gulmohar Avenue (Samina
Mishra, 2005, India)

L'Inde fantome (Phantom India) (Louis Malle,
1970, France)

I for India (Sandhya Suri, 2005, UK/India)

An Inconvenient Truth (Davis Guggenheim,
2006, US)

Intervista (Federico Fellini, 1988, Italy)

Italianamerican (Martin Scorsese, 1974, US)

Le joli Mai (Chris Marker, 1963, France)

JLG/JLG: autoportrait de décembre (JLG/
JLG: Self-Portrait in December) (Jean Luc
Godard, 1995, France)

Joyce at 34 (Joyce Chopra and Claudia Weill,
1972, US)

Khel (Saba Dewan and Rahul Roy, 1994, India)

King of Dreams (Amar Kanwar, 2000, India)

KShE, 'Komsomol Patron of Electrification'
(Esfir Shub, 1932, USSR)

Kumar Talkies (Pankaj Rishi Kumar, 1999, India)

Landslides (Sarah Gibson and Susan Lambert,
1986, Australia)

The Leader, His Driver and the Driver's Wife
(Nick Broomfield, 1991, UK)

Lettre de Sibérie (Letter from Siberia) (Chris
Marker, 1957, France)

Lightening Testimonies (Amar Kanwar, 1997,
India)

Local Angel (Udi Aloni, 2002, Israel)

Lost, Lost Lost (Jonas Mekas, 1976, US)

Manhatta (Paul Strand and Charles Sheeler,
1921, US)

The Many Faces of Madness (Amar Kanwar,
2002, India)

Más allá del espejo (Beyond the Mirror)
(Joaquín Jordá, 2006, Spain)

La memoria interior (Interior Memory) (María
Ruido, 2002, Spain)

Mixed Greens (Michelle Citron, 2004, US)

Monos como Becky (Monkeys Like Becky)
(Joaquín Jordá, 1999, Spain)

Montoneros, una historia (Montoneros, a
History) (Andrés Di Tella,1994)

My Brother (Yulie Cohen, 2007, Israel)

My Grandmother's House (Adan Aliaga, 2005,
Spain)

My Mother India (Safina Oberoi, 2000,
Australia).

My Israel (Yulie Cohen, 2008, Israel)

My Land Zion (Yulie Cohen, 2004, Israel)

My Terrorist (Yulie Cohen, 2002, Israel)

Nadar (Swimming) (Carla Subirana, 2008, Spain)

Nana, Mom and Me (Amalie Rothschild, 1974,
US)

Night Movie #1: Self-Portrait (Diana Barrie,
1974, US)

A Night of Prophecy (Amar Kanwar, 2001,
India)

Nobody's Business (Alan Berliner, 1996, US)

N.U. Nettezza Urbana (Michelangelo Antonioni,
1948, Italy)

One Minute Memories (Vito Acconci, 1971–74,
US)

Out for Love... Be Back Shortly (Dan Katzir,
1997, Israel)

Out of Reach (Annie Griffin, 1994, UK)

A Palestinian Journey (Osama Qashoo, 2006
UK/Palestine)

Papá Iván (María Inés Roqué, 2000, Argentina)

Paradise on the River of Hell (Abir Basheer and
Meenu Gaur, 2002, India)

Pashportrets (*Self-Portrait*) (Andris Grinberg, 1972, Latvia)

Pashportrets. Testaments (*Self-Portrait. Testament*) (Andris Grinberg, 2003, Latvia)

Los pasos de Antonio (*Antonio's Steps*) (Pablo Baur, 2007, Spain/Argentina)

Port of Memory (Kamal Aljafari, 2009, Palestine/Germany/France/UAE)

Porto Da Minha Infância (*Porto of My Childhood*) (Manoel de Oliveira, 2001, Portugal)

Postal desde Buenos Aires (*Postcard from Argentina*) (Ricardo Iscar, 2008, Spain)

The Red Tapes (Vito Acconci, 1976, US)

Retrato (Carlos Ruiz, 2004, Portugal/Spain)

Ritorno a Lisca Bianca (*Return to Lisca Bianca*) (Michelangelo Antonioni, 1983, Italy)

Roger and Me (Michael Moore, 1989, US)

The Roof (*Al-Sateh*) (Kamal Aljafari, 2006, Palestine/Germany)

Roof – Shower – Underwater 3 BandW Hand Developed Film Prints (Anja Czioska, 1994, Germany)

Los Rubios (*The Blondes*) (Albertina Carri, 2003, Argentina)

Sans Soleil (*Sunless*) (Chris Marker, 1983, France)

SCALE: Measuring Might in the Media Age (Alexandra Juhasz, 2007, US)

Scénario du film 'Passion' (*Script for the film 'Passion'*) (Jean-Luc Godard, 1982, France)

A Season Outside (Amar Kanwar, 1998, India)

Self Portrait (Chuck Hudina, 1972, US)

Self-Portrait (Jonas Mekas,1990, US)

Self Portrait (Maria Lassnig, 1973, Austria)

Self Portrait 2 (Lin Qiu, 2006, US)

Self Portrait '92 (Vilgot Sjöman, 1992, Sweden)

Selfportrait/Autobiography: A Work in Progress (Chantal Akerman, 1998, France)

Self-Portrait as Kaspar Hauser (Brian Frye, 2000, US)

Self Portrait Post Mortem (Louise Bourque, 2002, US/Canada)

Serious Undertakings (Helen Grace and Erica Addis, 1983, Australia)

Lo sguardo di Michelangelo (*The Gaze of Michelangelo*) (Michelangelo Antonioni, 2004, Italy)

Shadows of Freedom (Sabina Kidwai, 2004)

Sherman's March (Ross McElwee, 1985, US)

Sicko (Michael Moore, 2007, US)

Sita's Family (Saba Dewan, 2002, India)

Snapshots from a Family Album (Avijit Mukul Kishore, 2003, India),

A Song of Air (Merilee Bennett, 1988, Australia)

The Space Between the Teeth (Bill Viola, 1976, US)

Speaking Directly: Some American Notes (Jon Jost, 1972, US)

Summer in My Veins (Nishit Saran, 1999, US/India)

Tales of the Night Fairies (Shohini Ghosh, 2002, India)

Tarnation (Jonathan Caouette, 2003, US)

La television y yo (*Television and Me*) (Andrés Di Tella, 2003, Argentina)

Tell Them, 'The Tree They had Planted Has Now Grown' (Ajay Raina, 2002, India)

Le Temps et la Distance (*Time and Distance*) (François Gurgui, 2001, France/Spain)

Testament (James Broughton, 1974, US)

Le testament d'Orphée (*The Testament of Orpheus*) (Jean Cocteau, 1960, France)

Tren de sombras (*Train of Shadows*) (José Luis Guerín, 1997, Spain)

Three Transitions (Peter Campus, 1973, US)

Of Time and the City (Terence Davies, 2008, UK)

Uncle Yanco (Agnés Varda ,1967, France/US)

Visit Iraq (Kamal Aljafari, 2003, Germany)

Waiting for Fidel (Michael Rubbo, 1974 Canada/Cuba)

Waltz With Bashir (Ari Folman, 2008, Israel)

Way Back Home (Supriyo Sen, 2003, India)

Yo soy de mi barrio (*I Am From My Neighborhood*) (Juan Vicente Cordoba, 2002, Spain)

Yoman (*Diary*) (David Perlov, 1973–83, Israel)

Yom Huledet Sameach, Mar Mograbi (*Happy Birthday, Mr. Mograbi*) (Avi Mograbi, 1999, Israel)

INDEX